The THIMBLE RIGGERS

JAMES KELLY

The Dublin Arms Trials of 1970

James Kelly is author of:

Orders For The Captain (Kelly-Kane Ltd) : an account of the Dublin Arms Trials of 1970.

The Genesis Of Revolution (Kelly-Kane Ltd) : an analysis of the violence in Northern Ireland 1969/1976.

The Courage Of The Brave (Kells Publishing Company Ltd) : a politico-military analysis outlining a plan for peace in Ireland 1989.

The Marrow From The Bone (James Kelly) : a novel, 1987.

James Kelly was editor of *An Cosantoir,* the journal of the Irish Defence Forces in the sixties and has written extensively on politico-military affairs.

Captain James Kelly

Published by James Kelly
30 Curzon Street, Dublin 8

Printed by Sarsfield Press

ISBN 0 9535992 0 5

Thimblerig: A swindling game in which the operator apparently covers a small ball or pea with one of three thimble like cups, and then, moving the cups about, offers to bet that no one can tell under which cup the ball or pea lies. A swindler, esp. one operating such a game; also **Thimblerigger** — to cheat or manipulate by or as by the thimblerig.

(Webster Dictionary)

INTRODUCTION

On May 6, 1970, the Irish Taoiseach, Jack Lynch, sacked two of his most senior members, Charles Haughey, Minister for Finance, and Neil Blaney, Minister for Agriculture and Fisheries. On May 28, both men were arrested and charged at Dublin District Court with conspiracy to illegally import arms into the State. Also in the dock were a Belfast Republican, John Kelly, Albert Luykx, a Belgian born Dublin businessman, and the author, James Kelly, a former Irish Army Intelligence officer. All of us, except Neil Blaney, were sent forward for trial to the High Court.

This series of events was a sensational development on the Irish scene, with sensation following sensation as the trails got under way. In fact, there were two trials, the first having been abandoned after the presentation of the prosecution case, because of a capricious decision by the trial judge.

In 1971, I published an account of the arms trials under the title, *Orders For The Captain*. A documentary work, essentially based on the court evidence, with the minimum of comment, it was a best-seller. The current book is a much more substantial work, covering the two trials in greater detail and the subsequent parliamentary enquiry into the money that paid for the arms, which, perhaps inevitably, developed into a third trial. Conducted largely without rules, it sometimes degenerated into a free-for-all. Nevertheless, despite its shortcomings, it played an important role in clarifying aspects of the two trials, which the more legalistic approach of the courts made impossible.

A good test of good government and of good politicians is the degree of honesty and the sense of justice that informs their actions and decisions. The ideals of truth and integrity are the keystones of which the democratic system of government is based. If this principle of good government is not put into practice, we are left with a society where the rights of the individual are debased and sacrificed under such as an alleged and false concept of *State Security*, which has more in common with fascism and dictatorship than democracy. This is precisely what happened under the Irish Government of 1970, when to a background of official double-dealing and deceit, it mounted the arms trials of that year. Basically, loyal servants of the State should not be put in such an invidious position.

Apart from the grievous wrong perpetrated against the defendants, who were brought to the bar of the court on false evidence, a much greater wrong was perpetrated upon Irish society. The trust that had existed between the Government of the State and various functionaries of that Government, such as members of the army, the police and the civil service, was undermined. To sustain the false prosecution case, members of all three organisations were called upon to equivocate and shave the truth by economising with it. I knew many of them personally and I accepted them as men of authority and character, but when placed on the knife-edge of decision, where the balance between shading the truth in the alleged public interest and their innate honesty as individuals posed a major moral dilemma, they faltered. With careers at risk, maybe this was understandable, especially as most of the individuals concerned did not know the full story and the defendants had been portrayed as outlaws by the Dáil Éireann shenanigans of some grossly malign politicians during May 1970.

When *Orders For the Captain* was submitted for publication to Collins of London in early 1971, it was classified as "the most explosive book for some time" in the London media. Obviously, it was too explosive for the British Government, which blocked publication by Collins. Back in Ireland, Michael Gill, Managing Director of Gill and Macmillan in Dublin, stepped into the breach and took on publication. The work was dispatched to Cahills of Dublin for printing. A long established and well known firm, it had some valuable Government printing contracts and this was the soft underbelly that gave the Irish Government its chance, with word coming down from George Colley's Ministry of Finance to halt printing or else! As far as both Governments were concerned, *Orders For the Captain* was not going to see the light of day and they nearly succeeded.

I approached several printers with the intention of publishing myself, but "the word had got out" and they were not prepared to print in the face of official opprobrium. All the gates had seemingly banged closed, but I was saved by a phone call. A man, who refused to identify himself, requested that I meet him in an office in Jervis Street in Dublin's city centre. He indicated that he might be in a position to help solve my printing problem.

In Jervis Street, I climbed one or two flights of stairs in the designated building and found myself in a dark, dingy office. An apparently sturdy figure of average height sat hunched behind a small bare desk. He gestured towards a chair. Reiterating that he did not want to be identified, he requested that I should forget our meeting once it was over. To this day, I have not met the man again nor do I know who he was, but somehow or other I got the impression that he was a lawyer.

He told me that there was a small printing machine, operating on the photographic system around the corner in Abbey Street, which I could rent. We discussed the "ins and outs" of the matter and it was agreed that I should print 2,000 copies of the book initially, sell them and then pay the rent of the machine and the wages of the operator; and carry on from there. We shook hands on the deal and I went straight to the printing shop, where I introduced myself to the young machine operator and explained what I intended doing. Obviously, he had been briefed to expect me and I arranged to bring in the plates on the following week. Without hesitation or payment, Michael Gill instructed Cahills to release the plates to me, while the printing firm, despite the official *dictat* not to print, agreed to collate and bind the book. On the due day, I arrived in Abbey Street; the machine was set up, and we were ready to go.

"As I'm hiring the machine and your services, I'm the legal printer and I must press the starter button," I said to the operator, moving to do so.

"You can't do that," he objected,

"It's against the Union rules. You're not entitled to start it."

We debated the issue for a few minutes and I suggested that he turned his back. He walked towards the window looking out on Abbey Street, and as he did so, I pressed the button, putting into effect the instructions of my Jervis Street friend. The operator came back to the machine and the printing operation was under way.

The first 2,000 sold out in days, but my method of production militated against speed and I was short of books when the clamour for them was at its highest. Nevertheless, I spent a year producing and distributing the books, considerably relieving the impecunious position I and my family found ourselves in after the trauma of the trials. Efforts were made to block distribution by members of Fianna Fáil, the Government party. One of my best outlets, eventually selling hundreds of books, was Gills in Dublin city centre. One morning, shortly after the book came on the market, I found a parcel of books on my doorstep, ostensibly returned by this firm on the grounds that they were not selling.

On enquiry I learned that on the contrary they were selling like hot cakes. What had happened was that an assistant in the shop, a member of Fianna Fáil, felt that it was his duty to block the sale of "this treasonable book". Consequently, he intercepted a parcel of books I had delivered and dumped them on my doorstep, with a note attached on the firm's note paper, indicating that they were not selling. The subterfuge might have succeeded, if the demand for copies of the book had not prompted the firm's manager to ring me a day or two later, demanding to know why I was falling down on deliveries.

Even fifteen or so years later, having reprinted a short run of the book, I found the reaction of two Fianna Fáil County Councillors to it so extreme as to be bizarre. Both are still well-known public figures in Cavan, my native county. I met them in Drogheda one day, where they were on Local Government business. We had a friendly chat as I walked to my car. We continued talking as I opened the boot and offered them a complimentary copy each of *Orders For The Captain*. Immediately, the bantering conversation ceased and they backed away, each with a grin of embarrassment fixed on his face.

"No... No... We'd be ruined if we were seen with that," one of them explained and I suddenly realised that they were deadly serious.

I knew that the Fianna Fáil party gauleiters had done a good job of brainwashing, involving vilification of me, in Cavan, but I was still surprised at the reaction of two would-be sophisticated public representatives.

The British Press had described the book as explosive in 1971. Obviously, it was still a deadly weapon in 1986, as far as my two Cavan friends were concerned. One can only wonder how they will classify the current work, a much more comprehensive chronicle of the chicanery and betrayal that was the hallmark of the Lynch Fianna Fáil Government of 1970 and after.

TABLE OF CONTENTS

ACKNOWLEDGMENTS

I am grateful to my family for taking time out from their busy lives to concentrate on reading the manuscript of a story, which was possibly all too familiar to them. To each of my children, Suzanne, Jacqui, Sylvia, Sheila, Peter and Justin, my heartfelt thanks, with an especial thanks to a most loyal helpmate and friend of over forty years, a woman of wit and good-humour, my wife, Sheila. The suggestions put forward by them were invaluable.

Peggy Hefferon had no hesitation in giving me access to the papers of her late husband, Colonel Michael Hefferon. They are important corroborative documents and I am grateful to Mrs Hefferon and her son, Colm, for arranging that they be made available for my perusal.

My thanks to Comdt Peter Young of Army Archives, who was unfailingly courteous in dealing with my many enquiries.

My thanks also to Katrina Bouchier and Geraldine Walsh whose support in preparing and typesetting the book for publication was invaluable.

Matt O'Dea, an old friend, having read and reread the text, made some very pertinent recommendations, which I was only too happy to take on board. Thanks, Matt.

Thanks also to Charles Foster, whose expertise in print and design was at my disposal. He was responsible for the cover design.

LIST OF PRINCIPAL CHARACTERS
(Status at time of trials)

Neil Blaney	Former Minister for Agriculture.
Kevin Boland	Former Minister for Local Government.
Colonel PJ Delaney	Director of Intelligence.
James Gibbons	Minister for Agriculture, formerly Minister for Defence.
Charles Haughey	Former Minister for Finance.
Colonel Michael Hefferon	Former Director of Intelligence. Retired 9 April 1970 to be replaced by Colonel Delaney.
Captain James Kelly	Retired Intelligence Officer.
John Kelly	Citizens' Defence Committee organiser from Belfast (not related to Captain Kelly).
Albert Luykx	Belgian born, Irish citizen, acted as interpreter for Captain Kelly.
Jack Lynch	Taoiseach.
Desmond O'Malley	Minister for Justice.
Micheál Ó Moráin	Former Minister for Justice – replaced by Desmond O'Malley in May 1970.

CHAPTER 1

Under the British Government of Ireland Act 1920, the six north-eastern counties of Ireland were retained as part of the United Kingdom of Great Britain and Northern Ireland, while the remaining twenty-six counties went on to become the Republic of Ireland. This formalised the control of a Loyalist/Unionist self-perpetuating hierarchy, committed to British rule, in the six-county area, which led to injustice and discrimination being the lot of over half-a-million Irish people in the six counties of Northern Ireland.

As the British Prime Minister, Edward Heath, described the situation in his autobiography, *The Course of My Life*:

> "Those who have never visited the province cannot appreciate the bitter, tribal loathing between the hard-line elements in the two communities, springing from an atavism which most of Europe discarded long ago. This chasm in Northern Ireland inspired the Protestant majority to discriminate shamelessly against their fellow citizens for almost half a century. Denied adequate housing, jobs and social services, and poorly represented as a result of gerrymandering, the Catholic minority in the north had eventually formed a Civil Rights Association in 1968…
>
> Sadly, Protestant extremists who objected to the reforms had responded by violently attacking Civil Rights marches…"

In September 1969, a report of a Commission appointed by the Governor of Northern Ireland to enquire into that injustice and discrimination was presented. Commonly referred to as the Cameron Report, it unequivocally indicted the Stormont Government of Northern Ireland as a discriminatory regime and fully justified the efforts of the Civil Rights Movement to have the injustices, endemic in society in the area, righted.

One-man-one-vote had become a particularly effective cry of the Civil Rights Movement. This was in relation to local government elections, but the Stormont Government hesitated to grant the full right of franchise, unhindered by gerrymandering. In pursuance of this aim, together with the righting of such wrongs as discrimination in the fields of housing, education and employment, Civil Rights took to the streets to be hammered into the ground by the strong-arm police action of William Craig, as Northern Ireland Minister for Home Affairs.

It was against this background, that Terence O'Neill, the Prime Minister, decided to meet some of the Civil Rights demands in December, 1968, although, to quote Andrew Boyd in *Holy War In Belfast:*

> "At the same time he did not conceal his motives. He hoped that in an improved community the Catholics would become reconciled to Unionist rule, accept Northern Ireland's connection with Britain, and relinquish for ever their desire to live in an united Ireland under the government of the whole island."

Conceding that the claims of the Civil Rights Movement had some justification, O'Neill sacked Craig, promised to appoint an Ombudsman and advocated a points system for the allocation of local authority houses. On January 15, 1969, he announced the appointment of the Cameron Commission.

It seemed to Loyalism that if O'Neill was allowed to go ahead he might upset the Loyalist power base with its dependence on a "Protestant government for a Protestant people" concept. It was too much for Brian Faulkner, O'Neill's Deputy Prime Minister and Minister for Commerce. On January 23, 1969, he resigned, to be followed within hours by William Morgan, Minister for Health and Social Services. Within three months, the first bomb exploded in Northern Ireland. An electricity supply station was blown up at Castlereagh on March 30. On April 20, an electricity pylon was blown up at Kilmore and, on that same night, the outlet from the Silent Valley Reservoir – which met three-quarters of Belfast's water needs – was destroyed.

The Royal Ulster Constabulary (RUC) announced that the Irish Republican Army (IRA) was behind the blasts. It was not true. In fact, it was the extreme Protestant organisation, the Ulster Volunteer Force (UVF), that was responsible. The misleading police statement was calculated to consolidate Loyalism in the face of the spectre of a reactivated, militant IRA. Another related purpose was to exacerbate the rising tension between the communities in Northern Ireland. The misleading statement was exposed only towards the end of the year when it had done much to achieve its sinister purposes.

The immediate object of the explosions, however, was to remove Terence O'Neill from office by portraying him as a weakling, pandering to vicious and violent people. Meanwhile, O'Neill's Minister for Agriculture, James Chichester-Clark, had resigned. Increasingly isolated, O'Neill resigned on April 28, to be succeeded as Prime Minister by the most recent defector from his Cabinet, Chichester-Clark. Ian Paisley, an emerging Loyalist politician at that stage, exulting over the fall of "the traitor" O'Neill, even if that fall was ultimately achieved by exploding bombs, said: "We see this as the hand of God".

Chichester-Clark soon declared where he stood with the Orange Order, when, on May 23, at Bellaghy, Co. Derry, he told an Orange meeting that he was proud to be one of them. The Orange Order and political Loyalism, as represented by the Unionist Party, were as firmly integrated as they had been at any time since 1886. In that year, modern Loyalism was born, when Randolph Churchill came to Belfast's Ulster Hall and with unmatched and cynical disregard for Ireland, welded Orangeism to Loyalism in the interest to British Conservatism. His sole purpose was to return the Conservative Party to power in Britain through the manipulation of an Irish minority.

Churchill, waving the flag of Empire and stirring up anti-Catholic feeling, may have been successful in breathing life into a dormant Orange Order and establishing it as a sectarian vehicle of support for the economic well-being of the few, but he was also successful in introducing over a century of discontent in Ireland. As his son, Winston, British Prime Minister during the Second World War, saw it:

> "From that moment the excitement in Belfast did not subside. Eventually, dangerous riots, increasing in fury until they almost amounted to warfare, occurred in the streets between the factions of Orange and Green. Firearms were freely used by the police and combatants. Houses were sacked and men and women killed. The disturbances were savage, repeated and prolonged… "

In 1969, over eighty years later, Chichester-Clark saw fit to play the same Orange trump, stirring the same atavistic passions on which the elder Churchill had so cynically played.

On July 12, the day Orangemen celebrate William of Orange's victory at the Boyne in 1690, at Moneymore, Co. Derry, Chichester-Clark, with all the weight of the office of premiership behind him, castigated Irish Republicans as murderers, while, on the same day, Ian Paisley, speaking near Belfast, told the assembled Orangemen that they were engaged in "the great battle of biblical Protestantism against Popery". In the statements of both men, repeated by others at many venues throughout Northern Ireland, was revealed the Loyalist strategy of 1969. Unite Protestant Loyalism in an anti-popery campaign against Catholic Nationalism, which was planning to back a militant IRA in a war to overthrow Stormont.

As Cameron later made clear, religion was not an issue on the Nationalist side and there was absolutely no question of a militant IRA, but Chichester-Clark and Paisley had mastered the art of black propaganda. The aim was to assert the superiority of one group over another. In Northern Ireland, the aim, through the machinations of Chichester-Clark, Paisley and others, found expression in maintaining Protestant Ascendancy rule. In this manner, anti-Catholic feeling was revived, with Catholic families being driven from their homes on predominately Protestant Belfast streets. A parade of Junior Orangemen on August 2 sparked off two days of fierce rioting on the Shankill Road in Belfast. Again, to quote Andrew Boyd:

> "That week-end, Catholic families were ruthlessly driven from their homes in predominantly Protestant areas by gangs of armed Paisleyites. In the Ardoyne district, Catholics were told that they would be shot if they did not clear out within an hour."

The Shankill Road riots brought renewed demands for the banning of all sectarian marches, as it was widely believed that the annual Apprentice Boys' march, due to take place in Derry on the 12th of the same month, could only lead to further trouble. Despite the tense situation, the march was allowed to take place. In commenting on this, the editor of the London *New Statesman*, Paul Johnson, wrote:

> "Officially supported Orange parades have been a fertile source of disorder even in times of sectarian calm. To permit one to take place during the present crisis – and above all in Derry, where corrupt and gerrymandered local boundaries keep the Catholic majority in resentful subjection – was clear proof that Major Chichester-Clark and his colleagues are not fit to hold office.
>
> The truth, of course, is that the Chichester-Clark regime is weak, divided, vacillating and incompetent. It was conceived in confusion and likely to end in disaster."

On August 12, in Derry, the barricades in Catholic Bogside were strengthened as the music of the Orange bands wafted down from the walled city above, and that evening the battle was joined. Petrol bombs and stones, police advancing and retreating with a Protestant mob howling in support, were the pattern of the day. Night came and the blaze from the burning buildings reached towards the sky, while from the roof of the high-rise flats youths hurled petrol bombs at the police below.

Chapter 1

Tortuously, canisters of CS gas curved upwards to land on the flat roof and, momentarily, the youths disappeared to come back hurling further petrol bombs. Next day, the battle continued. The pattern was the same as the stalemate was finally resolved when British troops moved between the combatants.

CHAPTER 2

In August 1969, I was an Intelligence Officer at Army HQ in Dublin. I was on leave and, on the 11th, I travelled to Belfast to meet a friend of mine, Peter O'Brien. We intended going to Derry on the following day to see the Apprentice Boys' parade. Peter telephoned a friend of his who lived in Creggan, the Derry housing estate that straddles the high ground sweeping up from the valley of the Foyle and Bogside towards the Donegal border.

We were invited to spend the night in Creggan, an hour and a half or two hours' drive away. It was close to midnight, but Peter was a good driver and we crossed the big, square-angled bridge in Derry shortly before half past one. There were some policemen about, but otherwise the city centre was deserted. Down through Butchers' Gate, and we were in Bogside. There was not even a policeman on the deserted streets here, but, as we turned up towards Creggan, figures appeared in the car's headlights. Civilians, small and shadowy in the half-light, one armed with a heavy stick, blocked the road. Peter slowed to a crawl and as the figures came closer they emerged as strong, sturdy young men. Peter turned down his driving window, but the car was still moving.

"Move it another yard and you'll have a petrol bomb under it," a voice threatened and Peter stopped. Peter gave them the Creggan address and named the family.

"No family of that name living there," someone said. "Anyhow, who's your friend?"

"I'm just a visitor," I said casually.

"With a southern accent?"

As a Cavan man, it was strange to hear my accent described as southern.

"Any one of you fellows living in Creggan?" Peter shouted into the darkness. "Someone must know the family."

Someone did and we were allowed to pass. Up the hill, and we were ringing the doorbell of the terraced house. I felt somewhat guilty bursting in on an unknown family so late at night, but I need not have worried. There were other visitors there and we were made very welcome. Two extra made no difference, the woman of the house assured us, and it didn't. The conversation went on until four or five o'clock in the morning. The subject, of course, was the Northern Ireland situation and to me, as an Intelligence Officer of the Irish Army, it was interesting and informative to listen to articulate and well-informed comment on the crisis that had been developing for some time. The mood of the people in Creggan and Bogside, buoyant yet fearful, was caught in that terrace house in Creggan as we finally retired with the first streaks of dawn etching the uniform rows of houses overlooking the ancient and, for the moment, peaceful city of Derry.

Next day, as I looked down on a blazing Bogside, two elderly Derry citizens leaned on the railings beside me.

"Fifty years and nothing has changed," one of them said.

"Aye, after fifty years they're still making a mess of it," the other replied.

"We'd be better off with the Free State." The first speaker dropped the words slowly, watching for their effect.

"Aye, we wouldn't be worse off anyway. I wonder will they move?" His companion's words were carefully measured also.

"I hope they do. We'll only have peace when we're all one," and the first man spat over the railings.

"Aye, you're right," the other agreed.

On the morning of August 13, more petrol was slopped from open tins into hundreds of Bogside bottles, but three police tenders came in a zig-zag charge and the Bogside defenders scattered. It seemed as if the police had won the day, but a youth on the flank lobbed his petrol bomb straight into the right-hand tender and a policeman was out on the ground, clothes alight, rolling in agony. His comrades came to the rescue and the impetus of the attack was broken, leaving the Bogside lines intact. It was back to the CS gas and as a mere observer I stood well out of range of its nauseous, irritating fumes. People were making their way back to the first-aid station, faces blotchy and eyes streaming. A woman tapped me on the shoulder. All the men were needed up front, she indicated severely. Other women were looking at me and I went forward. Within minutes I was back and my running eyes were my protective badge of honour.

For me the battle of Bogside was a unique experience. During two years' service with the United Nations, I had witnessed the occasional firefight, and, on one occasion, halfway up the Golan Heights, I had lain with an Italian companion in a rocky crevasse, while the Syrians on the escarpment above and the Israelis in the valley beneath, exchanged heavy and prolonged bursts of fire. We were not in danger and we did not feel in danger but, certainly, in the chaos of Derry's Bogside, I felt much less secure. For me at least, the disorganised savagery of civil riot had a much more chastening effect than my first burst of machine-gun fire. Probably, the reason was psychological. As a United Nations observer in a foreign the reason was psychological. As a United Nations observer in a foreign country, it was essential that one should take a detached and objective stance, whereas in Derry, one was on home ground and the combatants on both sides were fellow-Irishmen.

That afternoon, police reinforcements, B Specials, a part-time, locally recruited police reserve, Protestant and Loyalist to a man, could be seen looking down from the city walls. With a deserved reputation of antipathy towards Catholics, most of whom they considered enemies of the regime, they instilled their own unique brand of fear, while simultaneously increasing the Bogside determination to resist.

The situation looked extremely serious and the Bogsiders consoled themselves that, if the battle continued, the minority Nationalist population would take to the streets in other areas of Northern Ireland. In this way, it was hoped that the necessary concentration of security forces to overrun Bogside and Creggan would not be feasible. Then word came through that the British army was on its way and the people of Derry heaved a collective sigh of relief. Shortly afterwards, with the battle of Bogside virtually at an end, I left Derry for Belfast.

The atmosphere there was very different from that in Derry. In Belfast, the Catholics were vastly outnumbered, geographically divided and surrounded by some of the most militant Protestants in Northern Ireland. The Catholics were afraid. Evacuations and house-swapping – Protestants and Catholics in hostile areas exchanged houses – had begun earlier in the month. The news poured in from Derry and the Catholics became more and more apprehensive. That night, Jack Lynch, the Irish Taoiseach, made his famous "not stand by" speech on television and radio, hinting at support for the beleaguered Nationalists.

Paddy Kennedy, MP for the area, and a friend of mine of some years standing, and I were driving along the Newtownards Road listening to the radio, when the speech was announced. We pulled in off the road the better to hear it. In Northern Ireland's Belfast, the Taoiseach's accent, with intonations from his native Cork, was unmistakably southern.

> "It is with deep sadness that you, Irish men and women of goodwill, and I, have learned of the events which have been taking place in Derry and elsewhere in the North in recent days," he began with the hesitancy of emotion lending dignity to his words. "The Government have been very patient and have acted with great restraint over several months past... but it is clear now, that the present situation cannot be allowed to continue. It is evident that the Stormont Government is no longer in control of the situation... The

> Irish Government can no longer stand by and see innocent people injured and perhaps worse."

Mr Lynch said that he had requested the United Nations to send peace-keeping forces to Northern Ireland immediately. He announced that the Irish army was to establish field hospitals along the border. His speech may have been received with consternation in Westminster and Stormont, but, in Northern Ireland, the minority felt reassured that if the worst came to the worst, the southern Government would come to their aid.

Some time later, Paddy and I drove up the Falls Road. Police tenders were there, but otherwise it was deserted. Our way was blocked by a wall of flame. A garage had been vandalised and its contents used to form a blazing barricade. We turned down into a narrow street. There was a woman in a doorway. Paddy called out to her. Soon the car was surrounded.

"Did you hear the Lynch speech?" he asked.

"Aye, we did. The Free State might be goin' to do something."

"I doubt it. I wouldn't bank on it," Paddy said.

"It's time something was done. Fifty years is too long," was the reply, followed by a general murmur of agreement.

The B Specials were mobilised in Belfast also and the city became still more tense. As Martin Wallace in *Drums and Guns: Revolution in Ulster* put it:

> "The whole truth will never be known, but one factor was certainly the decision to mobilise the B Specials and deploy them in the tangle of streets separating the Catholic Falls Road and the Protestant Shankill Road. The Catholic reaction was to throw up defensive barricades constructed of sawn-down telegraph poles, old furniture, paving stones, anything that burned. Not long after the public houses closed at ten o'clock, the fighting began. Police armoured cars drove into the barricades, and were met with petrol bombs. Protestant crowds, spoiling for a fight, massed behind the police and B Specials. Petrol bombs and bricks flew across the ill-defined changing no-man's land, which separated Protestant and Catholic mobs.
>
> Well before midnight, firing began... the morning brought evidence that rows of Catholic houses and flats had been raked with bullets from automatic weapons. In Divis Towers, a high block of flats, one of many bullets killed nine-year-old Patrick Rooney. His

> into a back room for safety. Trooper Hugh McCabe, on leave from Germany, was also shot dead in Divis Towers. Mrs Marie Skinner later said he died pushing her and another woman down as police fired at the flats. 'The armoured car came flying down Divis Street from the direction of the barracks. He was taking pot luck. He was firing at anything he could see.' She said Trooper McCabe had been making petrol bombs – their only means of defence."

Basically, the Protestant mob, supported by gun-firing police, some using Browning machine-guns mounted on armoured cars, had run riot during the night. Several Catholic families were burned out, with six people gunned down and many wounded. After a Catholic boy of fifteen was shot dead on the afternoon of Friday 15, an entire Catholic Street, Bombay Street, was razed. On the same evening, more Catholic homes were burned out in Belfast's Ardoyne. British soldiers arrived at 6.30 pm and forestalled another Protestant invasion from the Shankill Road, but sniping continued. By midnight, eighty-seven people had been shot.

One aspect of this genocidal attack was the practically complete absence of a Nationalist defensive mechanism, giving the lie to any militant intentions on the part of the IRA. In fact, lack of any capability to give even a minimum of defence became a subject of ridicule in the Belfast streets, with *IRA – I Ran Away* scrawled on many walls.

CHAPTER 3

I had returned to Dublin in the early afternoon of August 14 and, although technically on leave, I reported immediately to my superior officer, the Director of Intelligence, Colonel Michael Hefferon. He instructed me to develop further the various contacts I had established in Belfast and Derry and to concentrate on Northern Ireland affairs for the foreseeable future. From then until my retirement from the army on May 1 of the following year, my duties were concerned solely with the situation in Northern Ireland.

On August 17, a group of Northerners came to my house in Dublin straight from a week of terror in Belfast. Two of them were Belfast MPs, Paddy Kennedy and Paddy Devlin, and, as representatives of the people under attack, they were looking for arms for defence if violence should break out again. I told them that as a mere Captain in Intelligence I could do nothing except report their visit and, having consulted with Colonel Hefferon, I advised them to make contact with members of the Government.

My final visit to Belfast was in the second week of September 1969. On this occasion, I was accompanied by Seamus Brady, Director of a Dublin public relations firm, who at that time was working with the Propaganda Unit formed by the Dublin Government to bring to international notice the events in Northern Ireland and the background to them.

I had first met Seamus some days previously at a luncheon in McKee Barracks, Dublin, arranged by Colonel Hefferon. A Derry man with over thirty years journalistic experience, Mr Brady was well acquainted with the northern scene and, on Colonel Hefferon's suggestion, he had agreed to introduce me to various people in the North.

On the first two days of our visit, Seamus made the promised introductions, after which I was left to my own devices, while he concentrated on his Propaganda Unit duties. One of the people we met was Senator Paddy Wilson, a close friend of Gerry Fitt, MP. Paddy was later to meet a horrible death in a quarry outside Belfast, where he and his girlfriend were tortured before being done to death. He advised that we meet Gerry Fitt. I told him that I intended doing so, before returning to Dublin.

A meeting was arranged for Fitt's house on the night of Saturday, September 13. An initial get-together was arranged between Fitt, Billy Kelly, his brother, John, and others. This took place in the Fitt sitting room, overlooking the Antrim Road. Mr Fitt had returned from London that day and told me that the Kellys escorted him in from the airport, as he no longer trusted the Royal Ulster Constabulary (RUC). He shoved a gin and tonic into my hand and I sat in an armchair, as he stood at the mantelpiece, a drink in his hand, expounding on Republicanism and quoting Pearse and Connolly. When I got a chance, I told him that all the people I had met right across from Derry to Belfast asked for arms to defend themselves and their communities. I suggested that at that stage, there might be a period of calm in which to organise and put a case to the Irish Government, saying something to the effect that governments are slow to move. Mr. Fitt responded with passion:

"You're wrong. You say we have time to work out something. I tell you we haven't. We're sitting on a tinder-box here. Violence could break out at any time, today or tomorrow, tonight, even tonight, it's not too late yet. It could happen any minute."

At that moment, the room door burst open and Mrs. Fitt stood there.

"It's on, Gerry. It's on, Gerry," in a half-whispered shout.

"Where?"

"Round the corner, the New Lodge."

"What did I tell you? It's not next month we need arms. It's now, now, in the next five minutes maybe. Come on, come with me." Mr Fitt led the way out.

He stopped in the hall to pick up a red phone. He rang Lisburn (British Army HQ in Northern Ireland) and demanded the immediate dispatch of soldiers to the scene. Outside, a couple of hundred yards away, two mobs faced each other down a narrow street. The RUC lined up in front of the Protestant mob while vigilantes, with linked arms, held back the Catholics. Stolidly accepting the occasional punch from the more fanatical of their co-religionists, the vigilantes successfully contained the heaving, screaming mob until the arrival of the British army. The soldiers took up position in front of the Catholics while an officer negotiated with their representatives. He handed a loudspeaker to Gerry Fitt, who did an excellent job in calming down the crowd. Finally, with police and military forming a dual security screen between the rival factions, passions cooled and confrontation was avoided for another night.

All further meetings that night were effectively disrupted, but the Fitt demand for immediate arms had been dramatically emphasised. I had a quick talk with him and the Kellys and I said I would head for Dublin on the following morning and stress the urgent need for arms. I wrote out my report in longhand the following evening, had it typed by the confidential typist in Intelligence early in the week and gave it to the Director. It was of major interest that Gerry Fitt, perceived as the main political voice of Irish Nationalism in Northern Ireland at the time, should have endorsed the request by so many right across the Six Counties that the Irish Government should supply arms. As was usual with all my reports, Colonel Hefferon brought this report to the attention of the Minister for Defence.

I met John Kelly for the first time that evening at the Fitt house. In his early thirties at the time, he came from a staunch Belfast Republican family and was imprisoned for six years for his involvement in the 1956 IRA campaign. During the August violence, Citizens' Defence Committees were formed all over the Six Counties to co-ordinate defence and provide general organisation in areas where law and order had broken down. John had been one of the defence organisers in Belfast in that August week of violence and, when I met him in September, he was the Central Defence Committee organiser on a six-county basis.

In a calm and logical way he explained the seriousness of the situation which he and the other minority representatives wanted to communicate to the Dublin Government – a government to whom he and others felt they were entitled to look for assistance.

About a week later I was in the Derry area and, once again, it was evident that the Nationalists there looked to the South for assistance. I reported on my various meetings to the Director of Intelligence and, on his instructions, I did not enter Northern Ireland again during my army service. It seems that the identity of other intelligence officers who had visited the Six Counties had come to the notice of the authorities there and, in the circumstances, Colonel Hefferon issued an order that in future no intelligence officer was to enter Northern Ireland without his specific permission – a permission which I had never any necessity to seek. In fact, I had already made arrangements to meet my Northern contacts on the twenty-six county side of the border if and when required – a system which worked well and from which I never had cause to deviate.

Apart from Colonel Hefferon, I also reported on my September visit to Belfast to Neil Blaney, then Minister for Agriculture, who, I understood, was a member of the sub-committee appointed by the Cabinet to deal with Northern Ireland affairs. I had a general discussion with Mr Blaney who arranged that I should meet Charles Haughey, then Minister for Finance, another member of the sub-committee, that same evening. I covered the same ground with both Ministers, conveying to them the sense of urgency and the emphasis laid by the minority in the North, endorsed by Gerry Fitt, on the necessity of arms for defensive purposes. This did not take either Minister by surprise, because, since August, many deputations had come south seeking arms as a first priority, but what possibly did surprise them, as it had certainly surprised me, was the virtual unanimity among a very representative cross-section of the Nationalist community that some type of defensive weaponry was necessary and should be made available.

The other members of the Northern sub-committee were Joseph Brennan, Minister for Social Welfare, and Padraig Faulkner, Minister for Education, neither of whom I met and, in fact, it later emerged that the sub-committee met as such on only one or two occasions.

Mr Blaney was the only member of the sub-committee I met on a more or less regular basis, probably on an average of once a week. This arose because of the many contacts Mr. Blaney had in the Six Counties, resulting in a flow of information which in many ways helped to fill out the intelligence picture. In effect, our meetings resulted in an exchange of information useful to me as an intelligence officer and, I expect, to Mr Blaney as a member of the Cabinet sub-committee, which I presumed was reporting to the Cabinet as a whole. At all times, I kept Colonel Hefferon informed of my contacts with the Ministers.

Some time in the months before Christmas, Mr Blaney was informed that there was a possibility of surplus arms, offered for sale by the Defence Forces, being bought on behalf of the Ulster Volunteer Force (UVF), an extremist Loyalist organisation. When I checked this information with the Director of Intelligence, I discovered he was already aware of the situation and that the agent representing the company interested in buying the arms was a resident of Northern Ireland. When told of what was happening, James Gibbons, Minister for Defence, cancelled the sale, firstly, because of the possibility that the arms might come under the control of the UVF or a related organisation and secondly, and of more significance, because it was considered that they should be held in reserve in case it became necessary to distribute them to a defenceless minority in Northern Ireland at some future date. Thus, a contingency to be formalised by the Government Directive to the Defence Forces on February 6 of the following year was clearly foreshadowed at an early stage.

In late September 1969, a party of men, all residents of Northern Ireland, was arrested in suspicious circumstances in the midlands. It seems that the local Gardaí rang the RUC to verify the names and addresses of the arrested men. As the men were Republicans from a particularly exposed area in Northern Ireland, this effective identification of them to the RUC in the uncertain circumstances of the time, caused understandable agitation in the Nationalist community concerned. An approach was made to me on the matter and, when I discussed it with Mr Blaney, I learned that, in view of what had taken place, the Gardaí in general had been instructed not to make contact with the RUC without reference to higher authority.

A continuation of this "softly, softly" approach was evident later when, around Christmas, a group of Derry men in possession of firearms was arrested in County Donegal. What was obviously a training camp had been uncovered, but the full weight of the law was not used against the participants. Rather, through discreet official action, the men were allowed to return home after spending a few days in Dublin's Mountjoy Prison – admittedly without their arms, which were confiscated. In effect, it was the minimum action that could be taken against them, consistent with the publicity surrounding the arrest and subsequent trial. Such a denouement could only be construed as Government policy, especially when the previous training of Derrymen in the use of arms under official auspices, and how and why it had been discontinued, were taken into account.

In September, a serious situation had arisen in Derry city. The local Unionists were putting pressure on the British army commander in the area to take drastic action to bring the Bogsiders to heel. Eventually, a leading Unionist threatened that if the army did not act, his constituents would take the law into their own hands, stating that if something was not done "the streets of the city would run red with blood". Word leaked through to the Bogside and a decision was taken to fight in the event of any such attempted pogrom. Little or no arms were available and, even if there were, there were no men trained to use them. Accordingly, three people sought a meeting with Colonel Murt Buckley of the Irish army in Letterkenny, Co Donegal. Their request was simple: urgent facilities for training men, and arms to be made available close to the border in Donegal.

Colonel Buckley was sympathetic to the plight of the Derry men, but not inclined to meet such a request. He was bluntly asked to put the matter to higher authority. A week later, word came down that the training was to take place, with the first intake reporting to Fort Dunree, at the northern tip of Donegal overlooking Lough Swilly. The training, authorised by the Minister for Defence, was an intensive week's course in small arms, grenades and mortars, with a section or two, ten or twenty men, reporting each week over a period of several weeks. The men were to be drafted into An Forsa Cosanta Aithiuil (FCA), the local territorial force, providing a Donegal address to meet with army regulations.

Nine men enrolled for the first week's training and were due to return to Derry on Friday, October 3. On that day, I was in the office of the Director of Intelligence in my capacity as Personal Staff Officer when word came through that the training at Fort Dunree, which was a secret and undercover operation, was likely to be the subject of newspaper comment over the weekend. The Director attempted to contact the Minister or the Chief-of-Staff, but when neither was available, he decided on his own initiative to postpone further training for the moment. On his instructions, I attempted to contact two officers of the Intelligence Section who were in the Donegal area, but did not succeed because they were travelling between army posts at the time. Eventually, Colonel Hefferon contacted the Intelligence Officer based in the area and issued the necessary instructions for the postponement. He arranged with the officer that the issue or otherwise of the instructions should be confirmed by a telephone call at ten o'clock that night.

The call was made from the office of the Garda Chief Superintendent in Letterkenny to the office of the Director of Intelligence, because both phones were fitted with scrambler devices. It was confirmed that the group of about twenty men due to arrive in Dunree on the following morning would not leave Derry. On Monday morning, Colonel Hefferon reported on his action to the Chief-of-Staff and the Minister, James Gibbons, was subsequently informed.

The only reason for the interruption of the planned training of a considerable number of Northern Ireland citizens in the use of arms was the fear of publicity and, in fact, at the time I got the strong impression that Colonel Hefferon's decision to interfere with the training was not received altogether with favour at a higher level. In the event, the training was not resumed, but, a month or two later, I was summoned urgently to the office of the Director of Intelligence in connection with it. The Scarman Tribunal, another British inquiry, was sitting in Derry at the time and the Minister for Defence had been informed that the training might come under scrutiny by the Tribunal. When I arrived in the office it soon became obvious that the Secretariat of the Department was worried that this possibility might become a reality. I was instructed by the Director of Intelligence to get some information on the matter. I made a phone call and, within minutes, I was able to inform the Minister, through an Assistant Secretary in the Department, that the training would not be mentioned at the Tribunal.

Looking back, it is significant that the Government was not concerned about the training itself, but only about the possibility that it might become public knowledge. If the training had been the subject of enquiry at the Scarman Tribunal it could only have embarrassed the Government, because it took place after the Taoiseach's speech in Tralee on September 20, when he put forward the long-term policy of "seeking unity through agreement in Ireland between Irishmen".

> "Let me make it clear too," the Taoiseach said on that occasion, "that in seeking re-unification, our aim is not to extend the domination of Dublin. We have many times down the years expressed our willingness to seek a solution on federal lines, and in my most recent statement I envisaged the possibility of intermediate steps in an approach to a final agreed solution... It would remain the Government's most earnest aim and hope to win the consent of the majority of the people in the Six Counties to means by which the North and South could come together in a re-united and sovereign Ireland earning international respect both for the fairness and efficiency with which it was administered and for its contribution to world peace and progress."

Mr Lynch went on to state that he was not seeking the overthrow by violence of the Stormont Parliament or Government, but rather to win the agreement of a sufficient number of people in the North to an acceptable form of re-unification. In a reference to the Northern minority, he stated that they and his Government had accepted as a practical matter the existence of a government in the North of Ireland exercising certain powers devolved on it by the British Parliament. There were many fruitful contacts with that Government on matters of mutual concern, the Taoiseach said, and expressed the hope that such co-operation between North and South would continue.

It was a speech which unequivocally advocated peaceful means as a solution to the problem of re-unification. It may seem strange that the training of citizens of Northern Ireland in the use of arms should be undertaken within the same week as such a declaration of peaceful intent and, certainly, if such an apparent gap between words and deed had been ventilated before the Scarman Tribunal, the credibility of the Lynch Government would have been weakened, especially in the eyes of Unionists at whom the speech was so obviously aimed. It might have been difficult to argue that the speech and the training were compatible, although this line of reasoning was in fact largely sustainable.

In common with the vast majority of the Irish people, Jack Lynch's most earnest wish was that the six-county problem be solved by peaceful means, but governments have to be prepared for contingencies, the pertinently obvious one in the Irish case at this time being a complete breakdown of law and order in Northern Ireland, with a renewal of violence, again sparking off murderous attacks on the Nationalist minority – Irish citizens by definition and desire, many of them carrying Irish passports.

To me – an intelligence officer who knew what was taking place on the ground – this was the only way in which the apparent advocation of a policy of peace and the preparation for armed intervention, however low-key, could be reconciled.

For reasons already explained, the Dunree training was brought to an abrupt end on October 3, but the indication was that it would be resumed. On the weekend of October 4 and 5, I had a meeting with representatives of the Defence Committees from most areas in Northern Ireland at a hotel in Bailieboro, County Cavan. Two days previously, on Thursday afternoon, I had accompanied my Director, Colonel Hefferon, to a meeting at Charles Haughey's home. The proposed Bailieboro meeting and the question of how much it would cost was discussed. I suggested that £150 should cover it. In the end, Mr. Haughey arranged that I be paid £500 to cover the meeting, with any balance to be used for other subsequent expenses.

The purpose of the Bailieboro meeting was to meet and get the view of those on the Defence Committees, who would be responsible for the use and control of arms that might be issued by the Dublin Government. If, however, as was the intention, the Dunree training should resume, the cadre of men trained in the use of arms attached to the Committees would be greatly augmented. In fact, a major portion of the meeting was taken up with a discussion on the Fort Dunree training and, particularly, the reason for its abandonment. My explanation, for what was looked upon then as its postponement, was accepted, but the meeting emphasised that it would have to be resumed, if necessary, under some other guise. Very rationally, all present considered training essential before there could be any question of distributing arms.

There was considerable debate on what arms might be used for, but the meeting was unanimous and very adamant that they would only be used for defensive purposes. Many were aware of the promise of money by Dublin, which they understood could be used to fund the purchase of arms. Understandably, there was some mistrust of the Irish Government intentions expressed. I submitted a report on the meeting to Colonel Hefferon on the following Monday, making it clear that I was dealing with the Republican element of the Defence Committees on this occasion.

Some time later, probably in November, Colonel Hefferon checked with me again concerning the Bailieboro meeting. He had been approached by James Gibbons, the Minister for Defence, who told him that he had received a complaint from the Taoiseach concerning the meeting. It was conveyed to me that Peter Berry, then Secretary of the Department of Justice, had intimated to Jack Lynch that the meeting had some peculiar features about it. There was talk of a table and of my moving money across it or over it. There was a suggestion that there was a

Oct 6th 1969 — Northern Ireland

1. The N.I. Republican Movement is now a 6-county org. Its present first priority is the acquisition of arms for defensive purposes. It has the finance to accomplish this and it is the intention to import arms through the SOUTH

2. The second priority of Northern Republicans is that of training and they see this as of extreme and immediate urgency. Training required could be classified under the following headings

   a. Weapon Training – an intensive one-week course.

   b. INT Training – selected men – 2 to each county – to undergo an intensive course of some days' duration.

   c. Demolition Training – groups from each area to undergo a week's course.

   d. Communications Training – selected men to train in RT primarily.

3. Above Training is seen as given by the Defence Forces here. It is realised, however, that there may be problems, in view of which it is accepted that a., as a reluctant alternative might be left in their own hands to take place in Southern camps.

4. The defensive aspect of operations is genuinely stressed but there is a definite feeling that in the final analysis, the Defence Forces will have to come to the rescue.

5. In certain circumstances, Republicans see themselves holding such areas Belfast, Derry, Coalisland and Dungannon, Armagh and Newry for a period, which would indicate that planning here would need to take into consideration a drive to consolidate these areas, with BELFAST, the capital, as the main objective.

6. Republicans are insistent that training, if agreed to, must start immediately. Otherwise, events will overtake them.

Copy of original MS Report of Bailieboro meeting, Oct. 6, 1969 surfeit of alcohol consumed. In general, the substance of the complaint seemed to be nothing more than that some undefined attempt was made to subvert the conference for some undefined reason.

Even the factual details were wrong. As far as I recollect there was no table available in the room, and I certainly sat on a chair in the corner without the benefit of a table. There was no money whatsoever produced and, as regards a surfeit of alcohol, the cost of the meeting alone indicated otherwise. Fifteen people attended, some of whom stayed overnight, while there was a meal available for those who required it. The total bill came to £35, which did not give much scope for extras – this apart from the fact that those at the meeting were all mature individuals who had come long distances on very serious business and to whom the availability or otherwise of alcohol was of minor consequence.

Colonel Hefferon reported back to Mr Gibbons, who, I assume, reported back to the Taoiseach. Hearing nothing to the contrary, the only conclusion I could come to was that Mr Berry's complaint had been rejected by both Mr Gibbons and the Taoiseach. As far as I was concerned it was of major consequence that in November 1969 the Taoiseach and his Minister for Defence were aware of a meeting which was the genesis of a later attempted importation of arms.

CHAPTER 4

Once the Northern crisis erupted, with the Nationalist minority under attack, money was subscribed all over Ireland for the purchase of arms. Weapons were smuggled, singly and in small numbers, by air and sea. Old weapons were dug up and transported across the border. Groups of men, ordinary civilians not connected to any organisation subversive or otherwise, collected whatever arms were available, mostly shotguns and .22s, and headed north, willing to fight if necessary. One such group from the Dublin area headed for Letterkenny, and with some ex-soldiers armed with rifles in their midst, they were capable of giving a good account of themselves. They made one foray across the border, but it quickly dawned on them that, unfamiliar with the terrain, not knowing friend from foe and with no one to direct them, they were more of a hindrance than a help. They returned home after a couple of days.

In November, word reached Dublin that a considerable quantity of arms was available in London. John Kelly became aware of this. While the source of the information was suspect and it was felt that it might be some type of entrapment operation characteristic of the M5 and M6 British security agencies, John, accompanied by a Dublin man, Paddy, headed for London. John briefed me on what was afoot on the night before their departure.

The two men were shadowed from the time they arrived in England and were photographed as they left Oxford Street tube station in London. John, well acquainted with the methods of surveillance teams from his experiences in the Belfast streets, spotted a man at a bus-stop, standing on his toes looking after them, with a radio to his ear. Further down, he saw a woman standing at the tailgate of a station-wagon. When they passed, she pulled a radio from her bag and seemed to say a few words before replacing it. Paddy returned to Ireland first, with John, having met the contact, returning the next day, fully convinced that it was a "set-up".

Back in Dublin, I met John in Buswell's Hotel. He rang London and informed his contact that he was called back to Dublin suddenly and asked if negotiations could be resumed there. After some delay, this was agreed and the man said he would fly into Dublin Airport that night and meet John in the Gresham Hotel. He did not fly into Dublin, because, armed with his description, I monitored several London flights into the airport before and after his expected time of arrival. When I got back to the hotel, he was there. John and I could only assume that he had flown into Belfast, probably on a military plane, and had travelled down by road. This strengthened our suspicions.

When the small, dark-haired, goatee-bearded man finally got down to talk with John in an upstairs bedroom, he claimed to be a former British army officer, introducing himself as Captain Markham-Randall. Whatever he was, he turned out to be very well informed on behind-the-scene events on Ireland, throwing around the name Kelly in an obvious manner, which John took to refer to me. He was also very interested in Ministers Haughey, Blaney, Boland and Gibbons, whom he intimated were strong supporters of Northern nationalism. This was based on information straight from the heart of Government, as Kevin Boland later indicated in *Up Dev*, when he stated:

> "When the Bogside, initially, and, later, other nationalist areas came under murderous attack by the security forces, Blaney, myself, Haughey and Gibbons insisted that the safety of the people, whose lives and homes were under attack was our (Irish Government) responsibility."

The Kelly reference, on which Markham-Randall harped, also indicated inside knowledge which could only have come from an Irish source. The spy explained that he was well acquainted with Irish history, stating that there were many parallels with the Arab experience.

"You may notice I look like an Arab," he said. "But what is not so obvious is that I feel like an Arab; think like an Arab. My father may have been an Englishman, but I am one of my mother's people. I served with the British army. So did many Irishman. That does not make them any less Irishmen, as it does not make me any less an Arab... I trust you understand me. There are many Irish and many Arabs who do not like the English. I am Captain Markham-Randall and I am here to help you."

The Captain claimed to be an expert in guerrilla war and to have completed many courses in counter-revolutionary warfare. "I could be a big help to you people," he told John. "If I visited one or other of your training camps I would be very useful: small arms, fire and movement, tactics and that sort of thing."

"It is arms we are interested in at the moment." John cut across him.

"Arms, okay, okay." he shrugged his shoulders. "A consignment of automatic weapons, grenades and LMGs for thirty thousand. It's cheap. It's the market price. But I am on your side. You may have the lot for three thousand."

This was after several hours of talking. The haggling over price first and then the introduction of the friends of Ireland piece. John's suspicions increased by the minute. He was worried also by the small, rectangular, flat-topped case, which the Captain kept close on the table in front of him. In all the spy films, the enemy agent had such a case, but it was the price reduction that clinched it.

"You're not a dealer! You're an agent!" John challenged.

"Maybe I am, but what difference does it make to you? You get the guns and you can keep the money. All I want is access to the training camps," the agent's hand eased under the lid of the case.

"Don't chance it, My back-up is not too far away." John stood up, expecting a gun to appear in Markham-Randall's hand.

"Is it a deal? I want an answer now," Markham-Randall demanded.

"I'll have to think about it. I better see the lads. We're here a long time. They might be getting nervous." John turned and quickly left the room.

Three Northern men and I sat downstairs in the lobby of the hotel awaiting the result of the negotiations. When John voiced his belief that Markham-Randall was a British agent, the immediate reaction of the three men was to eliminate him.

"We'll show him training camps, but he won't come back," one of them said.

"You're right. That's what Michael Collins did in 1920. He shot the British spies and saved the day," a second man agreed.

I argued against this on the basis that it would only embarrass the Dublin Government, which had been extremely co-operative to-date. Some heated discussion ensued, but, in the end, it was accepted that the British agent should go free. Probably completely unaware how close he had come to losing his life, Markham-Randall remained around Dublin for a day or two at least, penning a letter from Buswell's hotel on November 30. It was left at the hotel desk to be collected. It eventually ended up at the Munster and Leinster Bank in Baggot St., Dublin, addressed to G. Dixon, the named arms account holder at the bank.

I reported on the episode to Colonel Hefferon, who had inquiries initiated on the matter with the Garda security section. Word came back that Markham-Randall was a person of ill-repute; some type of underworld figure, who was not particular how he made his money; just the type of person who would involve himself in selling arms or any other underhand activity for that matter. Later, in February 1970, it was brought to my attention that a large file on the attempted arms sale had been sent to Garda Headquarters. I was given sight of the file which had a photograph of John Kelly and Paddy "Dublin," as some of the Belfast men referred to him, coming up the steps of the London tube station.

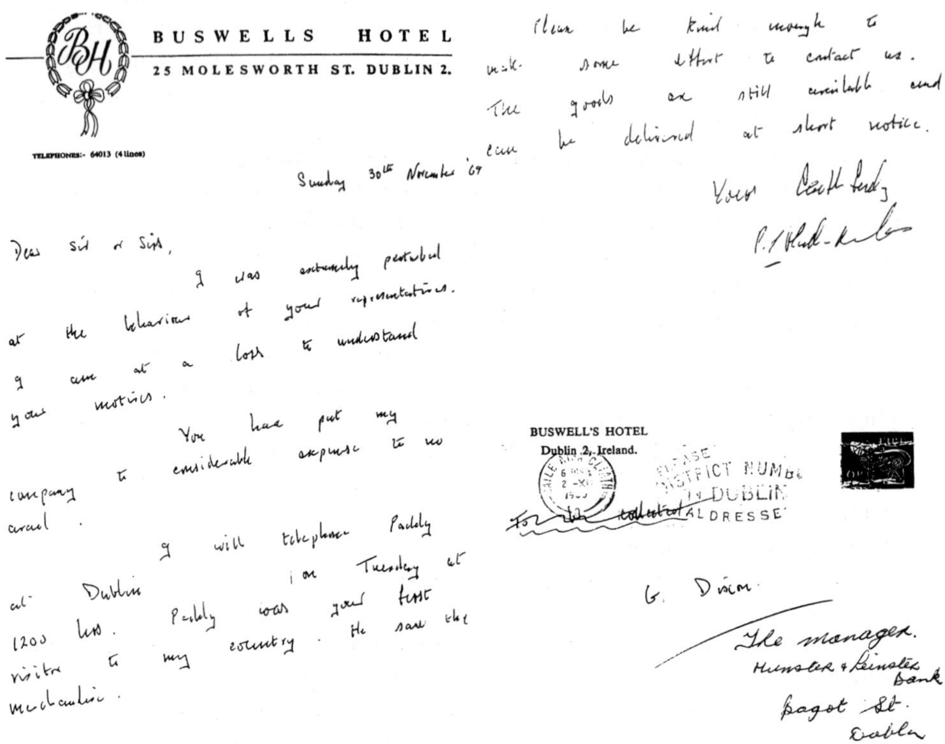

BUSWELLS HOTEL
25 MOLESWORTH ST. DUBLIN 2.
TELEPHONES:- 64013 (4 lines)

Sunday 30th November '69

Dear Sir or Sirs,

I was extremely perturbed at the behaviour of your representatives. I am at a loss to understand your motives.

You have put my company to considerable expense to no avail.

I will telephone Paddy at Dublin on Tuesday at 1200 hrs. Paddy was your first visitor to my country. He saw the mechanism.

Please be kind enough to make some effort to contact us. The goods are still available and can be delivered at short notice.

Yours faithfully

BUSWELL'S HOTEL
Dublin 2, Ireland.

G. Dixon.
The manager.
Munster & Leinster Bank
Baggot St.
Dublin

Copy of letter, together with envelope, written by Markham-Randall from Buswell's hotel on November 30.

Obviously, the Irish police had been briefed on the affair by their British counterparts. Interestingly, while the Gardaí recognised Paddy, they did not identify John Kelly. Presumably, neither did the British. Apart from filing the information, the security agencies here took no action on the matter, but the file confirmed that Markham-Randall was a British agent.

One aspect of the affair puzzled Colonel Hefferon. How could a British agent be so well acquainted with security details about members of the Irish Government and their attitude to the North, which could not and should not have been officially communicated to the British? For some time, he had a strong suspicion that there was leak in C3, the security section of the Gardaí at their Dublin Phoenix Park Headquarters. As he saw it, the finger pointed at the chief clerk there, who "was always creeping around the place, permitted to listen in to even the most confidential conversations and with apparent unrestricted access to information and files". The Colonel had nothing concrete to back up his suspicion and as the Garda in question was obviously a most trusted individual, probably the most trusted and best informed in Garda intelligence circles, there was little the Director of Military Intelligence could do about it. He would very quickly have been told to mind his own business.

Three years later, however, on December 21, 1972, Colonel Hefferon's judgement was fully vindicated. On that day, John Wyman, a British MI6 agent, was arrested in Dublin's Burlington Hotel. Arrested with him was his main Irish contact, Hefferon's security *bête noir*, Patrick Crinnion, the chief confidential clerk in C3. Both were charged under the Official Secrets Act, but, in the new year, both were freed and allowed to leave the country. When the case came to hearing, the extraordinary position arose that the prosecution refused to bring forward evidence, because the information which Crinnion was handling was too "top secret" to be put before an Irish court, not even to the extent of conveying it to the trial judge. Yet, Crinnion, a veritable repository of intelligence, both top secret and otherwise, on all aspects of security, was sent out of the country into the arms of the British to be debriefed by them at their leisure.

The investigation that led to the exposure of Wyman and Crinnion took place after a visit by Mr Lynch, the Taoiseach, to Mr Heath, the British Prime Minister, when Mr Lynch was taken aback to find that Mr. Heath was in possession of information that could only have emerged from a source close to the top of the Irish security organisation. This incongruous situation, with the Garda security apparatus so compromised that it had become a mere adjunct of British security, was made all the more incongruous by the handing over of Crinnion. Such a development was inconceivable except in some extraordinary circumstances where another factor took precedence over State security. Crinnion's access to "top secret" information was only half the story. The real factor was the credibility of the Lynch Government itself.

Crinnion, because of his work, was in a position to expose the full extent of official co-operation between the Irish and British security services, including co-operation in relation to Northern Ireland if he had been forced to defend himself. Further, the chicanery involved at various levels from the Cabinet down, when Lynch mounted the arms trials of 1970, would have been brought to light. Consequently, Lynch, with two embarrassing prisoners on his hands, one of them a potentially explosive witness, was very happy when Britain gave him a way out.

Britain, of course, was anxious to get Wyman, one of its more effective agents, back under its wing. It was also anxious to take Crinnion off Dublin's hands. On January 3, 1973, between the arrest and scheduled trial of Wyman and Crinnion in Dublin, the British Government notified Mr Lynch that the Littlejohn brothers, whom they were holding in England, could be exchanged for the two Irish prisoners. The Littlejohns had been recruited in London as British agents, because of alleged contacts one or other of them had made with the IRA during periods they spent in Ireland. As agents in Ireland, they came under Wyman's control, but they seemed to be more trouble than they were worth. One of their extra-curricular activities, for example, in conjunction with their spying mission, was participation in a major bank robbery in Dublin.

They sought refuge in Britain, but the Government there was not willing to accept responsibility for any such activity. The upshot was that a few days after the British message to Lynch, the British Director of Prosecutions came to Dublin where he met the Attorney General, Colm Condon, and the Minister for Justice, Desmond O'Malley. The purpose of his visit was to secure a sworn affidavit from the Attorney General in connection with the extradition of the Littlejohns to Ireland.

On August 13, 1973, Mr Lynch issued a statement consequent on the background to the Littlejohn affair having come to light. In it he described the conditions on which the Irish Attorney General issued the affidavit sought by Britain:

> "The Wyman case was pending at that time, and the first of these conditions was that an assurance be given that neither of the Littlejohn brothers had been employed by the British Government to suborn any member of the Irish security forces.
>
> Secondly, that neither of the Littlejohn brothers had passed to the British Government any information obtained from the Irish security forces.
>
> Thirdly, that the British Government would not seek to use the fact that Mr Condon, as Attorney General, had given an affidavit to the effect that the Littlejohn brothers would not be prosecuted for political offences, as an argument against proceeding with the prosecutions against Wyman.
>
> Fourthly, that there was no connection between the Littlejohns and the Wyman case."

The third condition was the core of the affidavit. In it, the Irish Attorney General deposed to the effect that Ireland would not prosecute the Littlejohns for political offences, if Britain agreed not to expose the fact that the Irish had entered into such an agreement. The *quid pro quo*, of course, was that Ireland would not prosecute Wyman. As regards the other conditions, the fourth one was shown to be false when it emerged that there was a connection between the Littlejohns and Wyman, in that the Littlejohn brothers, in their intelligence capacity, had worked through Wyman, whom they knew as Douglas Smythe. On the first two conditions, it was easy to answer in the negative whatever the reality. In the event, Wyman was not prosecuted by the Irish Government. The denouement to the Littlejohn affair came shortly afterwards when Fianna Fáil, Mr. Lynch's party, went into opposition. At that stage, Mr Lynch denied that the Littlejohns had been British agents, presumably on the basis of the conditions sought from Britain by the Attorney General in return for his affidavit. In *Up Dev*, Kevin Boland described why the Lynch denial was not true and why Mr Lynch knew it was not true:

> "Still more striking was the infamous Littlejohn affair. Again, after Fianna Fáil had gone into opposition, it came to light that the Littlejohn brothers, who were charged with a spectacular bank robbery in Dublin, were at the time British agents. Mr Lynch categorically denied any knowledge of this. Eventually a departmental file was produced to prove that the Secretary of the Department of Foreign Affairs had gone specially to his office to inform him of this fact, which had been confirmed by the Irish ambassador in London. There was now no option but to admit the truth and, in his confusion, Mr Lynch resorted to the schoolboyish excuse that he forgot! Did anyone ever hear such nonsense? The Secretary of the Department of Foreign Affairs had come into his office for the specific purpose of giving him this very important information and he forgot. He could not possibly forget. He did not forget; what he did forget was that there would be a file in a civil service office establishing the fact that he was told."

The fact is that the Irish Government was glad to get two embarrassing prisoners, Wyman and Crinnion, off their hands, regardless of their depth of knowledge, especially in Crinnion's case, of the national security service; not to mention the treason Crinnion had committed in selling out that service to a foreign power. To take the Littlejohns off British hands in return was considered to be a good bargain by the Irish authorities. The spy, Wyman, and his Irish agent, Crinnion, were shipped off into the maw of the British security services, while the less fortunate Littlejohns, also British spies, were extradited back to Ireland to serve several years in an Irish prison for their opportunistic bank robbery.

Agents of a different hue also surfaced in Ireland in the period prior to Christmas 1969. There were at least two and they were Sinn Féin or IRA men reporting to the Special Branch. They were not informers in the strict sense of the word, but skilled and clever infiltrators working on behalf of their own organisation. Over a period, they had provided enough solid information to establish their credentials with the Special Branch, but in doing so, they were quite adroit at slanting it to forward the Marxist oriented ideology of Sinn Féin at the time.

Over the years until 1962, Sinn Féin had been a traditional Republican party with the aim of having Britain withdraw from Ireland. In the 1956/1962 period, its military wing, the IRA, took up arms to achieve this. The campaign was a failure. In the aftermath, the Republican Movement was forced to reconsider its approach and the result was an adoption by Sinn Féin of a new Marxist policy. This expressed itself in the bringing to light and exploiting of social grievances in both parts of Ireland, with the declared final aim of establishing a thirty-two county Socialist Republic. Axiomatically, this called not alone for the overthrow of Stormont, but, also, the "Green Tory Government" in the South. Through agitation and protest against, in many cases, undoubted social inequalities and injustices, Sinn Féin hoped to achieve the necessary state of anarchy, North and South, to allow the IRA stage a *coup d'état* and establish a Socialist dictatorship.

The security agencies in the State looked askance at Sinn Féin with its Communist philosophy and all that it implied in the sixties. Military Intelligence was no different and we were fairly well briefed on developments and the likelihood of such ploys as infiltrating and influencing State agencies. Accordingly, when the content of the Berry report on the Bailieboro meeting with its slanted information, was brought to Colonel Hefferon's notice by Minister Gibbons, he suspected the hand of Sinn Féin. On one of his visits to C3, Crinnion's eyrie in Garda HQ, he suggested to the officer-in-charge that they had a Sinn Féin or IRA source.

"You're wrong, we have two," the Garda officer replied with some pride.

The activities of the Sinn Féin infiltrators seemed to finish at Christmas 1969. It is also interesting to note that the Sinn Féin split occurred over the Christmas period. Whatever the reason, the Sinn Féin sources dried up at that time.

Meanwhile, the search for arms continued and representatives of the Citizens' Defence Committees travelled to America in December 1969 to enquire about arms, but there was no indication that arms could be obtained there at that time. If secret agents were around they did not impinge. Meanwhile, rumbling away in the background like a vague rattle of thunder on the horizon, a rumour gained momentum that there were arms available on continental Europe and, where else, but in Hamburg, that ancient city on the Baltic that had clinging to it something of the unsavoury reputation of the battered old port that had seen it all. It had a particular resonance for Ireland. From there, prior to Irish independence, both Nationalists and Unionists had run guns in the second decade of the century.

Neil Blaney, Minister for Agriculture, had, through his continental contacts, unearthed the potential source of arms and he advised that, if people wanted arms, Hamburg was the place to go. There was talk of a Baron lurking in the background, but, it was claimed at one stage that he was really a Corporal with the Canadian forces in Europe, probably involved in intelligence work. When the American trip proved abortive, the European possibility was investigated and, around the start of the new year, £3,000 was paid to the account of Otto Schleuter, a Hamburg arms dealer, by a representative of the Citizens' Defence Committees. This was on foot of a consignment of pistols that was allegedly available. This deal was to culminate in the arms trials later in the year.

CHAPTER 5

In August 1969, the Dublin Cabinet debated the Northern Ireland troubles. Kevin Boland, who was present, wrote in *Up Dev*:

> "When the Bogside, initially, and later other nationalist areas came under murderous attack by Orange mobs orchestrated by the security forces, Blaney, myself, Haughey and Gibbons insisted that the safety of the people, whose lives and homes were under attack, was our responsibility.
>
> Hour after hour we argued doggedly that what was happening was as much our concern as if it were in Dublin or Cork. I, certainly, had enough common sense to see that interference by the Irish army would be disastrous.
>
> Places contiguous to the Border could obviously be assisted effectively but to do so would mean the wholesale slaughter of Nationalists (or Catholics) in other areas where there was no defence available. I feel reasonably certain that the others also saw this and that none of us visualised an actual incursion. We realised that we must not spark off what Gibbons later described as a 'doomsday situation', but our point was that it appeared extremely likely that this situation was going to develop very rapidly. In the meantime we must make the best possible arrangements for such an eventuality, which I think everyone, at the time, agreed was more likely than not..."

The eventual outcome of the conclave was a decision that the Minister for Defence, Mr, Gibbons, and the Minister for Finance, Mr Haughey, would confer with the army authorities and make the best arrangements possible. Mr. Boland has confirmed that this delegation of authority was made by the Taoiseach at a full Government meeting. In fact, this was also confirmed by Mr Gibbons and by the Minister for Justice, Michael Ó Moráin.

Haughey and Gibbons did not waste time, but arranged a working lunch that very day with the Army General Staff in Dublin's McKee Barracks. The result of that meeting was a recognition that although the Irish army, as such, was powerless to do much by direct intervention, it was accepted that "a purely local resistance, with minimum training facilities and supply lines could, if sufficiently determined, hold out indefinitely and, of course, if the Government should at any stage decide, that the situation justified assisting such resistance, then it would be all the more effective".

The Government consultation with the Defence Forces gave rise to a Contingency Plan, which inevitably led to:

1. The training of Derry citizens in the use of arms.
2. The Bailieboro meeting to assess likely resistance and how it might be accommodated.
3. Arrangements for the supply of weapons to the proposed resistance.
4. The movement by Mr Gibbons of arms to the Border town of Dundalk, when the armed attack on Ballymurphy occurred.

Following a Government decision taken on August 16, 1969, that "a sum of money – the amount and the channel of the disbursement of which would be determined by the Minister for Finance – should be made available from the Exchequer to provide aid for the victims of the current unrest in the Six Counties," Charles Haughey, the Minister for Finance, was authorised to fund individuals and organisations in Northern Ireland, or concerned with Northern Ireland.

I had learned through a contact in Belfast that, shortly afterwards, Mr Haughey had promised £50,000 to a three-man Belfast delegation. This promise of money from the Dublin Government was announced at a gathering of Defence Committee people in Belfast in a matter of days. It was also stated at the meeting that the money was for the purchase of arms. I informed Mr Haughey of this development. He was very annoyed that the matter of the money should be bruited around in such an indiscreet way and instructed me to inform the Central Defence Committee that money would not be forthcoming from his department until a proper and reliable finance committee was formed in Belfast. An eminently respectable committee was quickly put in place. Those operating the account and signing the cheques under the aegis of this committee were three of the more eminent men in the Northern Ireland Nationalist community. Mr Haughey was quite happy with the new arrangement and moneys from the "aid fund" were paid into a bank account in Clones, County Monaghan. This was the birth of the Belfast Fund for the Relief of Distress, which was eventually allotted £70,000 or thereabouts by the Irish Department of Finance.

On November 12, the account was moved to the Munster and Leinster Bank, Lower Baggot Street, Dublin, with the same account holders using pseudonyms. Two days later, two subsidiary accounts were opened in the fictitious names of George Dixon and Ann O'Brien. The Dixon account was to be used as an arms account, while the O'Brien account was used primarily to finance a weekly newspaper, The Voice of the North. The Distress Committee was not responsible for either of the two subsidiary accounts, but there was an inter-relation between the three accounts in that the subsidiaries were funded from the main account. This evolved from an agreement between various elements of the Defence Committees. Security was the main reason for this arrangement, as it was the reason for the use of false names – a security that was to be largely undermined by a Dáil Committee of Enquiry which opened in Dublin early in 1971 as a follow-up to the arms trials.

The £3,000 paid to Otto Schleuter came from the Dixon account. A week or two afterwards, I was formally requested to assist in the proposed Continental purchase. I agreed to help on condition that the Dublin Government approved. Accordingly, I put the proposition to Colonel Hefferon, who approached the Minister for Defence, and my understanding was that my active co-operation with the Northerners had the full and unequivocal approval of the Minister. A very pertinent point, especially in view of later events, was that Colonel Hefferon suggested that possibly a serving army officer, and especially a GHQ Intelligence Officer, should not be involved in such work and that, maybe, I should be given a job in some other branch of Government service while continuing to assist in the import operation. I appreciated the Colonel's reticence on the matter. I knew, that as Director of Intelligence, it was part of his duty to co-operate with British Intelligence on matters relating to the Cold War. Consequently, I could appreciate why he might feel, if not compromised, at least uneasy, if it emerged that one of his officers was central to an undercover operation, which, in the last analysis, was related to British occupation of part of Ireland.

He and I discussed the matter and, in the end, I filled in a form, seeking retirement on February 13, the 21st anniversary of my joining the Army. I chose that date on the grounds that some extra benefits would accrue to me after twenty-one years, but I saw it as a very tentative application, which the Colonel felt he should have when he approached the Minister. As it turned out, the Minister rejected the proposal that I retire out of hand, while accepting full responsibility for my involvement in the impending arms importation. This was not surprising as the interview between Minister and Director took place shortly before the former instructed the Defence Forces on behalf of the Government to prepare for incursions into Northern Ireland.

More money was paid to the arms dealer at the end of January, and, in mid-February, I drew the necessary money for the Defence Committee man, who was scheduled to travel to the Continent to pay the third instalment. Some days before his departure, I was told that he could not make the journey. I informed Colonel Hefferon and suggested that I should travel in his stead to find out, firstly, if arms really were available and, secondly, what exactly was going on. We discussed the question of security and decided on a cover story. I had a sister living in Frankfurt at the time and, it was agreed, that I should say I was visiting her.

The Director went to see the Minister, advising him both of the real purpose of the trip and of my cover story. The Minister gave his assent, and, to support the cover story, my wife rang an officer on the Intelligence Staff to inform him of my sister's supposed illness.

My passport was out of date, but, within hours, I obtained a new one and, on February 19, I went to the Continent with £10,000 on my person, and the name and address of my contact man in my head. As I boarded a plane at Dublin Airport, I was secure in the knowledge that the Minister for Defence was fully briefed on this, my first direct involvement in the proposed arms importation.

My contact man met me in Dusseldorf and brought me direct to Dortmund where in my presence he lodged the £10,000 in a bank, handing the receipt to me. Two days later, I met Otto Schleuter in Dortmund. He assured me that there were arms available, including pistols, bullet-proof vests and machine-guns, but I was somewhat disappointed to find that I could not inspect them. We discussed transport and prices; there was still some money outstanding; and I returned to Dublin having seen neither arms nor ammunition.

On March 3, I sat with the Minister for Defence for three or four hours in the Parliamentary Secretaries' dining-room in Leinster House, while he entertained a Northern delegation. They were looking for arms and Mr Gibbons's attitude to me and to the others was that he would do all in his power to assist them. In fact, when he got up to leave for his Kilkenny home at about ten o'clock that night, he was challenged by an older member of the delegation, a well-known Republican from Derry, who made a remark to the effect that he hoped the meeting was "not so much water under the bridge," with the clear implication that Northern Republicans had been hoodwinked by previous Fianna Fáil governments. The Minister's reaction could only be described as restrainedly aggressive. Apparently grievously insulted by this questioning of his integrity, he came back from the centre of the room where he was settling into his overcoat and, standing over the table where we were sitting, he vehemently declared that he was not that sort of man; that his word was his bond and, that what he said, he would stand over.

The delegates accepted Mr Gibbons's assurance and, in fact, some of them felt that there had been no need for one of their number to adopt such a cynical attitude to a Minister who had been so forthcoming. The incident had the effect of reinforcing the delegates' confidence that Mr Gibbons would do everything possible to meet their requests. Indeed, the delegates and I left Leinster House that night convinced that the Dublin Government, as represented by its Minister for Defence, would provide arms to the minority in the North, if the matter was up to him.

I had an appointment to meet Mr Gibbons on the following day, March 4, in his office in Leinster House. On his uncluttered desk, he had two paperbacks, biographies of Padraig Pearse and James Connolly, two of the signatories of the 1916 Proclamation, part of a series by Mercier Press in Cork. I said that I had read them and we had a short discussion on their merits. He then went on to refer to his Republican background, mentioning, in particular, an uncle of his of whom he was apparently very proud. He seemed genuinely concerned about the plight of Nationalists in the North, declaring that his greatest ambition was to see the Irish Tricolour floating over Belfast's Ulster Hall. I was reminded of my meeting with Gerry Fitt at his Belfast home some months previously, both were so vehement about their Republicanism. I briefed him about the Schleuter arms, expressing some doubt about their existence at all and informing him that I would probably have to go to the Continent again to follow up the matter.

A week later, I was in Antwerp where I met Herr Schleuter. The arms, I was told, were crated at the docks, and I was assured that they would be shipped to Dublin on March 17. In the event, The City of Dublin, the vessel on which the arms were to be transported, arrived in Dublin on March 25. That morning early, John Kelly and I were on the quayside, where we contacted the Customs Surveyor. Only forty bullet-proof vests, the importation of which was perfectly legal, had arrived. The Surveyor arranged with the shipper to have a telex message sent to Antwerp asking what had happened to the arms. Some time later we were shown or given a copy of a telex message explaining that because of a procedural technicality the arms cargo had been off-loaded at Antwerp.

The lorry to transport the goods was supplied by a Dublin Fianna Fáil man. The intention was to transport them to the yard of another Fianna Fáil man in the West of Ireland. The three Northerners, who had come down to accompany the load, were lolling at the front of the truck, when they were apparently surrounded by a section of fully-armed Irish soldiers who jumped from an army lorry that had pulled up beside them. The leader of the Northern trio, an IRA man of the fifties, had an old revolver in his possession.

"My first reaction was to pull it," he said later. "Then, I saw all the big shiny guns and all the brass buttons and I said to myself: 'F..k this, you haven't a chance'."

"What did you do?"

"I popped one of Blaney's wee white pills."

He had been on a delegation visiting the Minister for Agriculture on the previous evening and when he said, "I'm on a job in the morning," Blaney, who knew quite well what was going on, handed him four small pills that he had fumbled from his breast pocket, saying in his usual jocose manner: "One of these will calm you down if anything goes wrong".

The soldiers, moving at the double, took up position guarding The City of Dublin. I knew the Sergeant in charge. I went over to him and shook hands. "What's up?" I asked. "Some munitions for the army" he replied. It was a mere coincidence that a routine consignment of army stores should be on the ship scheduled to carry our less routine cargo.

The Northerners, with worried faces, white in the morning light, stood peeping around their truck. I went over to reassure them, telling them what had happened.

"Give us one of them f..kin' pills," one of them demanded of the leader.

A few days later, a message arrived saying that the arms would be shipped from Trieste at some future date, information which I conveyed to the Minister. Each day I grew more dubious about the whole operation and felt that I should go back to the Continent to investigate. Towards the end of March, I was told by an NCO in Intelligence that I was on twenty-four hour regimental duty at Army Headquarters on April 4. As it seemed that I would be on the Continent then, I approached the Director of Intelligence to have me excused this duty, and he, in turn, approached the Minister for Defence.

During my previous visits to the European mainland, I had come up against the language barrier and felt that I should provide my own interpreter on future visits. When I returned to Antwerp on April 1, I was accompanied by an interpreter, Albert Luykx,* a naturalised Irishman who had been introduced to me by Neil Blaney. He came with me on the clear understanding that I was on official business, which had the complete approval of the Minister for Defence.

On our flight to Brussels we were accompanied by an Irish Army Athletic Team on its way to an international meeting in Belgium and I

* *Albert Luykx had been imprisoned in Belgium for his activities as a Flemish Nationalist during World War 2. He escaped and came to Ireland in 1948. He was barred from entering Belgium.*

chatted amicably with a Commandant, whom I knew well, as we approached the immigration desk at Brussels Airport.

Albert was stopped by the immigration people; he explained exactly who he was and that he was acting as interpreter for me, an Irish army officer in Belgium on official business. While officialdom sorted out the matter, Albert and I had a beer in the airport lounge, where within a short time we were approached by a policeman, who apologised for the delay and told Albert he was free to enter Belgium.

When we arrived in Antwerp, we learned that the arms had already left en route to Trieste. Next day we went to Dortmund, intending to stay overnight before travelling to Hamburg to see Otto Schleuter. When we had settled into our hotel, I rang my wife in Dublin. Later, during dinner, I was called to the telephone. It was my wife. She told me that Colonel Hefferon had issued instructions that I should come home immediately because of the situation in the North – it was feared that serious rioting in Ballymurphy in Belfast might escalate. She further informed me that weapons were being sent to Dundalk for possible distribution in Northern Ireland and that I would have to supervise their distribution. I asked her if Mr Gibbons was still in his office. She told me that she did not know, but she knew that Neil Blaney was at home. Accordingly, I booked a call to Blaney's house.

When I got through to Mr Blaney, he told me that the situation in Belfast had improved. I, therefore, suggested that it was not necessary for me to rush back to Dublin immediately and, after some discussion, agreed with Mr Blaney that I would complete my mission on the Continent. I requested him to inform Colonel Hefferon of this decision.

When Albert Luykx and I arrived in Herr Schleuter's Hamburg office the following day, we enquired about the situation in Belfast and were told that British soldiers had been shot there. I have often wondered since if Schleuter had been pulling the long bow or if he had actually been misinformed. As it turned out, he had extra weapons available at that time. To me, the news of the deaths in conjunction with the Ballymurphy incident made it more imperative that the arms deal be brought to conclusion as quickly as possible. The arms were on their way to Trieste, but Herr Schleuter assured me that he could have them stopped at Vienna. I made arrangements there and then to charter a plane to fly the consignment to Dublin. It was at this point that Schleuter announced the availability of four hundred more machine guns. It may have been slick salesmanship on his part, but I decided to take them, telling him that I could not pay for them immediately. Neither could I pay for the charter of the plane. Mr Luykx intimated that he might be able to help and, when I assured him that he would be reimbursed when we returned to Dublin, he gave the arms dealer a cheque for £8,500. Herr Schleuter agreed that, as soon as the cheque was cleared, he would send the arms and ammunition to Dublin in a chartered plane. He set a tentative date for the flight on thc following Tuesday, April 7.

Before leaving Schleuter, Albert suggested that he should become his Irish agent and arrangements were made for Herr Schleuter to give a demonstration of anti-riot equipment and some new types of guns to the Department of Defence in Dublin on a date in early May, to be arranged by Mr Luykx. Within a week or two, Schleuter shipped two prototype weapons to Dublin Airport, which he was to collect himself on his arrival in Dublin in May. He did not come to Dublin, having been informed that Albert Luykx and I had been arrested on May 1, but his two guns became the basis of a newspaper report on May 28 that there had been a new attempt to import arms illegally. It seems that the Special Branch had seized the guns at the airport and someone had jumped to conclusions. Aer Lingus issued a statement saying that the weapons, the property of the Department of Defence, had been sent abroad for overhaul nearly a year before.

Shortly after our return to Ireland on April 4, I had a further meeting with the Minister for Defence and briefed him on the position to date. In the event, the charter fell through and Herr Schleuter's agent in Vienna, on his own initiative, decided to send the arms and ammunition on regular scheduled flights. John Kelly learned of this when he was making arrangements for the customs officials at Dublin Airport to meet the expected charter. Airline officials then became involved and they agreed to transport the weapons on routine Aer Lingus flights. International air regulations, however, prohibit the transport of ammunition on regular flights and the arrangements with Aer Lingus were cancelled. Tentative plans were then made with John Squires, Managing Director of Aer Turas, an Aer Lingus subsidiary, to bring in the total consignment by charter.

On Friday, April 17, Albert Luykx and I went to Vienna to complete arrangements there. Herr Schleuter, however, was not licensed to handle such items as sub-machine guns in Austria and only the pistols and about one-third of the ammunition were in Vienna. We made arrangements to collect the missing part of the cargo en route to Dublin. As it was Saturday, the arrangements could not be finalised until the following Monday, but, as we sat down to a meal that evening, it seemed that all our problems were sorted out and that John Squires could collect the consignment early in the following week. I booked a call to Dublin, satisfied that one aspect at least of a rather difficult mission was close to completion; but, when I eventually got through to my wife, I was given very disturbing news.

"There is something wrong," she said. "Colonel Hefferon called. No one seems to know what is going on at this end, but the Special Branch have got the wrong end of the stick. They are waiting to seize the goods and arrest you. Stay where you are and John Kelly will fly out to meet you tomorrow morning."

It was Brian Lenihan, Minister for Transport and Power, who had informed Colonel Hefferon that the airport was surrounded and the goods would be seized. He suggested that the importation should be postponed until the matter was sorted out.

Next morning, Sunday, April 19, Mr Luykx, Herr Schleuter and I were at the airport, Herr Schleuter on his way back to Hamburg and Mr Luykx on his way to Dusseldorf, where he was to complete some private business. John Kelly arrived but he could add little to what my wife had told me on the phone the previous night. We were both mystified. Neither of us could understand what was happening in Ireland. Herr Schleuter and Mr Luykx departed and John and I stayed overnight in Vienna.

Next morning, I had a call from Mr. Haughey's office instructing that the operation be called off. Immediately I rang the agent in Vienna and told him that the operation was cancelled – for the time being at least.

On Tuesday, April 21, John Kelly and I returned to Dublin, arriving on the same flight as Albert Luykx. We were obviously expected and were directed to a special desk, where an individual, with all the characteristics of a policeman, perused our passports. They conveyed no information about our travels, but it was not the usual procedure.

Next day was Budget Day in Ireland, but the Minister for Finance, Mr. Haughey, did not appear in Dáil Éireann. Instead, the country was startled to hear that he was ill in Dublin's Mater Hospital, having fallen from his horse that morning. Through the day, rumour fed on rumour and fantastic theories circulated about what had taken place. The news reports indicated that Mr. Haughey was not in a grave condition, but those close to him knew that he was much more seriously ill than had been made public.

Mr Haughey did fall off his horse, but the rumour-mongers were not to be denied, with the top echelons of the Department of Justice not immune. As the published diary of its Secretary, Peter Berry, shows, the Garda Commissioner, Berry, Minister O'Malley and the Taoiseach, Mr. Lynch himself, were exercised by the rumours well into May. On the day after the Haughey accident, Mr Berry, as published in *Magill* magazine, wrote as follows:

"The (Garda) Commissioner telephoned me to say that the Minister for Finance, Mr. Haughey, had had an accident... the Commissioner phoned me again to say that a strange rumour was circulating in North County Dublin that Mr Haughey's accident occurred on licensed premises on the previous night... I informed the Taoiseach of the rumour... He said: 'Oh no, not that, too', and he went on to agree that there should be no police enquiries: he was emphatic on that. I conveyed the Taoiseach's view to the Commissioner.

Within a couple of days there were all sorts of rumours in golf clubs, in political circles etc., as to how the accident occurred with various husbands, fathers, brothers or lovers having struck the blow in any one of dozens of pubs around Dublin. In short, the accident served a Rabelaisian purpose without anybody really believing that it was other than a fall from a horse.

One anecdote: 'Did you hear the real story: Charlie did not fall off the horse, he fell off the groom'. There was nothing much to it; the rumour was partly in affection for a public figure who was attractive to women.

But when a new Minister, Mr. O'Malley, was appointed in May he questioned me as to the rumours and I told him of the Taoiseach's view that there should be no enquiry and that I had so informed the Commissioner. The Minister said: 'I ORDER you to tell me of any information which you were given and I ORDER you to tell the Commissioner that I want to know any information that has come to the notice of the local Gardaí.' I told the Minister one of the most far-fetched yarns that had come to my ears (which no man in his senses would believe) and I conveyed what he had said to the Commissioner who replied, dryly, that if the Minister were to give him an order in writing he would consider it. That ended that."

It is a sad commentary on the operation of a major Department of State, and especially on the Minister, who on the basis of salacious rumours and the usual slick anecdotes, was ordering the collection of baseless trivia, involving a waste of Garda time, in respect of an accidental fall from a horse.

On April 23, I attended a meeting in Mr Blaney's office, at which Mr Blaney, Mr Gibbons and Colonel Hefferon were present. The two Ministers did most of the talking; both seemed to be puzzled as to why the Special Branch should have mounted the week-end operation to seize the expected arms. At one point, Mr Gibbons suggested to me that I was "in the hot seat" – the first intimation I got that he was going to deny authorising the arms importation. I reacted somewhat aggressively and the Minister for Defence referred to me as "a brazen bastard". I did not take too kindly to this, but the matter could not be clarified there and then, because both Ministers were scheduled to attend a ceremony in Rathfarnham, County Dublin, where St. Enda's, the school founded and run by Padraig Pearse, the executed 1916 leader, was being handed over to the nation.

As the Ministers rushed to their waiting cars, it was decided that the meeting should reconvene later in the day. It did not do so and I was left wondering what exactly Mr Gibbons meant by telling me I was in the hot seat.

However, after a further meeting on April 27 in Leinster House, when the Minister indicated that the arms could still be imported provided secrecy was maintained, I felt that his attitude at the earlier meeting must have been an aberration. As the meeting concluded, he told me that to maintain secrecy he was having me transferred from Intelligence to an undemanding army position in Dublin from where I could carry on my work, reporting directly to him.

I left him that night reassured that there was to be no change in the contingency plans and the related importation of arms. Next morning, my complacency was only slightly dented when I was virtually arrested by two comrades from Intelligence and placed under a definite form of restraint. Colonel Hefferon had recently retired and Mr Gibbons had assured me that his successor, Colonel Delaney, knew nothing about the arms importation. I felt, therefore, that there had simply been a breakdown in communications and made an appointment to see Mr Gibbons that evening.

Once again the meeting took place in the Minister's office in Leinster House and he immediately announced that there had been a misunderstanding between himself and the army authorities; that, not being in the picture, Colonel Delaney had obviously overreacted.

"Yes," I said, "overreacted to the extent of blocking some leave I applied for this afternoon!"

"That was probably my fault," the Minister said softly and I sat up with a jolt.

"Why?" I asked.

"Because I said that you were not to get leave."

"In the circumstances I could understand the army overreacting," I told him. "They could only assume that I am persona non grata."

He still insisted that Delaney, through ignorance of the true situation, was overreacting.

"He gave me a very definite and formal order this morning," I said. "For instance, part of it was that I should break all my Northern contacts."

"No," he came back with some vehemence, "there's no necessity for you to do that. You must keep your Northern contacts".

"What about Colonel Delaney's order, then? If I disobey it, he's perfectly entitled to court-martial me."

I could still meet my Northern contacts, the Minister insisted. He was obviously playing his cards very close to his chest. Whatever his intentions, he did not want the Northerners to know at that stage that there might be a Government about-turn on the arms.

"Will you guarantee there won't be a subsequent court-martial?" I asked. I could not get a straight answer.

I left the Minister's office that evening convinced that I was to be a pawn in a very devious game. I was certain that the Minister was changing his stated policy *vis-á-vis* the Northern situation and that he was attempting to place me in a compromising position with the army authorities; in a position where I could be court-martialled for disobeying a lawful order.

But even if I did not walk into the rather obvious court-martial trap, my position as an army officer was still virtually impossible. I was already under partial restraint and it would have been easy to hold me totally incommunicado, debarred by military law from giving my interpretation of events.

In such circumstances, it was conceivable that I could be made to support Mr Gibbons's policy switch by enforced silence, or better still from his viewpoint, by corroborating what was, inevitably, to be untruthful evidence.

Leaving Mr Gibbons's office on April 28, I knew that I had to retire and retire quickly. That night, my wife and I sat up for hours discussing the advisability of retiring. We had five children; I had been in the army all my working life... but I really had no choice, the decision was inevitable. Next morning, I applied for retirement to take effect two days later, on May 1. I was not surprised when I was called to Mr Gibbons's office that evening. He did not want to sign my retirement forms, but as he could give no good reason why he should not, I insisted that he sign and sat opposite him until he had done so.

CHAPTER 6

Twenty-one years' service – a long time, a large slice out of one's life, but, in retrospect, it did not seem so long. Still, the first day of retirement was a relief, a relief in a strange sort of way, even if the circumstances were peculiar.

A lazy breakfast, followed by a reflective sit in an easy chair. A knock at the door. The man was a stranger, tall with bushy hair; even in civilian clothes the square, solid look of a policeman. Inspector Doocey of the Special Branch and he had a warrant for my arrest.

I was arrested under the Offences Against the State Act. I had heard of it before; something de Valera had brought in to counteract the IRA in the early days of the Second World War. No specific charge need be brought and, at that stage, I was not charged with any offence, but arrest under such an Act sounded ominous – an enemy of the State.

I could bring my own car, the Inspector said, the boys were up the road. I could see them, two or three doors up along the tree-lined suburban street; two or three men in a black car. They pulled in behind me and followed closely, while I, at the wheel, and the Inspector in the passenger seat made polite conversation.

Yes, the Renault 4L was a good car, economical and still with surprising room. Yes, quite an amount of baggage could be stored behind the back seat. It suited me fine. It had only one fault as far as I was concerned. The cables, especially the clutch cable, were inclined to fray. Probably city driving, changing gears too often. Still, it was easy to have them replaced.

The Bridewell! I had heard of it often. Where exactly was it? Down behind the Four Courts. We passed Christ Church Cathedral, where Strongbow was entombed, one of the first Norman freeloaders eight hundred years ago. The Cathedral still stood firm and, as the lights changed, we eased under the arch and down the hill towards the river. On the right, desolation: a car park on cleared rough ground, where the Corporation offices now stand. The traffic policeman waved me on. Across the river, with its sulphurous smells, and the policeman on the other side gave me a clear passage also. The dome of the Four Courts green against the sky and, then, the building tall and grey on our left. Behind the building and, then, right, through the high, iron gates and we were in the Bridewell yard.

"Lock the car, it's not safe here," the Inspector said.

In the back way, through a dingy hallway and we were within an enclosed square – it could not be called a room – in the heart of the Bridewell – a heavy, iron-barred gate and cold steps running up. Two young policemen, cold but not indifferent; jailers and the place felt like a jail. At this stage, the Inspector of half-an hour's acquaintance began to seem like an old friend, if only because of the massive impersonality of the place. I was ushered into a rectangular room, two barred windows, a table and a few chairs. A man came in and sat down as the Inspector left. We were to sit looking at each other for an hour or more, talking in a desultory fashion, killing time. A uniformed jailer came in with a plate in his hand. There was a wedge of fish in the packed, mashed potatoes. It was my lunch, dinner, call it what you will. I was a prisoner in the Bridewell and I was under guard, despite the barred windows and the jailers and heavy gate outside. The hammered-down fish and spuds brought it home to me. I pushed the plate to one side.

"I'm not too hungry," I told my friendly guard.

His smile was sympathetic. A mug of tea next and a small packet of bread and butter. I ate the bread and drank the tea. A smoke and relax again – at least look relaxed.

The door opened. The big chief, a tall man, Chief Superintendent Fleming, head of the Special Branch, with the smaller Inspector Doocey at his shoulder entered. My guard nodded and left. The newcomers did not even sit down. They went into the attack from a standing position. Maybe, it gave them a psychological advantage. Maybe that was how they reasoned, but they were standing and I was sitting. I did not feel at a disadvantage. The ace up my sleeve.

"You're in a spot. A statement."

"No statement."

"We know all about it. You're up to your neck in it."

They were going well. One cutting in on the other. A well-coordinated duo. Interrogation! It must be a special skill.

"What do you know about the Garda Fallon murder?"* Doocey shot out the question.

"What the hell are you trying to suggest?" my eyes spiked the policeman's closed face.

They had gone too far. The Chief Superintendent withdrew the allegation. So did Doocey. It was time to call a halt.

Swing it across their bows. Privilege! Claim privilege.

** Garda Fallon had been shot at the Dublin Quays some weeks previously, when he confronted armed bank robbers.*

"I claim privilege."

"Nonsense. You can't be serious."… But I was.

"You're a civilian. You haven't the protection of the army behind you now."

A certain animosity there, an inter-service rivalry maybe – we've got one of the bastards where we want them… it surprised me but not too much.

"I was in the army until midnight last night. What I did, I did as a serving officer. Get the Minister for Defence down here."

"The Minister for Defence!"

"Yes, the Minister. Get him down here."

Disbelief. Insistence and a gradual dawning.

"You don't really mean… He won't come. Do you seriously think the Minister would come down here? Do you mean to say you did everything with his authority?"

"I mean to say nothing. He can talk for himself."

Doubtful, but they were gone and my guard was back. Higher authority had to be consulted. As Justice Secretary Berry reported in his diary of that date, quoted in *Magill*:

> "Captain Kelly asked to see the Minister for Defence, Mr Gibbons. Chief Superintendent Fleming informed me of the request and I conveyed it to the Taoiseach and it was arranged that Captain Kelly would be brought to Chief Superintendent Fleming's office in Dublin Castle, where he would be confronted with Mr Gibbons. I warned Mr Fleming that as Captain Kelly was in custody there could be no question of a private meeting between the two and that after Mr Gibbons had indicated to Captain Kelly that he should speak up – as he said he would, if instructed by the Minister – the Minister should be politely shown the door."

My guard and I sat twiddling our thumbs for an hour or more, before Inspector Doocey came back, alone. Friendly and smiling this time. We were going for a little drive. Across to Dublin Castle. The Minister was coming there. I was Jim now, very palsy-walsy.

"We arrested you with tact now, Jim, didn't we? You have no complaints, have you?"

"I have no complaints, Inspector."

Doocey drove and I was now in the passenger seat. Back across the river and up towards the Christ Church arch in the sunshine. Nice, pleasant, inconsequential little chat. Into the Castle yard, much of Ireland's history within its confines. Another archway and the door of the Chief Superintendent's office a dark oblong in its shadow. I was Jim to the Chief now too. The Minister was coming to see me in that very office.

A chair, make yourself comfortable. A cup of tea? Nice tea.

I had been in the office before in the time of Chief Superintendent McMahon, Mr Fleming's predecessor. Circumstances were slightly different then. I was not under arrest then, just an intelligence officer about my official duties. A group outside in the sunshine. Tourists, visiting the State apartments. I must visit there sometime. Yes, it is well worth visiting. I understand the ceilings in St. Patrick's Hall are magnificent. The Board of Works did a good job of restoration.

The Chief was on his feet.

"He's here."

The Minister's lopsided smile was boyish, yet hesitant, the sleek hair in place over the hooked nose and brown eyes. He knew me, he assured the Chief. He was sorry to see me in the present circumstances, he added, taking a seat on my left, while the Chief went back to his desk on my right.

I had refused to make a statement, the policeman explained.

The Minister thought that was a mistake. He suggested that I make a statement, a full statement. Tell everything, was his advice.

"Everything?"

"Yes, everything."

"Why?"

"Because it is now a Taoiseach's investigation, isn't that right, Superintendent Fleming?"

"That's right, Minister."

"A Taoiseach's investigation, you must do everything possible to assist him," the Minister told me.

"But you realise the implications, Minister?"

"I can understand why Captain Kelly should have reservations," he told Mr Fleming. "He has reason to have them."

"But the situation has now changed," he turned to me.

"Could I speak to you in private for a moment, Minister?"

A quick glance between the Minister and the policeman, and the policeman had the last word. I was under arrest and could have no such privilege. I could not even talk to my Minister of twenty-four hours previously.

"You're in a spot," he said, "now is your chance to get out of it."

I watched him and the flickering smile came and went. In a spot! At the meeting in Agriculture Minister Blaney's office seven or eight days previously, the Minister for Defence's grin was more cocky, but he had told me then that I was in "the hot seat". Good-humoured man-to-man stuff some might say, but it had cast its shadow of doubt.

The Minister was nervous, worried, twisting on his seat, but apparently sincere.

"Are you sure of your ground, Minister?"

He was and his advice was to tell the full story. After all, it is now a Taoiseach's investigation.

"If you put it that way, Minister, I suppose I must accept your advice."

The best all round, but doubt lingered. Time to think needed.

"Thanks very much, I appreciate your coming, Mr Gibbons." A handshake! The Minister and the policeman were shaking hands also.

"Treat Captain Kelly well, Superintendent. He was a very good and competent officer. He got caught up in the changeover of Directors of Intelligence."

Changeover! Colonel Hefferon had retired as Director three weeks previously, a normal retirement on reaching the age limit, Colonel Delaney replacing him on the following day, April 10. The Minister was muttering something about policy change. The Superintendent seemed to understand. His nod indicated as much. The Minister was in the doorway, the slanting sunshine brightening the archway behind him. Goodbye and good luck. The Minister had succeeded in his mission. It seemed as if the Taoiseach was going to get his statement, but the undertones of deceit darkened the sunshine as the door closed behind the departing Mr Gibbons. The "sneering brazen bastard" comment of a few days earlier in Blaney's office came to mind and I wondered why the Minister had not told the Taoiseach that he knew all about the matter; that he had authorised the operation. Why was I in custody? If Mr. Gibbons was playing it straight and not acting to some hidden agenda I should not have been arrested. It was Gibbons who should be making the statements.

The Chief was back behind his desk, pen and paper ready. The fire in the office grate burned steadily, the incandescent coals in its centre a swirling, fiery glow.

"Now, Jim, some background information first."

Mr Fleming was friendly and polite. I hesitated. But the Minister? Age, service particulars? Two years and two months with the United Nations in the Middle East. Yes, in Intelligence since 1960. Probably the longest serving officer there. That's right, one of the more prestigious postings. The swirling gases in the recesses of the fire burned faster and the redness was more vivid, more intense.

Chapter 6

Change of policy and I caught in between: arrested under the Offences Against the State Act: a Taoiseach's investigation. What's the Taoiseach playing at? What's the Minister playing at? The Minister knows all about it. Let him make the statement.

" How far have we got, Superintendent?"

I am a native of Bailieboro, County Cavan, where I was born on 16 October 1929. I joined the army in 1949 and was a cadet in the Military College, Curragh Camp, until 1951, when I was commissioned and took up duty as a subaltern in the 5th Infantry Battalion, based in Dublin. In 1956, I went as Training Officer to the Boyne Area, FCA, and remained there until 1960, when I was transferred to Intelligence Section, GHQ.

I have been with Military Intelligence since then, except for a period from 1963 to 1965, when I was an Observer with UNTSO in Palestine.

I returned from Palestine in 1965 and resumed my duties with Military Intelligence. After the outbreak of the trouble in Northern Ireland in August 1969 I became involved in military intelligence duties on both sides of the border.

"That's as far as we've got, Jim," the Superintendent said. "Are you ready to go on from there?"

"I acted as liaison officer *vis-á-vis* the North, with various authorities of State in the Twenty-Six Counties."

"Namely?"

"No names, that's as far as I go."

"That's no good, Jim, you must name the authorities."

"You may add a further sentence if you wish, Superintendent, something to round it off, something like I feel in conscience bound to go no further with this statement."

"It's not a statement at all and you told the Minister for Defence you would make a statement."

"I've reconsidered and I've nothing further to add."

Names, the Superintendent would settle for names: names of Cabinet Ministers.

"That's a matter for the Taoiseach and his Cabinet."

"But this is a Taoiseach's investigation."

"It's still a matter for him and his Cabinet."

"You're foolish, Jim," but I got the strong feeling that he thought I was right; that he was merely going through the motions.

"I have my reasons," I said.

Twisting the pen in his hand, eyes on what he had written, the Superintendent asked if I would talk to the Taoiseach.

"I would talk to anyone," I told him.

Peter Berry was the man in the gap again and Mr Fleming made his predictable phone call. Mr Berry recorded the contents of the call in his diary, giving himself a little pat on the back for his perspicacity in assuming that I would ask to have a private word with the Minister. One good reason why he should have made that assumption, of course, was a prior knowledge or suspicion that Mr Gibbons had more knowledge of the arms importation attempt than he was prepared to admit. Berry wrote, in *Magill*:

> "It happened as had been anticipated: Captain Kelly sought to see Mr Gibbons privately and when the Minister had instructed him to make a full statement, the Minister proceeded to settle himself comfortably to listen-in, but it was indicated to him that he should leave. The Chief Superintendent reported that there was a rapport between the Minister and the Army Officer which was very evident: he strongly suspected from all his enquiries that Mr. Gibbons had pre-knowledge of the attempts to import arms. He also reported that having begun a statement, Captain Kelly desisted, saying that he would name names if he saw the Taoiseach."

Mr Berry then noted: "I so informed the Taoiseach who agreed to see him".

CHAPTER 7

Green seemed to be the prevalent colour; green, soft and enveloping, permeated the Taoiseach's suite. The man himself, pale, powdery pale, gentle voiced and uncertain, rose from behind his corner desk. "Is this Kelly?" in a murmur to the Superintendent and it seemed strange and slightly sinister to have dropped one's rank for the first time since my arrest. He hesitated slightly before he took my automatically proffered hand.

Did I wish to speak to him in private or would I prefer to have the Superintendent present?

I did not mind, I told him.

The Taoiseach had ordered the investigation and consequent decisions were his also. But I was under arrest and the Taoiseach seemed in some doubt as to the propriety of speaking to me alone in such circumstances. But was it doubt or was it gamesmanship? He checked with the Superintendent. Mr Fleming might know if he, the Taoiseach, was permitted to speak to me in private? The Superintendent demurred. What did I think? The Taoiseach deferred to me again. "It's your privilege, Taoiseach." The Superintendent departed. The Taoiseach had his secretary standing by.

If I was making a statement, there was a witness needed, he said.

"But I'm not making a statement, Taoiseach."

Impatience edged his voice: he was a busy man, he had a lot of important work to do. It was I who had taken the initiative in seeking an interview with him and the implication was that I would make a statement if he agreed to see me.

"No, I'm sorry, Taoiseach, I don't agree. When the suggestion was put to me that I talk to you, I agreed to do so, nothing more, there was no question of a formal statement."

The Taoiseach did not accept that. It was scarcely worth arguing about, I thought.

The circumstances under which I came here are not really important, I suggested to the Taoiseach. After all, he was the Taoiseach and there was no point in arguing about a triviality. It was a mistake. Trivialities can matter. The point conceded for the sake of peace would be used against me – used in Dáil Éireann.

My decision not to make a statement had crystallised and set as I probed the depths of the glowing coals in the Superintendent's office.

Uncertainty was eliminated then and the decision made before Mr Fleming casually dropped his suggestion that I might talk to the Taoiseach. No statement – Mr Lynch accepted the inevitable, but he still wanted information. It was not his function to act as an investigator or a policeman, he told me, but he was going to ask me some questions. He had experience as a barrister on circuit, a trained interrogator, but would his questions be answered?

That depended on the questions.

"You won't answer pertinent questions?"

"No, it's out of my sphere, it's a question for the Cabinet, a matter between you and your Cabinet colleagues."

"Yes... well now... memory, memory is a funny thing. One does not remember everything one hears. A lot goes in one ear and out the other. One only remembers what is relevant, what applies to a particular situation, what is necessary to achieve a particular objective."

A pause.

"I understand perfectly, Taoiseach."

A deadlock it seemed. But not quite.

A serious situation with international implications, the Taoiseach suggested.

I did not get his point.

"Too many people know about it, Departments of State, various individual functionaries, it cannot be swept under the carpet," he said.

"Possibly not but..."

"Members of the Cabinet involved?" he queried softly.

"Possibly."

"Two members?"

"Yes, possibly."

"Names?"

"No, it's not my business to name people in this situation."

He knew them anyhow, the Taoiseach indicated.

Then, why are you quizzing me? Why do you want me to finger them? What game are you playing? You know all about it since the Bailieboro meeting. Do your own dirty work, Taoiseach. That is what I felt like saying, but I held back.

"Then I think you should approach them yourself, Taoiseach," I said quietly.

"But I have approached them, they won't talk to me."

"I'm sorry, Taoiseach, I'm afraid I can't help but... but maybe I can. Why not stop this farce, this farce of my arrest and let me go? I could talk to some people, maybe something could be worked out even at this stage."

"Have you that much influence?"

"I don't know, but it's worth a try."

"But... but they wouldn't talk to me. Have you any reason, any reason to think that you will succeed?"

"No, no great reason, but it is the only possible way I can see out of the present impasse."

Not acceptable.

I did not know at that time that Mr Lynch had held a Government meeting before coming to question me, where he had told his Cabinet colleagues that the matter of the arms was swept under the carpet; that he accepted the denials of Haughey and Blaney that they were engaged in an illegal attempt to import arms.

Kevin Boland takes up the story in *Up Dev*:

> "After the Government meeting, I said to Blaney, 'I think I should go to the Mater and set Haughey's mind at rest'. Blaney said, 'No, I don't trust him'. I replied, 'He has told the Government that the matter is over and done with. Surely, he's not going to go back on that?' I, accordingly, went straight to the Mater Hospital and told Haughey what had transpired, but Blaney was right. While he was telling his Government the matter was finished, Captain Kelly, who unknown to the rest of us had been arrested that morning, was waiting in his office to be questioned by him – the Taoiseach – personally. So far from the matter being over, he assumed command of the investigation and was playing the role of District Attorney."

Back at the Taoiseach's office, the Taoiseach suggested that if I was let go free, I might leave the country. I could go anywhere. Cross the border, maybe?

Ridiculous! Is the man mad? Firstly, I have nothing to run from and, anyhow, I have a wife and five children. Nine months constant work for my country, weekends away from home, finish at midnight, one o'clock or three o'clock in the morning, awkward situations, disbelief in the sincerity of the Dublin Government, disbelief and doubt finally culminating in trust, a modicum of trust at least. Trouble, even shooting avoided on occasions, because the Northerners believed that, in the last analysis, the South would come to the rescue. No weekend trips for the children or visits to the supermarket for my wife. You bought a car, daddy, and you never let us ride in it, and now you, the Taoiseach, have the effrontery to suggest that I might leave the country, run like a rat. No, Taoiseach, but if that's how you see it, that's it."

"Names?"

"But you must understand, Taoiseach, I was only at the practical end and there is... there is another end."

"The policy end," Mr Lynch filled in. "Names of Ministers? One of them is sick," he suggested, "the other one, is he near here, could you get to him easily?"

"Yes, I don't see any problem. If I'm allowed to go free I could talk to various people."

There was no question of that, however. I might run away.

Not talking really, but thinking out loud, the Taoiseach was murmuring something about violence. Uncertainty seemed to be dominant.

How to avoid violence? Isn't that what everyone is working for? With some success too, but that doesn't invalidate contingency plans, the plans of the Government of which he is head. Delegations, deputations, if you accept the trust of suppliants, you take on obligations. What about all the intelligence reports presented to the Minister for Defence, verbal and otherwise? Is all the effort wasted? Was the order to the army by his Government to prepare for intervention in Northern Ireland all so much eyewash? Why does he not get his Cabinet together and thrash the matter out? The avoidance of violence does not mean being unprepared for eventualities.

The Taoiseach was back from his reverie, back to the cat and mouse game.

Tell. Tell what? Inform on the Government, which he runs? Inform on Jim Gibbons, Minister for Defence, the man to whom I was ultimately responsible until midnight on the day before? Why arrest me? Why not arrest Gibbons?

"No, Taoiseach, there's a more correct way of solving this problem. It's a Cabinet matter."

"Yes, but if I bring a man here will you talk to him? Talk to him in my presence?"

"Certainly, Taoiseach."

"I can get him here in a few minutes."

"But, Taoiseach, I'm not going to act as accuser."

That was not acceptable. It was still turn informer.

Would I talk to the man on the phone, the Taoiseach asked.

"Yes, but I must ring him privately."

That was not acceptable either. I guessed that the man was Blaney. This turned out to be true.

"Listen, Taoiseach, the position is simply this. As I see it, it's a matter to be sorted out between you and your colleagues in Cabinet. That's the level at which this affair should be handled and, anyway, I'm not going to be a stool-pigeon for you or anyone else. I am not going to be a stool-pigeon, Taoiseach," I reiterated, my forefinger tapping the table in an emphatic reflex.

Chapter 7

There was a visitor waiting to see the Taoiseach. He had a word with the Chief Superintendent who took a seat with me in the outer sanctum. Fifteen minutes or so later, the Taoiseach was back. The Superintendent left. No, the Superintendent and I had discussed nothing relevant. We just had a casual chat.

"I can't help but admire you, but..." the Taoiseach looked down at his fingertips on the edge of the table, then straightening up: "There's no point in carrying this any further?" A question, not a statement.

"No point, Taoiseach. I'm sorry, but that's the position."

Mr Fleming was back. The Taoiseach and he discussed the technicalities of my arrest. The Superintendent could hold me for twenty-four hours and for another twenty-four hours if necessary. This seemed to satisfy the Taoiseach. I might leave the country, skip the jurisdiction – he put his invidious suggestion to the Superintendent. He put the idea to me; a great man for consensus, the Taoiseach.

"You're right in theory, Taoiseach."

The cynicism may have been lost, but possibly not. Anyhow, it was take me back and hold me.

Merrion Street was deserted with all the office workers gone home when the Superintendent and I got outside, and we drove back to the Bridewell along comparatively deserted streets. I was handed over to a jailer – a man agog with disconcerting curiosity. What was I in for? The suggestion was soon clear. He believed I was in for the Garda Fallon murder. I could be arrested for nothing else under the notorious Offences Against the State Act. Such was his reasoning. I convinced him to the contrary. I felt it was necessary to reassure him, or I might have a rough time. He didn't really understand, an army officer until the day before, but he would get me a better cell. The better cells were aliens' cells, my jailer informed me.

In the new cell the walls were freshly painted, but the chug-chug toilet bowl in the corner and the iron bed – the only furnishings – were much the same, with the bedclothes equally filthy. There was nothing for it but to get into bed. Pick a clean place on the floor to put my clothes on and squeeze in between the dirty sheets. There was someone at the spy hole, It was the night man. The Superintendent had promised a meal on arrival back at the Bridewell, but it had not materialised. The night man, a decent man, promised me a cup of tea. It came, milky, but welcome. I turned over to go to sleep. "In a lonely Brixton prison, a hunger-striker lay," the brain blank, but the words went on whirling interminably, just the first line over and over again.

The cell door was open. I had fallen asleep. Chief Superintendent

Fleming would like to see me downstairs. I got dressed and went out into the passageway. A quick dash of cold water in the grimy sink in the corner of the passage, a run of wet fingers through my hair and I went down to the interrogation room. It was midnight at the end of a long day. Fleming and Doocey were there.

"We brought in Luykx," the Superintendent said. "He made a comprehensive statement."

"I hope you did not hold Mr Luykx. He's only incidentally involved in this," I said.

"No, he's gone home and if you make a statement you can go home too – we can all go home."

"I'm making no statement."

"Now, Jim, we got it all from Luykx, he made a very full statement, what's the point?"

"There's no need for to tell you anything then. Anyhow, you know my position. There are people more entitled than me to speak. Maybe that's not the correct phraseology, but you know what I mean."

Inspector Doocey seemed to know what I meant.

"You're right, there are people more entitled than you to talk, but save yourself."

Save yourself, that was the catch-cry. Save yourself, give us a statement, get off the hook, get us off the hook.

"There is no point in carrying this any further," I told them.

There was something peculiar going on and I was not talking until I had some idea of what it was. In the meantime, could I ring my wife? She probably did not even know where I was.

"She knows: wasn't she there when you were arrested?" the Chief showed his teeth in either a leer or a smile.

Nice fellows, not even a phone call permitted, not even a call to a woman waiting at home, waiting over twelve hours and midnight approaching, if not gone. I turned to go back to my cell. The Chief made a big concession. They would phone my wife, he assured me, and this consideration was appreciated. A friendly policeman doing his job, a mere functionary of the State with the solid ground imperceptibly slipping since the arrogant noon interrogation in the same room only twelve hours before. I was happy enough as I went back to the dirty sheets and the lavatory that went glug-glug of its own volition.

Next morning I had breakfast in bed, a wee parcel of dry bread and a mug of bad tea. Warm and comfortable, turn over and go to sleep again. What was going to happen next? There was not much choice in the matter. Might as well stay put, relaxing in the womb of the bed. Dozing, waking, dozing, in the euphoria of half-sleep, I heard the jailer enter my cell. I was required downstairs. A car was waiting and I was off for another drive across the river, to the office of Chief Superintendent Fleming again. It was another attempt, half-hearted this time, to obtain a statement. No response, it was becoming monotonous.

"You are probably right not to make a statement," the Superintendent took me by surprise.

Anyhow, he knew who was involved, so he said, and named three Ministers, Haughey, Blaney and Gibbons. He was not too happy about the Taoiseach either. How did I feel about him, he asked.

"What do you mean, Chief?"

"What do you think, did he know all along?"

"I don't know, but in view of my arrest it would seem as if he didn't unless...Well, he certainly knew about the Bailieboro meeting and..."

"I believe he knew," Fleming cut in.

"Then it's time you let me go," I suggested.

That seemed to be Mr. Fleming's idea also, but he wanted my word of honour that I would not leave the country without first consulting him.

I told him that I had no intention of doing so.

"Going North, are you serious, Superintendent? There is just one further point, Superintendent, this matter may be cleared up shortly and I don't think I should break my Northern contacts in the meantime."

The Superintendent seemed to agree, but he was not his own master. He made the predictable phone call. To whom? It was the Taoiseach's investigation, but perhaps the ubiquitous Peter Berry felt empowered to take the momentous decision, although if he ran true to form he probably had a word in the Taoiseach's ear. Whoever made the decision, the word came back. There was no reason why I should not meet my Northern friends: friends of the Government too until a day or too previously. It seemed, however, that, as Gibbons had indicated four days earlier, the authorities in general did not want the Northerners to know that there might be a breakdown on the arms issue. It seemed that the Taoiseach, playing the role of District Attorney, was still waiting to see which way the ball would hop. My arrest! How to explain that? Well, he was released, wasn't he?

I went home to Terenure and the house was a haven of welcome, with exuberant wife and family, well-wishers and friends. No, it wasn't so bad, the Special Branch men were kind enough, just ordinary fellows doing a job. No, I wasn't allowed to make any phone-calls; it seemed one had no rights under the Offences Against the State Act. It was a bad Act. Innocent until proven guilty was a misconception. Assumption of guilt was axiomatic. At least the initial attitude of the police would indicate as much, although there was a notable change when the Minister put in his appearance. What about the poor unfortunate with no Minister to call upon? There was no need to emphasise it, but I was glad to see Gibbons.

"But he didn't go down himself, Jim, he was sent," my wife said quietly.

"Who?"

"Gibbons."

"What?"

"Gibbons, he didn't want to go down, he tried to duck out of it, but the Taoiseach ordered him down."

So Jack Lynch saved the day.

"Maybe he and Gibbons have got together and sorted it out," my wife suggested.

"But Fleming intimated that Lynch know about it all along, and that's what I think too."

"What are you going to do, Jim?"

"I don't know. Today is Saturday. I'll go down to see my solicitor on Monday. We might as well relax for the weekend."

Joe Deane, a solicitor, had called to the Bridewell on the night of my arrest. In the event of my non-release on the following day, Mr Deane was to take whatever legal action was possible. It was Monday evening when I eventually got down to his office. His office had been broken into over the weekend, he told me, but it was no ordinary burglary. Only the files had been disturbed and, in particular, one relating to a Captain James Kelly, a seaman. Nothing taken, however. Obviously, Fleming's men had been out and about over the weekend, and not too worried about the legality of their operations, it seemed. The target was any file that Joe Deane might have opened on me. So much for police respect for confidentiality between solicitor and client.

It was only later I learned from Joe of the run-around he had been given on that night by the Gardaí. On calling at the Bridewell, he was told that the permission of the Special Branch was required before he could see me. He went to the Special Branch, who demanded formal identification before they would entertain this request. He had to go back to his office to get the necessary documentation before going back through the obviously obstructive Garda circuit merely to interview his client. "And then," said Joe, "after all that, this casual person appears on the scene and tells me not to worry, it'll all blow over in a day or two".

CHAPTER 8

I woke in the early hours of May 6, 1970 to the insistent ringing of the telephone in the hall downstairs. It was 3.15 am and I was still half-asleep when I lifted the phone, but the caller soon shook me wide awake.

"Did you hear the news?" he asked, "Lynch has sacked Blaney and Haughey, and Boland has resigned."

I had been expecting something of the sort, but it was still sensational news. A fourth senior Minister, Michael Ó Moráin, Minister for Justice, had resigned – officially on health grounds – two nights before. The Cabinet had lost four of its most able Ministers in the space of three days.

The timing of the official announcement was unusual to say the least. It was made at 3 am, in a statement by the Taoiseach.

"I have requested the resignation of members of the Government, Mr Neil T Blaney, Minister for Agriculture and Fisheries, and Mr C J Haughey, Minister for Finance, because I am satisfied that they do not subscribe fully to Government policy in relation to the present situation in the Six Counties as stated by me at the Fianna Fáil Ard Fheis* in January last. Mr Caoimhin Ó Beolain, Minister for Local Government and Social Welfare, has tendered his resignation as a member of the Government and I propose to advise the President to accept it."

The country buzzed with rumour: the Government was about to fall, the Taoiseach had discovered an attempted *coup d'état*; the sacked Ministers had been working with the IRA. Speculation fed on earlier events: did Charlie Haughey really fall off his horse on Budget Day, or had something more sinister happened? Had Ó Moráin really been sacked and were the health grounds merely an excuse? Leinster House, the focus of all eyes on that May morning, was alive with speculation. Mr Lynch was the man with the answers, but his first action when the Dáil met was to request the adjournment of the House in order that meetings of the Government and the Fianna Fáil deputies might be held. Mr Lynch's proposal was accepted and it was agreed that the Dáil would sit at ten o'clock that night.

The day of crisis was also, ironically enough, a day for the honouring of dead heroes. The 1916 commemoration ceremonies at Arbour Hill were held that afternoon, and a newspaper photograph the following day showed Mr Lynch, the Taoiseach, leading his Ministers to the gravesides

* *National Convention*

Paudge Brennan

of the executed leaders. Kevin Boland, now recognised as the conscience of Fianna Fáil, was also in the photograph, grim-faced, but no more so than his former Cabinet colleagues. His resignation, he had stated the night before, was in protest against the method of government and, in particular, the method of dismissal of the two Ministers. Another resignation had occurred by this time: Paudge Brennan, Parliamentary Secretary to the Minister for Local Government, a Wicklow Republican who had been heard to declare that the Fianna Fáil party was to him a second religion. Mr. Brennan, like Mr Boland, had not been asked; nor had his arm been twisted; nor had he been otherwise coerced into resigning. Both resigned on principle.

Four Ministers and one Parliamentary Secretary gone – I wondered why Mr Gibbons was still in office. To me, it was inconceivable that the Taoiseach was not aware of the central part played by Mr Gibbons, as the statutory authority, in the arms importation. If the Taoiseach did not agree with his actions, there was a obvious step to take: cancel the operation. Blaney and Haughey had been dismissed, however. It seemed that the Taoiseach was going to deny that the arms importation was backed by Government policy. Would Mr Gibbons deny his part in the affair? On the morning of May 6, I did not believe that he could, but if he did not, how could the Taoiseach claim that the importation was unauthorised? Were Lynch and Gibbons conspiring together to deny knowledge of the attempted importation, in which they were both involved, as indicated by Chief Superintendent Fleming? Was the Department of Justice in on the conspiracy, with its Secretary, Peter Berry, having been informed by Fleming of his suspicions about Gibbons? It was a morning of uncertainty for me, but, like everyone else, I had to wait until the Dáil assembled to possibly get some clarification.

Soon after the House met that night, the Taoiseach proposed the nomination of Mr Desmond O'Malley as Minister for Justice to take the place of Mr Ó Moráin. Referring to the dismissed Ministers, he said: "On Monday, April 20 and Tuesday, April 21, the security forces at my disposal brought me information about an alleged attempt to unlawfully import arms from the Continent. *Prima facie*, these reports involved two members of the Government. I decided to interview the two members of the Government – Deputy Blaney and Deputy Haughey. In the meantime I ensured that adequate steps were taken to prevent any unauthorised importation of arms."

Why the Taoiseach should have taken the action he did was difficult to understand. Was he misinformed or uninformed? It was interesting that when he was speaking of the security forces of the country he should qualify the reference with the words at my disposal. Was he aware that he was not using all the security information that was available. Was he being selective for his own purposes? Did Chief Superintendent Fleming not inform him about his suspicions of Mr Gibbons?

The Taoiseach continued:

> "On April 22, the day I decided to interview the former Ministers I received news of the accident to Deputy Haughey and as a result I was unable to interview him... I ultimately got the doctor's permission and I decided to interview Deputy Haughey in hospital on Wednesday, April 29... I then summoned Deputy Blaney to my room and interviewed him upon which I went to the hospital and interviewed Deputy Haughey ... Each of them denied he instigated in any way the attempted importation of arms. They asked me for time to consider their position. I agreed to do so. In the meantime I authorised the continuation of investigations and I made personal investigations myself, following which I decided to approach the two Ministers again and to repeat my request that they tender to me their resignations as members of the Government. I did so on the basis that I was convinced that not even the slightest suspicion should attach to any member of the Government in a matter of this nature... I may say that on the question of suspicion, Deputy Cosgrave came to me yesterday evening to say that he had some information from an anonymous source connecting the two Ministers concerned with this alleged attempt at unlawful importation."

The leader of the Opposition Fine Gael party, Mr Liam Cosgrave, spoke after Mr Lynch:

> "Last night at approximately 8 pm, I considered it my duty in the national interest to inform the Taoiseach of information I had received and which indicates a situation of such gravity for the nation that it is without parallel in this country since the foundation

of the State… I received information that an attempt had been made involving a number of members of the Government illegally to import a large consignment of arms from the Continent for use by an illegal organisation. Arrangements were made under the pretext that this consignment was coming as an official supply of arms to the Army, and that involved making arrangements with the Department of Finance for allowing this consignment through the customs without check at Dublin Airport. My information was that the arrangements involved an army officer. The affair came to the notice of the Garda authorities and the Garda officer in charge, a senior Garda officer, informed the Commissioner who sought a directive from the Department of Justice in view of a suggestion from an official in the Department of Finance that the Minister for Finance had authorised the passage through the customs of this illegal consignment.

When advice was sought by the Garda, no directive was given and when it appeared to the Garda that the situation was not being handled with proper seriousness, a further request for a directive from the Minister for Justice was made. At this stage the matter was notified to the Taoiseach and, eventually, after a lot of dithering, the authority from the Department of Finance was dropped. I understand that because of the linking up of certain Ministers, an Army officer, the brothers of two Ministers, one the brother of the former Minister for Finance and the other the brother of the former Minister for Agriculture and Fisheries, and some of their friends, with these highly dangerous and illegal activities, the question of dismissing the Ministers from the Government arose. No action, however, was taken until the resignation of the Minister for Justice on Monday last. Yesterday, when I received a copy of a document on official Garda note paper which supported the information already at my disposal and which also included some additional names, I decided to put the facts in my possession before the Taoiseach. This particular document says: A plot to bring in arms from the Continent worth £80,000 under the guise of the Department of Defence has been discovered. Those involved are a Captain Kelly, the former Minister for Finance, the Former Minister for Agriculture and two associates of the Ministers."

This was deception on a grand scale; deception by the Taoiseach and the leader of the Opposition with the apparent aim of permitting the Taoiseach to mount charges of illegal importation of arms against various individuals on a wholly false premise. The document on *official Garda notepaper* was real enough, but when Mr Cosgrave told Dáil Éireann, *this particular document says*, he went on to mislead the parliament of his country as the leader of the Opposition, by not naming the Minister for Defence, James Gibbons, whose name was included on the document in his possession as one of those involved in the importation.

Mr. Cosgrave was fully aware that Mr Gibbons was the statutory authority for the importation of the arms and the only conclusion one can come to is that he colluded with Mr Lynch in misleading the Dáil. This treachery by the two men was exposed two days later, again in Dáil Éireann, when Deputy Richie Ryan, a senior colleague of Mr Cosgrave in Fine Gael, the opposition party, announced to the House in relation to the Cosgrave document: "Deputy Gibbons' name was mentioned". To which Mr George Colley, the Minister for Industry and Commerce, replied: "Deputy Ryan's name might be mentioned in connection with something but that would not necessarily mean that Deputy Ryan was involved."

Deputy Ryan: "He (the Taoiseach) did not know, but he knows now, that Deputy Cosgrave and a Dublin newspaper received Garda Síochána notepaper with the name of Deputy Gibbons on it, associating him with this sordid transaction."
Minister Gibbons: "An anonymous note."

Neither Colley nor Gibbons, both members of Lynch's Government, denied the existence of the note, but, by their comments, supported Ryan's assertion.

Others, who knew the contents of the note were senior members of the Fine Gael party. As Stephen Collins described it in his book, *The Cosgrave Legacy*:

> "He (Cosgrave) decided to consult a few of his colleagues... Those present were Tom O'Higgins, Michael O'Higgins, Mark Clinton, Denis Jones and Jim Dooge.
>
> Cosgrave told his colleagues there was something important he wanted to tell them. He said he had received a tip-off about a plot to import arms.
>
> 'I want your advice, what should I do? Is this a plant? Is someone trying to plant this on me to make me go over the top?' he asked his colleagues.
>
> 'We (sic) argued first of all as to whether he could take it as being something he could bet on, because he feared the danger of just

being hoist on a petard. And we came to the conclusion that yeh, on balance, we had to act.' Having agreed to this, Cosgrave said he had a second question about the form of the action he should take. 'What do I do? Do I bring it up in the Dáil? Do I go to the newspapers? Do I go to the Taoiseach?' he asked.

Mark Clinton was the first one who spoke and he said: 'I think this is of such national importance, the only thing is to go to the Taoiseach, and to go to him tonight.' The others present agreed."

Two years or so later, at a debate in Trinity College, Dublin, Deputy Garret Fitzgerald, later successor to Mr Cosgrave as leader of Fine Gael and as Taoiseach, when asked by me, confirmed that Mr Gibbons' name had been on the note, from which Cosgrave purportedly quoted. In the meantime, I had obtained two copies of the note, one some months after the Dáil debate and, the second in response to a statement I issued on March 6 1971, which *The Sunday Press* headlined as CHALLENGE BY CAPTAIN KELLY TO COSGRAVE. In the statement I suggested that Mr Cosgrave should make clear whether or not Mr Gibbons name appeared on the document and that he should disclose the source of the document. The suggestion was ignored and I repeated my public challenge to Mr Cosgrave on March 19. There was still no reaction from the Cosgrave camp, but, on March 22, a heavily-sealed envelope arrived for me in the post. It contained a photostat copy of the document, which was identical to the copy I had already received from a friendly political source. It read as follows:

"A plot to bring in arms from Germany worth £80,000 for the North under the guise of the Dept. of Defence has been discovered. Those involved are – Captain James Kelly, I.O., Col. Hefferon X Director of Intelligence (both held over the weekend in the Bridewell) Gibbons, Haughey and Blaney, and the Jones Brothers of Rathmines Road and Rosapena Hotel, Donegal. See that this scandal is not hushed up.

GARDA"

It will be noted that, except for the words, "for the North," Mr Cosgrave in his statement to the Dáil on May 6 1970 used the exact phrasing reproduced in the first sentence above.

Who leaked the document to Cosgrave? Most people believed it came from former Chief Superintendent Phil McMahon whom John Fleming had replaced as head of the Special Branch and who had been retained on

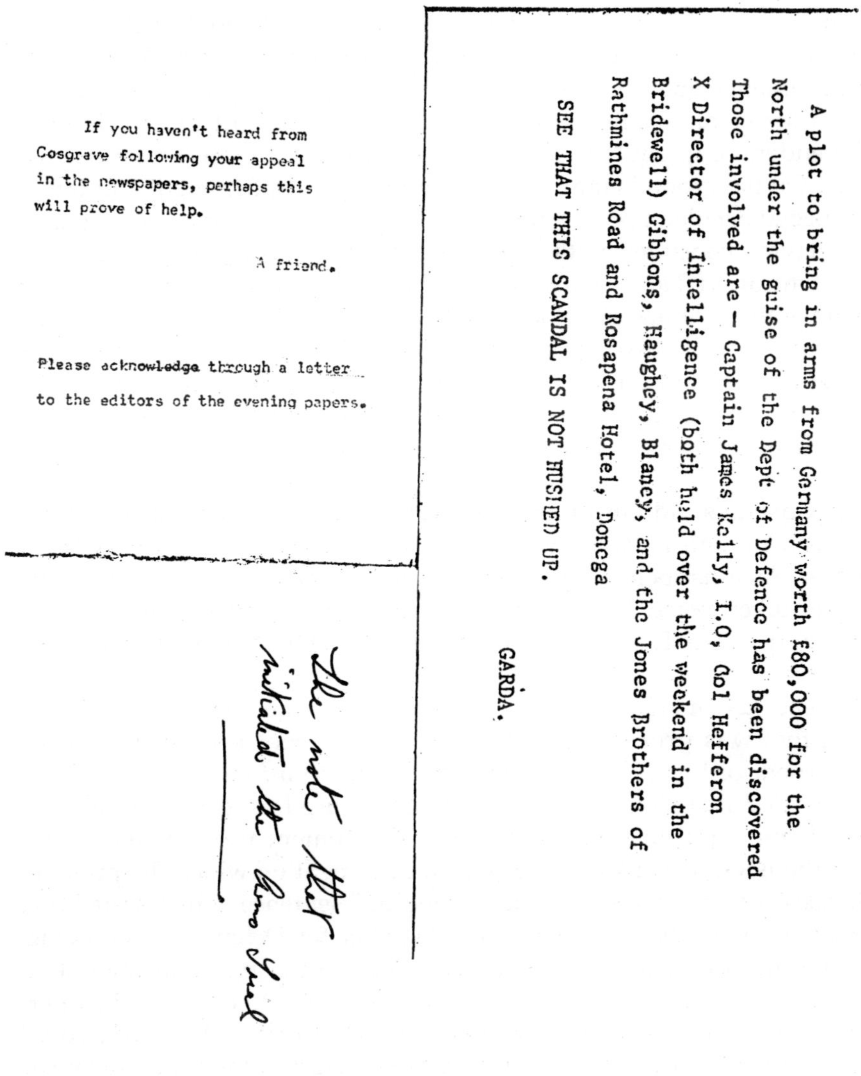

If you haven't heard from Cosgrave following your appeal in the newspapers, perhaps this will prove of help.

A friend.

Please acknowledge through a letter to the editors of the evening papers.

A plot to bring in arms from Germany worth £80,000 for the North under the guise of the Dept of Defence has been discovered Those involved are – Captain James Kelly, I.O, Col Hefferon X Director of Intelligence (both held over the weekend in the Bridewell) Gibbons, Haughey, Blaney, and the Jones Brothers of Rathmines Road and Rosapena Hotel, Donega

SEE THAT THIS SCANDAL IS NOT HUSHED UP.

GARDA.

The note that initiated the Arms Trial

Copy of original Garda document given to Mr Cosgrave

the Government payroll as a security consultant and advisor. Because of what Fleming has told me about the involvement of Haughey, Blaney and Gibbons in the arms operation, I suspected him initially, but knowing from my intelligence work that Cosgrave and McMahon were close friends, I concluded it was McMahon. Not that it really mattered which of them handed over the document, for they worked in unison. Either way, the document came from the same stable. It seems Cosgrave showed it to an old army man who was political correspondent of the Sunday Independent, Captain Ned Murphy, who brought it to his editor, Hector Legge. On the grounds that there was no way of confirming the information, Legge decided not to run with it. It found its way back to Cosgrave, who, having consulted with trusted members of his party, brought it to the attention of Taoiseach Lynch. What went on between Lynch and Cosgrave that evening is not known, but it is certain that they rejected the information of the two top security men in the country, the head of the Special Branch and the Government's own special security expert, Phil McMahon, and, contrary to the information available to Mr Berry in the Department of Justice, agreed to remove Gibbons from the arms equation.

Mr Cosgrave did not bring up Colonel Hefferon's name in Dáil Éireann even though he was mentioned on the document as one of those arrested. As it happened, the planned arrest of the Colonel by the Gardaí had not taken place, because of a change of plan at the highest level – after all, it was a Taoiseach's investigation, as Mr Gibbons had emphasised.

Instead, as emerged later, a statement was taken from the Colonel. When this was processed by the Gardaí and sent up the line in the Department of Justice, it was gone through with a fine comb. Finally, it was decided that Colonel Hefferon could be used as a prosecution witness, if the penultimate sentence in his statement was deleted. Thus, when the Book of Evidence, the official document on which the prosecution based its case, appeared, the "offending" sentence, which stated that I had acted with the authority of the Minister for Defence, was missing. The significance of this was that if I, as the central figure at the operational end of the proposed importation, was shown to be acting in a perfectly legal manner as Colonel Hefferon in effect deposed, nobody could be charged with attempting to import arms illegally. Instead, a case was fabricated by tampering with the evidence of the Director of Intelligence and producing a false and doctored Book of Evidence as the kernel of the prosecution case.

Whether unwittingly or not, Mr Cosgrave was party to the

Government plot by concealing the names of Mr Gibbons and Colonel Hefferon, two of the chief security figures in the State.

Next day, in Dáil Éireann, Mr Cosgrave continued in his best self-righteous manner, asserting that in this case not only was the security of this State involved but also that those drawing public money to serve the nation were attempting to undermine it.

> "The lives of the people not only in the greatest part of Ireland for which freedom was won at such great price have been put in peril... But, even worse than that, the people, particularly the minority about whom we are so concerned in the Six Counties, have their lives and their welfare put in jeopardy... So far as this situation is concerned these are criminal activities... This is the situation that those whom we commemorated at Arbour Hill today could never have visualised would have happened. I am privileged to speak from a family tradition that as far back as '98 gave lives in defence of the rights of the Irish people to govern themselves. This party asserted and defended and vindicated the people's rights to ensure that this sovereign authority and it alone would act and work and discharge its responsibility ...:

It was a bit difficult, if not indeed nauseating, to listen to this moralistic tub-thumping from a man who had just betrayed the integrity of the very nation and State of which he was so rightly proud, of which we were all proud, of which many of us had family traditions of serving back as far as '98 also. I was quietly proud of my twenty-one years army service, as I was quietly proud of my nine months service in relation to Northern Ireland, which Mr Cosgrave – a man incidentally, whom I had admired as a person of honesty and integrity – was setting at naught by misleading Dáil Éireann on the contents of the note which he allegedly quoted.

Mr Cosgrave's performance gives rise to the following questions:

Did he know that truth, honesty and integrity are the very bedrock on which democracy is based? ... Of course he did!

Did he not know that it was beneath contempt to drag the name of a loyal army officer into the public arena, designating him a criminal, while concealing the name of the person, who, under statute, was the authorising person for the operation in question and who was named on the same "police" document? ... Of course he did!

Did he not consider it a gross abuse of the privilege of the House to act in this manner? ... If he did not, he should have!

Did he not consider it grievously wrong to connive with a ruthless

Taoiseach in this manner to help promote a false trial? ... If he did not, he should have!

Did he not consider it his duty, at some time in the last thirty years, to apologise to the defendants, including the late Albert Luykx, whose reputation and freedom he wrongly put at risk? ...If not, he should reconsider!

Did he not owe an apology to the memory of Colonel Hefferon, with over forty years of unblemished and distinguished service in the army, whose character was assailed by the Lynch regime because he dared to tell the truth as a prosecution witness in the trials which Mr. Cosgrave helped to initiate by his false Dáil presentation? ... He did!

Did he not owe an apology to the families of those he wronged? ... He did!

On the same day that Richie Ryan exposed Mr Cosgrave as concealing Mr Gibbons' name, on the occasion of the appointment of three new ministers to replace Boland, Haughey and Blaney, Mr Cosgrave was his usual self-righteous self, even congratulating himself for his deception in colluding with Mr Lynch:

"It was not until I presented the situation as I knew it that the Taoiseach and those of his ministers who were left with him knew that the game was up and they could no longer conceal the true facts of the situation from the people" – this from the man who had helped to have a false representation of the facts in his possession put on the Dáil record.

He went on:

> "For the second time in the past half-century, in our long and chequered history, this country and our people may thank God that they have this party to maintain and defend and assert the people's rights. Only for this party there would be a real danger of civil war, civil war of the worst kind, of a religious character. This Taoiseach and this government must now resign and dissolve this Dáil and let the people elect a government in whom they can have confidence and who will guarantee their lives and liberties, their homes and hearths and show to the world that this country, this State established by Griffith and Collins, is fit to, and will, govern itself."

In the context of his misleading the Dáil two days previously, the rhetoric sounded somewhat hypocritical.

CHAPTER 9

It was nearly three o'clock on the morning of May 7 when the previous day's Dáil debate ended.

"Scuffles broke out in the lobbies while the Deputies were going through," *The Irish Independent* reported later that day. "In the crowded lobbies it was not clear who was directly involved, but some Deputies had to restrain others. Two pictures on the wall were knocked out of position before the Superintendent of the House arrived... Extra Gardaí were drafted in to deal with the hundreds of spectators outside of Leinster House. Many of the crowd had travelled specially from the Six Counties and a number of young people, realising that they had no chance of getting in without tickets, were huddled around transistor radios in an effort to keep up with the historic debate."

John Kelly stayed at my home that night, and, as a Northern Republican, he was particularly sad and disillusioned. Like the Leinster House people, he and I stayed up until after three o'clock in the morning, and our discussion was long and soul-searching. We went right through from Mr Lynch's "not stand by" speech of the previous August 13 to his reception of Northern Ireland delegations in the earlier months of 1970, the latest – to our knowledge at least – having been received on March 3. To none of the delegations had the Taoiseach or any of his Ministers gone back on the August pledge despite public utterances such as the much quoted speech made by the Taoiseach in Tralee on September 20, 1969.

Northern representatives whom the Taoiseach had met in February were left with the impression that he had made his Tralee speech merely to counteract possible evidence that might be given at the Scarman Tribunal. Mr Lynch felt it was possible that evidence would emerge linking his August 13 speech to the flare-up of violence on the following days.

The delegation which met the Taoiseach on March 3 also met, as already described, the Minister for Defence, Mr Gibbons, later in the evening. Afterwards, in the same room where John Kelly and I sat discussing the implications of the Cosgrave speech, a member of that delegation, enthused by the more than sympathetic reception accorded by the Taoiseach and his Ministers, made a remark which, two months later, had become a sick joke. "Gibbons is so Republican, he makes me suspicious," the Northern delegate declared with an instinct later to be proved so correct.

This was the Gibbons who had come to see me when I was in custody on May 1. What exactly was his part in the affair? What was the significance of a visit to my home by Tony Gallagher, a reporter for the magazine, *This Week*, a few days earlier – before Mr Cosgrave had made his Dáil "revelations" and before my name had become public knowledge?

Mr Gallagher had the real Gibbons story, he told me. He knew of my involvement and his suggestion was that if I told him my story it would be published alongside the Gibbons story. He intimated that in this way I could clear my name. His attitude did not appeal to me. He sounded too "know-all" and, anyhow, I did not feel I had to clear my name.

"Who gave you my name in the first place?" I asked.

"A Minister of Government."

"Which Minister?"

He would not give me the name of the Minister, claiming that it was against journalistic ethics to do so. I declined to give my story and Tony Gallagher left, leaving me to ponder the identity of the communicative Minister. I assumed it was George Colley, Minister for Industry and Commerce, soon to be appointed to Finance in place of Haughey in the reshuffle on May 8. He was known to be a friend and mentor of Gibbons.

In the early hours of the morning of May 7, John Kelly and I queried why the elected representatives of the Twenty-Six Counties should, by their inanity, stupidity and petty vindictiveness, jeopardise the delicate balance between Nationalist and Unionist, which had been maintained with some success in Northern Ireland through the long winter of 1969/1970 and the spring of 1970. There were no ready answers and the natural inclination was to expose the whole sorry mess. But that was the easy way out. Cosgrave was right in one thing, if wrong in almost everything else: lives could be involved, especially the lives of people in Northern Ireland.

People in the North had placed some trust in the Lynch Government; many of them believed that in the last resort they could look with some confidence to the South for help. It would be dangerous to do anything that might undermine that confidence, because as long as even a vestige of confidence existed, people would be less inclined to act rashly. Violence for the sake of violence only appeals to the psychopathic, but, if the cause seems hopeless, with all doors closed, even sane people are inclined to react with violence. In Northern Ireland the great specific fear of many of the Nationalists was of being defenceless in the event of an attack similar to that in Belfast in August 1969.

The British army came to the rescue, as it did in Derry's Bogside, but there were many Nationalists and Catholics, especially in isolated rural areas, who believed that the British army would not always be in a position to come to the rescue. Also, there were many who believed that the British army was too thin on the ground to withstand concerted attacks in many widely-spaced areas. It was against that background that delegations came South to the Government of the Republic looking for support. Having gone away feeling that, in the last analysis, the South would not leave them defenceless, they were psychologically prepared to withstand greater pressure without resorting to the extreme of violence. Indeed, many people in close touch with the situation in the North, were aware that this psychological link had already been effective as a restraining factor in some potentially ugly situations.

It might seem that Northern Republicans, committed to a thirty-two county Republic, would regard such an apparently negative form of support with little enthusiasm, but such was not the case. Republicans were not committed to violence per se and they, in common with most of the minority in the North, would grasp at any opportunity to achieve their objective by peaceful means. In this context, many Republicans saw the possibility of help from the South, if Nationalists were defenceless under attack, as a major step forward. To them it expressed rightful concern by the people of the South for the minority in the North – a concern which they saw being translated into diplomatic activity and international pressure on various levels to make Britain more aware of her responsibilities towards Ireland as a whole. The hope of many of them was that if the Irish nation were to speak out with one voice for a United Ireland, Stormont might be overthrown.

In seeking the overthrow of Stormont, it would seem that they were at one with Jack Lynch, for he told the February delegation that he was in a very strong position with the British Labour Government and asked if the delegation would be satisfied with the abolition of Stormont at that stage. He explained that he could not negotiate with the Northern Ireland Government because it did not represent a sovereign power, but that if Stormont fell, progress might be more easily made directly with Westminster. He then went on to discuss the economics of unity and the delegation went away convinced that he and his Government were working towards the ideal of a United Ireland. On the question of gas masks and arms, he said he felt that gas masks could be supplied for humanitarian reasons. On arms, he assured the Northerners that his heart was in the right place and that he would put the arms question to his Cabinet.

This was the background against which John Kelly and I discussed the advisability of making a public statement. It was three o'clock when we reached a final decision that it would not be in the country's interest. We reasoned that while a statement might clarify matters for people in the Republic, there was a grave danger that it might snap the tenuous lines of trust so painstakingly established between the minority in the North and the Government in the South. We still had some hope that the politicians might open their eyes and see the realities, but, within forty-eight hours, we were to be further disillusioned.

When the Dáil sat at half past ten on the morning of Friday, May 8 1970, the Ceann Comhairle (Speaker) announced:

"Before the order of business I would inform the Dáil that there was a defect in the bells, and at the last division at 2.30 am on Thursday, I extended the period of their ringing beyond the usual time on receiving complaints from the Chief Whips… "

This low-key, mundane introduction was the prelude to a debate in the Irish Parliament, which has gone into Dáil history as the "Marathon". The Opposition decided to filibuster and the debate went on for thirty-six hours. Much of the verbiage evoked was uninformed and speculative, while some of it was deliberately and positively misleading. The debate, with its mixture of hyperbole and falsehood, did not end until eleven o'clock on the following night, Saturday, May 9. In these circumstances, it was probably fitting that the proceedings should have opened on the farcical note of the bells that would not ring.

The motion before the House, in the formal words of the Taoiseach, was "that Dáil Éireann approve the nomination of the following members by the President to be members of the Government: Jerry Cronin, Robert Molloy and Gerard Collins".

New men had stepped or were stepping into the shoes of Blaney, Haughey, Boland, Ó Moráin and Paudge Brennan, and Jack Lynch and his reorganised Government were apparently willing and able to carry on. Mr Cosgrave, however, put the matter in perspective, when as the first speaker, he stated: "The motion that has now been brought forward to add additional names to the Government is really of no significance in the present circumstances," even though it sounded somewhat hypocritical coming from a man, who had misled the House two days earlier, to accommodate Jack Lynch and ensure Fianna Fáil remained in power. Other members of the House were of the same mind as Mr Cosgrave to judge by the debate when, rather than concentrating on any theoretical approval of the new Ministers, most of the eloquence and long-winded rhetoric were expended on the alleged "arms conspiracy," so dramatically sprung on the country by Mr Cosgrave.

In the reshuffle necessitated by the new appointments, Mr. Gibbons had gained promotion, stepping up the ladder from the lowly-rated

Department of Defence to the more prestigious Department of Agriculture and Fisheries. I was particularly interested in any contribution he might make to the debate. I was not at home when a summary of his speech was given on that evening's five o'clock radio news, but I was to learn about it in a sobering fashion. I arrived home at about ten minutes past five to find my thirteen-year-old daughter crying.

Normally well able to express herself, she was practically inarticulate.

"He told lies about you. Mr Gibbons told lies about you on the radio," she eventually blurted out. My wife came in from the kitchen. She was wiping tears from her eyes, a woman not normally given to tears. "He said you were under suspicion, he said terrible things about you, Jim."

I was shocked. I had expected something like this from Gibbons, but I was still shocked; that a man should stoop so low. I first met him on March 4, because, through some stroke of good luck, I had taken the momentous decision for an Army Captain to seek an interview with his Minister. I did it to ensure that there was absolutely no doubt at Government level, as represented by the Minister, about the plan to import arms later in the month. I had been reporting to my superior officer, Colonel Hefferon, all along and I knew that he briefed the Minister on a regular basis, but, because of the unique undercover operation in which I was involved, I felt it would be better to brief the Minister face-to face. From that very first meeting, when he seemed to be as well briefed as I was on the operation, and at several further meetings between the two of us, his sole interest, as he expressed himself to me, was in bringing the arms operation to a successful conclusion. Never, until the fateful meeting in Blaney's office on April 23, did he give any indication whatsoever other than that as Minister he was underwriting the operation, thus, as far as I was concerned, giving it the full seal of Government approval.

I sat, watched by a disconsolate wife and three young daughters, with the black hole behind my lower ribs expanding and contracting, but not for long. John Kelly and I had decided not to go public after Mr Cosgrave, in co-operation with Mr Lynch, had set the ball rolling by turning the signposts, but it was now Gibbons, the Minister responsible, who had picked up the ball of deceit and was running with it. It was time for me to go public. I phoned the news media. Dick Walsh of *The Irish Times* and Mike Burns of Radio Telefís Éireann (RTE) were among the first to arrive and they confirmed what Mr Gibbons had actually said. Having denied any "knowledge or consent" on his part in relation to " an attempt to smuggle arms", Mr Gibbons had gone on:

> "I was aware through the Director of Intelligence that attempts to smuggle arms were a constant danger, and these attempts were

> kept under surveillance at all times. I wish to say I discharged my duty to the full extent of my knowledge of the situation, I want to say also that in recent times I formed the opinion that Captain Kelly was becoming unsuitable for the type of work that he was employed on. I want to say that certain suspicions were forming in my mind. I was kept informed by the Director of Intelligence but nothing concrete emerged…"

The seeds of doubt he had planted in Blaney's office two weeks earlier, with his "brazen bastard" comment, had sprouted and were out in the open. He was now irretrievably committed to the road of deception and betrayal. Certainly, he was all set to betray me; sacrifice me for his sinister purposes. It was essential to nail his lies and do so in no uncertain terms. I dictated a statement to Dick Walsh at my dining-room table:

> "Under privilege in the Dáil Mr Gibbons has attacked me. All he said is a tissue of lies. Any work which I did I brought to the knowledge of Mr Gibbons at any and every opportunity.
>
> He is completely aware of anything I did prior to my leaving the army on Friday, May 1.
>
> I got home today to find my family in an hysterical condition on account of what had been said by Mr Gibbons in the Dáil. Other relations of mine who are throughout the country and who are not in touch with the situation are bound to be similarly affected.
>
> The man is an unmitigated scoundrel and I say that not under privilege of Dáil Éireann.
>
> I met him in his office in Leinster House as recently as Wednesday, April 29, and discussed the situation with him as it then existed, that is, in relation to myself. We parted on amicable terms.
>
> Mr Gibbons has indicated on various occasions that I was doing an excellent job for the country as an Intelligence Officer. When I was arrested by the Special Branch last Friday morning, I claimed privilege and asked that Mr. Gibbons be called. He came to the office of Chief Superintendent Fleming of the Special Branch, where we had a conversation in the presence of Superintendent Fleming.
>
> Mr Gibbons's advice to me was to tell everything I knew concerning my activities as an Intelligence Officer. In the event, I rejected his advice because of the implications involved.
>
> It was then suggested that I speak to the Taoiseach. I did so.
>
> Before he left the office of Chief Superintendent Fleming, Jim

> Gibbons, in my hearing, indicated that I was a competent and highly respected officer of the Defence Forces and that I was to be treated as such.
>
> What Mr Gibbons has done is nothing better than character assassination obviously intended to preserve his position at any cost to his honour and integrity."

I read the statement to a RTE television crew in my back garden. Later, I rang Seamus Brady, the journalist and PR man, who had accompanied me to the North in the previous September. A group of reporters and press photographers were encamped outside my house, on the front lawn and along the side of the road. Mr Brady's experience proved invaluable in controlling them and fielding their questions.

Mr Christopher Gore Grimes, a solicitor, had arrived to represent me and he helped me to draft a second statement in which I stated that everything I had done had been undertaken with the full knowledge and authority of Mr Gibbons as Minister for Defence, and that, because of the Officials Secrets Act, I could not say more than that. Mr Brady read this statement to the Press and arranged for the photographers to take their pictures. Satisfied, the Press departed. Seamus stayed until four o'clock next morning, entertaining us with his seemingly inexhaustible fund of amusing stories from his journalistic experiences and his PR dealings with various politicians.

Next morning, Douglas Gageby, editor of *The Irish Times* , arrived. An old friend of mine, he had served in the Intelligence section at GHQ during the Second World War. He was accompanied by Dick Walsh and the cool, calm appraisal and appreciation of events by both of them was a great source of comfort and support to Sheila, my wife, and me, at the end of eight days of what had been a very traumatic experience for both of us. They stayed for several hours and I briefed them fully on what had taken place. I was confident that, if events should block my giving my interpretation of events, they would do so.

CHAPTER 10

On the afternoon of May 8, PJ Burke, a Government deputy, ended his speech with the words: "Leave those who are not in a position to defend themselves alone". Admirable sentiments, making it all the more ironic that the next speaker should have been Mr Gibbons.

"I want to intervene in this debate," he began, "to clarify some points which have been raised and also to refer to a statement by Mr Patrick Kennedy, Belfast MP in the course of a Radio Éireann interview; he suggested that any participation by Captain James Kelly in an attempt to smuggle arms could only have been made with my knowledge and consent."

What Paddy Kennedy had said was, "I would be surprised – assuming there is any truth in the allegations – if any action he (Captain Kelly) took was not known to his superior officers and even to the Minister for Defence". This was a mere assertion of an opinion in defence of me and could not be construed in any way as an indictment of Mr Gibbons, and Gibbons was not the type of man to misunderstand it. It was more likely that another assertion by Mr Kennedy had forced the Minister's hand.

"As far as I know," Mr Kennedy had said, "Captain Kelly was not asked to resign. He tendered his resignation, so that it would be possible for him to tell whatever he had to tell rather than remaining muzzled within the army".

Knowing that Paddy Kennedy was a friend of mine, it is likely that Mr Gibbons saw him issuing a threat on my behalf to expose all and he decided to get in the first word.

"I wish emphatically to deny any such knowledge or consent (to smuggle arms)," he continued and went on to more or less repeat his May 6 denunciation of me.

Before making his attack on me on this occasion, he had gone one step further than previously. He had telephoned the recently retired Colonel Hefferon and, having intimated that he would be making a statement to the House, asked if it would be right to say that I, Captain Kelly, had not been reporting regularly on my intelligence activities for some time back. It was a clear attempt to drag the Colonel into his net of deception, but he was met with a contemptuous and very definite "NO". Shortly afterwards, Mr Gibbons walked into the Chamber and made his intervention, going on to claim:

"I am satisfied that at all times I honoured the obligation that was placed on me by the Taoiseach when he made me Minister for Defence."

He went on further with his remarkable version of events, making me wonder more and more what exactly was the obligation placed on him by the Taoiseach that he was so keen to be seen honouring. Certainly, they were birds of a feather, in that Gibbons had tried to suborn the former Director of Intelligence on May 8, just as Jack Lynch, in a more elaborate charade, had attempted to suborn me in May 1.

It was late in the evening of the same day, when John Bruton, a member of the Fine Gael Opposition and a future Taoiseach, read my statement to the media into the Dáil record.

"This statement implicates Deputy Gibbons in this affair," he said.

Referring to an earlier remark by Mr Lynch, he continued:

"Now, where do we leave the Taoiseach's statement that not even the slightest suspicion should attach to any member of the Government in a matter of this nature? How is the statement to be applied in this case? The Government may seek refuge behind the line adopted in the current edition of the periodical, *This Week.* They may seek to adopt this story to state that Deputy Gibbons covered himself by telling the Taoiseach at the end of last year of his knowledge of the matter. I quote from the current issue of *This Week:*

'The next development, coming up to the end of the year, must have been a bombshell to the Taoiseach. He was consulted privately by James Gibbons, the quiet, unflappable Kilkenny-born Minister for Defence, who had some very disturbing information.

Gibbons had reports from army sources that the connection between the IRA Army Council and the two Cabinet Ministers was still being continued. The reports were vague; there were no times, places or hard-and-fast details to back them up.

Unverified, the information he brought could not be acted upon immediately. Lynch was left in a lonely dilemma of doubt, which he had no clear way of resolving.

More concrete evidence was not too long emerging, however. Within the last two months, hints, rumours – and a lot of more factual material – snowballed.'

However, this is not conclusive evidence that Deputy Gibbons was not himself implicated in the plot. There is no reason to believe that he may not have been covering himself by going to the Taoiseach while in fact continuing in the plot with Deputy Blaney and Deputy Haughey, backing both horses at once. No matter what way we look at it, either of two situations must represent the true facts.

Either Deputy Gibbons did tell the Taoiseach at the end of last year as in the *This Week* story that he knew of the plot, in which case, the Taoiseach did nothing about it and has misled this House in saying that the first knowledge that he, the Taoiseach, had of this affair was on April 20, or – the second alternative – the Minister for Defence himself was involved in the plot behind the Taoiseach's back and did not go to the Taoiseach..."

It would seem that Mr Bruton was coming close to the truth. If Tony Gallagher had the "real Gibbons story," and there was no reason to assume otherwise, as his contacts were in the Colley-Gibbons camp. Because of the Lynch knowledge of the Bailieboro meeting, it would be surprising if he had not been on the look-out for future developments. The man to keep in touch with would have been the Minister for Defence and it is difficult to accept that Gibbons did not convey some inkling of the type of work on which Military Intelligence was engaged. It is interesting to note also that Mr Gallagher quoted army sources and that the only army source reporting to Gibbons at the time was Colonel Hefferon. This indicated that Gibbons was briefed on the situation by Military Intelligence prior to Christmas 1969. It was a good opportunity for either of them, Lynch or Gibbons, to shout STOP, if they did not approve of what was going on.

Mr Bruton must also have been aware of the special political relationship that existed between Mr Gibbons and Mr Colley, now to become Minister for Finance. When Sean Lemass retired as Taoiseach in 1966, Colley and Haughey were the two principal candidates for leadership, but when agreement could not be reached, Blaney's hat was thrown into the ring by Kevin Boland. This was followed by the drafting of the generally-accepted unwilling Lynch as candidate. In the final analysis, only Lynch and Colley remained in the field and, when the vote was taken, Lynch emerged victorious with an overwhelming majority. One of Colley's chief supporters, in what has been described as the succession race, was Gibbons and, as such, he was antagonistic to the Blaney/Haughey wing or wings of the Fianna Fáil party. Because of this, it was possible that Gibbons might have filtered his reports through his mentor, Colley.

In the event, the Taoiseach, in his winding-up speech to the House on Saturday May 9, did little to answer the questions so many people were asking, although he put great emphasis on a meeting he had with various security people on April 30.

"I had consultations jointly with officers of the Special Branch of the Garda and the Army Intelligence Service and the Attorney General and the Minister for Defence were also present at these consultations. The Minister for Justice, who would have been the other appropriate Minister, was not present because he had entered hospital some days previously. The purpose of that meeting was to co-ordinate as well as I could the evidence that was available from both of the specialist sources and also to receive guidance from the Attorney General...

... I have referred to the conference I had on April 30 with the Attorney General," he reiterated, "the two top security men from the Army and the Garda, and the Minister for Defence. I said that the reason was to co-ordinate some of the information that I already had and to get guidance about what might be done in respect of two individuals (Haughey and Blaney) whose names were mentioned in the course of the reports I had read".

In his *Magill* diaries, Mr Berry described this meeting:

"The Taoiseach phoned me that evening to have the Head of 'S Branch' at his home at 8.00 pm. I had assured him that this was the Garda officer who had the most knowledge of the arms conspiracy. I informed the Commissioner and, later, had a phone call from Chief Supt. Fleming for information as to the purpose of the meeting and who would be present. I told him that I knew no more than that he was to be at the Taoiseach's house at the time stated. 'But,' he said, 'you know more than anybody else. Will you be there?' I said that I had not been asked and that I did not know the purpose.

Later in the night, at about 9.30 pm, Chief Supt. Fleming called to my house. He said that he was bewildered as to why he was summoned to the Taoiseach's house as he had not been asked any questions or for an opinion. He told me that the Attorney General and the Minister for Defence, Mr Gibbons, were present as was Colonel Delaney, Director of Military Intelligence (only since 9th April, i.e. for three weeks) who was not asked any questions either — not, said the Chief, that he could contribute anything. He said that the Taoiseach and the Attorney General did most of the talking to one another with an occasional remark from the Minister for Defence, but it was inconsequential kind of talk which did not clarify any matter that he could see.

While the Chief Superintendent was speaking to me the phone rang and I answered it: it was the Taoiseach. He said: 'I have had a conference with... including Col. Delaney and Chief Supt. Fleming and I now have a better understanding of the position.'

I said: 'Mr Fleming called to my home after he had left your house and he told me that he was bewildered as to why he was present as he was not asked any question and his opinion was not sought; he also told me that Col. Delaney was not questioned. I think that you should know this as the Chief Superintendent will be making a report on these lines to the Commissioner.'

"There was an appreciable pause and then the Taoiseach said: 'why did he not ask questions if he was in doubt about anything'. I said that nobody had told him for what purpose he had been summoned to the Taoiseach's house. The Taoiseach's voice was angry."

Earlier on April 30, the Taoiseach had sent for Mr Berry. He told him that he had seen Mr Blaney and Mr Haughey and that the matter was ended. A day later, he had told his Cabinet the same thing. As Mr Berry noted: "As a result of the misstatements already recorded, with more to follow, I lost respect for the Taoiseach's credibility."

In the Dáil, the Taoiseach went on to state that I and "another individual"* whose name he would not disclose had been arrested under Section 30 of the Offences Against the State Act on May 1.

"At all events," the Taoiseach continued,

"Captain Kelly was interviewed on Friday morning, May 1, and some time before one o'clock I received a telephone message to say he refused to make any statement in the Bridewell Station, but that if he was confronted face to face – I think he said that in his own statement as published and therefore I feel free to say it here in the House – with the Minister for Defence, he would make a statement. The Minister for Defence went to the office of Chief Superintendent Fleming in Dublin Castle, to which place Captain Kelly had been brought, in the meantime having been given lunch."

The Taoiseach was very definite about lunch. There was no reason why he could not have been as definite about the contents of my published statement, especially as Mr Bruton had read it into the Dáil record. It did not say that I would make a statement if confronted with the Minister for Defence, and the Taoiseach was in a position to know that. Instead, he chose to confuse the situation by basing his comment on the ambiguous "I think", thereby conveying that my published statement read otherwise than was actually the case.

---

* *The "individual" was Albert Luykx. When he was arrested at his home on May 1 and brought to the Bridewell, Chief Superintendent Fleming's first action was to threaten him with deportation within twenty-four hours.*

> "The Minister told him that he should tell everything he knew and made some reference about his competence as an officer," the Taoiseach went on, "I believe the Minister felt sorry for the plight in which Captain Kelly found himself. However, the Minister then left and at about four o'clock or shortly before it I had another telephone call to say that Captain Kelly had begun to make a statement, but after the usual preliminaries, date of birth, occupation, address, decided to say no more. He said that if he was brought to me — and this is the message I got — he would name names. I readily agreed to see Captain Kelly and perhaps within twenty minutes or so he and Chief Superintendent Fleming arrived at my office."

The crocodile tears were good padding, even if they indicated that the Taoiseach had at least some acquaintance with my statement, but I had not said that I would name names if brought to him. I had merely agreed to the suggestion that I should talk to the Taoiseach. Despite his suggested bad memory, Mr Lynch may have had some recollection of my version of how I came to visit his office, given to him during our conversation on May 1. Referring to that conversation, the Taoiseach told the Dáil:

> "I said to him, 'you asked the Minister for Defence to go face to face with you in Dublin Castle and that you should make a statement then, and you refused. You asked permission to come to me and said you would name names and make a statement and again you refused.' He said: 'Well, that is the position.' I kept him for some minutes talking around the subject but he refused to give me any information whatsoever."

I had not, as a pre-condition to my meetings with either Mr Lynch or Mr Gibbons, promised to make a statement. Needing time to think, I had indicated to Mr Gibbons that I would make a statement as a consequence of his visit. When I changed my mind for the reasons outlined, it was Chief Superintendent Fleming who suggested, unconditionally, that I talk to the Taoiseach. By implying that the facts were otherwise, the Taoiseach was adroitly undermining my credibility. Mr Lynch seemed to have the facility of twisting facts, in themselves minor and not of great importance, but with an accumulative discrediting effect.

Mr Lynch continued:

> "Then I consulted with Chief Superintendent Fleming and I asked if he could leave. Captain Kelly did say that if he was let go free, peo-

> ple would come and make statements. I consulted Chief Superintendent Fleming. I told him this and Chief Superintendent Fleming said he had no authority to let him go free.
>
> In the meantime, I consulted the Attorney General. He told me the Chief Superintendent had authority to detain him for some further period and did in fact do so. I believe that ultimately Captain Kelly was released the following morning or early afternoon – not having made any statement."

We were in the realm of pure farce here. The Chief Superintendent had no authority to release me, but he had authority to detain me. We were in "Alice in Wonderland" country. There was no need to consult the Attorney General about the power to detain under the Offences Against the State Act. The dogs in the street could have told Mr Lynch about it, not to mention the Head of the Special Branch, with whom he had his fatuous conversation about holding me or otherwise in my presence on May 1, without any reference to the Attorney General. No wonder Mr Berry had lost respect for his credibility.

Asked by Dr Noel Browne, the Labour TD, why he did not sack Deputy Gibbons, as he had sacked Messrs Haughey and Blaney on the grounds of "slightest suspicion", the Taoiseach replied:

"It was somebody else, not I, who cast suspicion on Deputy Gibbons. I did not see any statement from Captain Kelly."

It was approaching midnight on Saturday, May 9, when the Taoiseach declared that he had not seen any statement from me. Yet, Mr Lenihan, Minister for Transport and Power, could state nearly twenty-four hours before that all the allegations in my statement had been taken into consideration.

"Asked early today," *The Irish Times* reported on the morning of May 9, "about the allegations by Captain Kelly against Mr Gibbons, the Minister for Transport and Power, Mr Lenihan, said that cognisance had been taken of all allegations. The Taoiseach had decided that no scandal whatsoever was attached to Mr Gibbons and he was retaining him in Government."

This Lenihan statement clearly indicated that the Government and the Taoiseach had taken my statement into consideration, contrary to what Mr Lynch told the Dáil.

As I read the Lenihan statement, I wondered if he remembered a meeting he attended in Dublin's Hotel Sutton House earlier in the year. Albert Luykx was present at that meeting and when the party were having a drink in the hotel bar afterwards, Mr Lenihan nudged him and said:

"Albert, I heard that you are doing a good job for the country."

"Well, I am doing my best," Albert replied.

"Keep it up, boy, keep it up," was the Lenihan rejoinder.

At the time, one could only speculate on how many members of the Government knew about the proposed arms importation.

Years later, Mr Lenihan told me on various occasions that he had opposed the arms trials and that Mr Lynch was a vindictive so-and-so to initiate them. On one occasion in Buswell's Hotel, a well-known political haunt in Dublin, Mr Lenihan introduced me to a political friend of his, reasserting that Mr Lynch should never have mounted the arms trials. He went on to tell his friend that my repeated condemnation of Mr Lynch over the years was fully merited; that, in fact, Mr Lynch was much more devious and sly than I ever portrayed him. Turning to me, he said, "I will tell you all about it some day". I asked him why he stayed in the Fianna Fáil party if Mr Lynch was such a villain. He replied that in his book loyalty to the leader and the stability of the party took precedence over other considerations.

I pointed out that as history demonstrated it could be a dangerous philosophy. He did not demur, but grinned and playfully punched my shoulder, suggesting that we should have a more in-depth discussion on another occasion.

In the Dáil on May 14, Michael Pat Murphy, a Labour deputy, stated:

> "Either the Minister (Gibbons) or Captain Kelly is telling lies… If the Minister for Agriculture is of the opinion that Captain Kelly's statement is not true surely he has the necessary machinery to deal with the allegation. He can go to the courts and have his name cleared… "

Mr Colley intervened at this stage to state:

"I doubt very much if those words are actionable" in a reference to my statement.

Later, Mr Colley said:

> "Deputy Murphy referred to a question asked by Deputy Corish (Labour Party Leader) at the conclusion of the debate last week and he repeated it himself. Summed up it could be: who is telling the truth? Is it Captain Kelly or is it Deputy Gibbons?… The assumption underlying what was said by Deputy Corish was that Captain Kelly had admitted publicly in a statement that he had engaged in illegal activities. To my knowledge, Captain Kelly said no such

> thing. What he said was that all his activities were known to the Minister for Defence. There is a great difference between those two things and a grave injustice is being done to Captain Kelly by those who have been making that point."

In appearing to defend me, Mr Colley was merely skilfully parrying an opposition assault on Mr Gibbons. I had accused Mr Gibbons of telling lies and if there was any substance in the "arms importation" with which both the Taoiseach and Mr Gibbons had associated me, I had certainly claimed that Mr Gibbons was aware of my activities, clearly inferring that Mr Gibbons had authorised the operation. On May 14, Mr Colley knew that, as did everyone else in Dáil Éireann and many outside of it.

Deputy Garret Fitzgerald, another future Fine Gael Taoiseach, spoke immediately after Mr Colley and referred to the *This Week* article, already quoted by Deputy Bruton. He compared it with the statement the Taoiseach had made on May 9:

> "'Deputy Gibbons came to me occasionally,' the Taoiseach told the Dáil on that occasion, 'sometimes of his own volition, sometimes at my request, and we discussed largely the operation of the military units along the border. We also discussed his information in so far as activities within the Six Counties were concerned. He came to me on occasions for advice about different matters, but on no occasion did he ask my advice or make any report to me about any other Ministers.'"

Deputy Fitzgerald found it difficult to reconcile the statement with the Gibbons story in *This Week.*

> "'It is not easy to reconcile these two statements,' he said, "I do not believe people on the opposite side lie. They try to make statements which are true if you read them very carefully. There are difficulties in reconciling this statement. One suggestion put to me for reconciliation is that Deputy Gibbons did not perhaps inform the Taoiseach at one of these meetings to which the Taoiseach refers. I am sure the Taoiseach is not saying anything which is untrue, even if we must pass over what was happening in the House last week.
>
> Deputy Gibbons would scarcely have said this week that he had let the Taoiseach know about this unless there was some truth in it. That certainly would have damned him with the Taoiseach if he had not only attempted to exonerate himself, but had done so by

> lying and saying he had tipped off the Taoiseach. What may have happened is that Deputy Gibbons may have communicated through an intermediary on this particular point, and may have covered himself by letting the Taoiseach know, through an intermediary, about the activities of these Ministers but not actually have spoken to the Taoiseach direct. The two statements can be reconciled on that presumption. There may be some other reconciliation. I am not prepared to accept that either person is not telling the truth."

Despite Dr Fitzgerald's amazing and unique interpretation of events to substantiate that "people on the opposite side" did not lie, the fact remained that between them, Lynch and Gibbons were misleading Dáil Éireann.

CHAPTER 11

The reaction of Northern Ireland Nationalists to what was to them the inexplicable and disastrous about-face of the Dublin Government was graphically portrayed at a Dublin press conference on May 8, 1970. Disillusioned and bitterly disappointed at what was described as foul betrayal of Irishmen by an Irish Government, a spokesman accused the Taoiseach of "throwing them to the wolves".

When, on May 8, Gibbons again intervened in the Dáil debate, the bitterness, particularly in Belfast, shifted more towards Mr Gibbons, whom they had seen as promising so much; a man seemingly so much more Republican than themselves – "so Republican he frightens me".

Still, I was surprised and shocked to find that a team of three Belfastmen had arrived in Dublin on the way to Kilkenny to shoot Mr Gibbons. I was apprised of what was afoot by a member of the team, who felt it might be to my detriment if the shooting was carried out.

"I'm damn sure it would," I remonstrated, "It's absolute madness to even suggest it. Making a martyr of Gibbons! No, you must call it off."

"I'm not so sure. He's an informer, worse than an informer. He's betraying the Nationalist people of the North. Another bloody Carey," he spat out the words.

James Carey was a name excoriated by many in Ireland, to whom he represented the lowest type of scoundrel; the man who betrayed his friends to save his own neck. He had been one of the chief organisers of the killing of Lord Frederick Cavendish and Mr TH Burke, the Chief Secretary and Permanent Under-Secretary of the British regime in Ireland, on May 6, 1882 in Dublin's Phoenix Park. The two men had been done to death by members of the *Invincibles* , an organisation opposed to British rule in Ireland, of which Carey was a founder member. At the subsequent trial nearly eight months later, Carey turned informer and, primarily on the basis of his evidence, five men, Brady, Kelly, Fagan, Caffrey and Curley, were hanged in Kilmainham Gaol, while other *Invincibles* were sentenced to long terms of imprisonment.

A few weeks later, Carey, his wife and family, whom Britain was relocating abroad, were aboard ship heading for South Africa. They travelled under the name of Power, but an Irish-American named O'Donnell learned of their true identity and shot James Carey dead. O'Donnell was arrested and brought to London, where he was hanged at Newgate.

"It's going a bit far, comparing Gibbons to Carey," I protested.

"More good men will die because of the desertion of Gibbons and the Irish Government, than ever died because of Carey," the Belfastman persisted.

"Forget about it. If nothing else, it would be sheer stupidity to shoot Gibbons."

After some further discussion, the proposed shooting was called off and I took possession of a small battered attaché case containing a short-barrelled revolver wrapped in cloth and five or six rounds of ammunition in a crumpled 20 cigarette packet. All I could do was store the case and its contents in my home. In the climate of the time, where I had been vilified as an enemy of the State under privilege by Cosgrave, Lynch and Gibbons in Dáil Éireann, they were not the best items to have in my possession. I was in something of a Catch-22 situation until they were collected by a friend of mine and brought back to Belfast.

Days passed, then weeks, and while I waited I wondered when and how the hammer would fall – if it ever fell. On May 25 Mr Haughey, who was by now out of hospital, issued a statement regretting that on medical advice he could not make a personal statement to the Dáil.

> "The Taoiseach informed the Dáil that he requested my resignation on the grounds that he was convinced that not even the slightest suspicion should attach to any member of the Government. I fully subscribe to that view.
>
> As far as I have been able to gather, the Taoiseach received information of a nature which, in his opinion, cast some suspicion on me. I have not had the opportunity to examine or test such information on the quality of its source or sources. In the meantime, however, I now categorically state that at no time have I taken part in any illegal importation or attempted importation of arms into this country."

On 27 May, Arthur Noonan, political correspondent of *The Irish Independent*, wrote a feature on the previous day's proceedings in the Dáil under the heading, "It was Stonewall Jack".

"Those who came to the Distinguished Strangers' Gallery, the Press and public galleries yesterday for a further exciting instalment in the gun-running saga left disappointed," said Noonan.

Jack Lynch's stonewall was as impregnable as ever.

> "The net effect of his answers to opposition questions is that the Attorney General has the matter in hand, that he knows the

> Taoiseach's desire to have it wrapped up as speedily as possible, but that Mr Lynch does not intervene to dictate to the Attorney General as to how he does his job… Anyhow, the Dáil had to be content to leave the matter for another week or two, when no doubt the questions will be pressed more firmly if nothing has happened by then… And there it rests-for another fortnight …"

At ten o'clock that morning John Kelly was arrested. Later in the day he appeared in the Dublin District Court on a charge of conspiring with people unknown to import arms and ammunition into the State in contravention of the Firearms Act between March 1 and April 24. He was remanded in custody until the following Wednesday.

At four o'clock that afternoon I was arrested, and Albert Luykx was brought in shortly afterwards. We were charged with the same offence as John Kelly. Cool and calm in the hurly-burlv of excited policemen rushing around the Bridewell, Mr Christopher Gore-Grimes, at that stage representing both Albert Luykx and myself, was as impeccable as ever, and the rosebud in his lapel seemed to retain its morning freshness when at seven o'clock in the evening the charges were formally put. Albert Luykx contented himself with a plea of "not guilty," while I stated: "I plead not guilty as charged and I wish to state further that anything I did while a serving officer I did with the knowledge and approval of the then Minister for Defence, James Gibbons".

Police, plainclothes and uniformed, were standing around. "I am going on hunger strike until I am released from custody," I announced, the words sounding unnecessarily dramatic in the silence that greeted them.

Within minutes I joined Albert Luykx in a room across the hall where my determination not to eat was soon put to the test. I had only a light lunch that day and when Tone Luykx, Albert's son, arrived with a magnificent packed supper which included a roast pheasant, I fully realised just how hungry I was.

"You must eat," Albert said, holding out a leg of pheasant with basted brown skin crinkling back. There were several good reasons why I should not go on hunger strike, Albert assured me, but I persisted, and next morning I did not eat my jail breakfast, in itself not a major sacrifice.

When I came downstairs from my cell, Mr Gore-Grimes was waiting with a fresh rosebud – a different shade – in his buttonhole. I followed him into one of the interrogation rooms. Had I any bailsman in mind, he asked. Yes, Seamus Brady said he would go bail for me, Seamus Brady or Gerry Jones, a Dublin businessman and friend of Neil Blaney's. I left the

Picket outside Dublin District Court at the preliminary hearing

room to phone my wife and ask her to make the necessary arrangements. Charles Haughey and Neil Blaney were in the main hall, under arrest and in the process of being charged. They were luckier than Albert Luykx or me in that they did not have to spend a night in a Bridewell cell – but perhaps the four of us would be joining John Kelly in Mountjoy before the end of the day.

We were brought by an underground passage to No. 4 District Court, where I was the first to be arraigned. Chief Superintendent Fleming opposed bail on the grounds of the seriousness of the charge and of the likelihood that I would interfere with witnesses. When questioned on the last point, Mr Fleming merely stated that from his investigations he believed that I would interfere with witnesses. When pressed for evidence by Mr Ernest Wood, then my defending counsel, Mr Fleming claimed privilege, a negative but major weapon in the armoury of State witnesses about which I was to learn more later. The Assistant State Solicitor sought a remand in custody, stating that he hoped to have further evidence in a week's time, and adding that the safety of the State could very well have been imperilled.

Neil Blaney and Michael Ó Moráin

My first time in court... it was a unique experience, especially when I was held up to public odium by the insinuations of the officials of a Government which to me had already shown itself to be dishonest and dishonourable. The Justice, Herman Good, could not see his way to remand me in custody, however. He felt that he was bound by a Supreme Court ruling that every defendant appearing in the District Court was entitled to bail unless there were outstanding circumstances. Mr Good did not consider that a withholding of bail was warranted, but in view of the serious nature of the charge bail would have to be substantial. He remanded me on my own bail of £500 and one independent surety of £1,000 or two of £500. Gerry Jones was on hand to act as bailsman. I was free to leave the court with the three others who were remanded on the same terms.

Chapter 11

While I was at home discussing the events of the morning and of the previous day with my wife, Kevin Boland, the former Minister for Local Government, was holding a post-mortem on the same events in his own typical way. He had called a press conference at his home a few miles away in Rathcoole, and at it, calmly and without equivocation, expressed his thoughts on what had taken place. He put the blame squarely on the shoulders of the Taoiseach and called for his removal. He was particularly incensed by the arrest of John Kelly, a man who "stood between the defenceless nationalist people in Belfast and slaughter last August, and who was permitted to go freely about his business in Belfast... and he comes to Dublin and is arrested by the Irish Government".

Mr Boland went on to say that he considered it to be "felon-setting by the leader of the Irish Government" and it appeared to him to be "a deliberate effort to deliver the Nationalist population of Belfast into the hands of their enemies". To his way of thinking, it constituted "the ultimate treachery of which an Irishman could be guilty".

When asked if the Taoiseach should give more information on the case, Mr Boland replied: "I would not be interested in whether he does or not. Whatever evidence he has does not interest me in the least. It comes from a source of a man of no honour. It is tainted evidence."

This may seem a harsh indictment of his leader by a former colleague, but to my wife, to me and to others who knew the background to the case, it was fully deserved. James Gibbons had denied knowledge of an operation which I had carried out under his auspices and with his approval and that, to me, made him a man of no honour. Equally his leader, who had countenanced the Minister's disavowal and who had supported it by his speech in the Dáil on May 9, was a man of no honour.

At his press conference, Mr Boland also called for the convening of a special Fianna Fáil Ard-Fheis or conference "to clear up the matter once and for all". That night the Government Information Bureau issued a statement on behalf of the Taoiseach in answer to Mr Boland. It read as follows:

> "While in other circumstances he would welcome a special Ard-Fheis, it would not serve any purpose at this point. The action that he had taken was his sole responsibility as Taoiseach.
>
> The Fianna Fáil Parliamentary Party had unanimously endorsed his right to take this action and his nomination of members of the Government to replace those now out of office.
>
> He had passed the papers in his possession to the Attorney General who, having made further investigations, decided on his

The matter was therefore *sub judice* and an Ard-Fheis could not discuss the issue."

Having accepted responsibility for his action, Mr Lynch thus shifted it to the Attorney General a few lines later. This approach enabled him to resist criticism by pleading *sub judice* when challenged to explain what he had done.

John Kelly was not granted bail until June 10, having been held in Mountjoy Prison from his arrest on May 27. It. was a particular mockery of Irish justice that he, a representative of the minority in Northern Ireland whose only crime was that of coming South to seek assistance from the Dublin Government, should have been incarcerated. It was left to the Assistant State Solicitor, Mr EJ Durnin, to introduce the proper farcical note when during the bail proceedings he asked the potential bailsman, Gerry Jones again, if he were prepared to go bail for £10,000. Jones, however, was equal to the occasion, stating that he would consider it an honour to go bail for John Kelly even if it were for £10,000. The justice showed some sense of proportion when he said that it was an exaggerated figure, but he still placed a high price on John Kelly's freedom when he fixed bail at one personal surety of £1,000 and an independent surety of £5,000, accepting Mr Jones as bailsman.

Thirty or forty Belfast men cheered John Kelly from the court. They burst on to a startled Dublin street, joyous and elated that their fellow Northerner had secured a modicum of freedom; that he was now at least as free as his co-accused from the South.

On July 2, the other four accused and I were once again before the Dublin District Court, the prosecution having completed its case and presented the various statements of evidence on which it proposed to rely.

Informations were refused against Neil Blaney who left the court to be mobbed by a crowd of well-wishers.

The four remaining, Charles Haughey, Albert Luykx, John Kelly and myself, were remanded on continuing bail. The case proper was not to open until September 22 in the Central Criminal Court. Meanwhile it was *sub judice* as it had been since May 28. Mr George Colley, the new Minister for Finance, however, was not greatly inhibited by this restriction on comment.

Speaking at a Fianna Fáil dinner in Carlow on June 19, Mr Colley said: "I know that a concentrated effort for base tactical reasons is being made to denigrate Mr Jim Gibbons. Because of his legal position his hands are tied. In due course he will tell the people of this country the whole story. I tell you, do not believe one word you hear denigrating Jim Gibbons".

Mr Colley was an effective mouthpiece for the silenced Mr Gibbons. On May 28 Mr Lynch had accepted no responsibility for the preferring of charges, stating that the Attorney General had done so on his own initiative. Mr Colley's calculated reference to the potential evidence of a witness on a question then before the courts was presumably also a matter for the Attorney General.

On July 24, the President of the High Court, Mr Justice Andreas O'Keeffe, startled the country by announcing, with reference to the impending arms trial:

"I would be reluctant to take this case myself. There are other judges who are also reluctant to take it. However, I would be prepared to do so. It is a question of finding a judge who is not reluctant..."

The consternation caused by Mr O'Keeffe's remarks found expression in the public press and *Hibernia* of August commented:

"If Mr Justice O'Keeffe found the reaction of the national press to his expression of reluctance to try Mr Haughey hysterical he has no one to blame but himself. It is easy to understand his personal position since as Attorney General he had been closely associated with Mr Haughey for three years. In the circumstances, his reluctance is quite understandable."

It was an added irony, therefore, that Mr O'Keeffe should have been named subsequently as presiding judge in the arms trial.

Before the case got to the High Court, it was necessary that I obtain independent legal representation. Mr Gore-Grimes had been an excellent representative during the preliminary phase of the case, but he was fully committed to another defendant, Albert Luyxk, for whom he had worked for many years. Somewhat casually, thinking it was only a matter of form, I sought around for a solicitor, but it soon impinged on me that there was a strange reluctance to take me on. Undoubtedly, the Dáil Éireann blackballing had its effect. Eventually, a complete stranger, Frank Fitzpatrick, head of the Dublin-based branch of James Fitzpatrick & Co, Solicitors, sent me a message, requesting that I call to his office. After a short introductory conversation on the first visit, he appointed a young woman solicitor, Pat Moynihan, to deal with me. It was an inspired choice. She turned out to be a bright, competent, dedicated and hardworking person, who left no stone unturned in her contribution to the presentation of my defence.

Some days after Pat's appointment, an attempt was made to nobble Frank Fitzpatrick by a representative of the Government party, Fianna Fáil. A well-known solicitor and equally well-known Fianna Fáil activist called to Frank's office and made the invidious suggestion that it might be better if the Fitzpatrick firm did not associate itself with my defence. It called to Frank's office and made the invidious suggestion that it might be better if the Fitzpatrick firm did not associate itself with my defence. It was made clear to Frank that this message came from the very top echelon of the party, which also meant the very top echelon of Government.

Frank, in his own understated style, rebuffed the ignoble approach. It is timely, nearly thirty years after the event, that I should acknowledge the debt I owe to the Fitzpatricks for their support during that critical time. At the first briefing of my legal team in an office on the Dublin Quays, I remember a tall, straight, elderly man standing quietly in the background.

It was James, the founder of the firm and Frank's father. He left shortly before the briefing ended and I did not see him again, but I understood that, as a result of what he heard, he fully endorsed Frank's decision to represent me.

The time-serving solicitor was thwarted with relative ease. But Charles Haughey, my co-defendant, who, before his sacking, probably had been the most powerful Minister in Government, was a different matter. Out of the blue, he told me he was going to deny that he knew that arms were involved in the alleged illegal importation; that as far as he was concerned it was a purely Military Intelligence operation within the bailiwick of the Minister for Defence; that he had merely supplied the money to accommodate the purchase of whatever military stores the Ministry of Defence might require; that he did not interest himself in what those stores were; and that he certainly did not know that it was proposed to import arms.

It was a clever, but dishonest ploy by Haughey. It was clever, in that he knew I was defending my part in the proposed arms importation on the basis that it was authorised by the Minister for Defence; that the defence of John Kelly and Albert Luyxk was also based on authorisation, largely coming through me as the representative of the Minister for Defence. If this defence succeeded, Haughey, like the rest of us, was in the clear. If it failed, the rest of us would be convicted, while Mr Haughey would almost certainly go free. It was dishonest, because Mr Haughey was willing to deny any knowledge of arms to save his own neck, while leaving the rest of us in the lurch.

Haughey did know, of course, that arms were involved and did so from the start. His governmental colleague, Kevin Boland, has since made public that Mr Haughey had discussed the pending arms importation with him in some detail in late March or early April, several weeks before the aborted attempt at Dublin Airport. In fact, I met Mr Boland for the first time that morning. I was sitting in the Parliamentary Secretaries' dining room in Dáil Éireann, probably waiting to keep an appointment with Mr Gibbons. The door to the passageway was open and I saw Mr Boland rushing past, followed by an aide, who glanced at me and nodded. Seconds later, Mr Boland came bustling into the room, obviously informed of my identity by the aide, and stood over me at the table, demanding:

"What's going to happen with these arms? Who's going to distribute them? Are proper arrangements made with the people up there? Will they be in the right hands?"

"As far as I know, yes," I answered. "It's an awkward situation you know, but there are plans in place."

"I'm glad to hear that," Mr Boland turned and left.

The Haughey defence was mean and selfish, if not in the Gibbons category. Unlike Gibbons, who not only tried to save his own neck, but gave false evidence in an attempt to secure the conviction of his erstwhile friends, Haughey only tried to save his own neck. leaving his erstwhile friends to fend for themselves. In fact, apart from denying knowledge of the arms, a crucial factor, Mr. Haughey's evidence generally was supportive of the defence.

The most low, mean, rotten and despicable act of vindictiveness committed against me and my family, during that traumatic summer of 1970, however, was the refusal of the Lynch Government to pay to me the gratuity and pension to which I was entitled after twenty-one years service. Penniless, with a mortgage overdue, my wife and I watched for a cheque at the end of May. When it did not arrive, I borrowed a few pounds to literally keep bread on the table for our five children. I rang the Department of Defence to find that any payments due to me were blocked by the Government. Relief came in the form of a £100 note, given to my eleven year old daughter, Sylvia, by a strange man, as she played in front of the house. "Make sure you give that to your father," he warned. It was years later that I found out the identity of the family benefactor. He was a Captain O'Shea, a merchant seaman, and one of my regrets is that he died before I had an opportunity to thank him for his generosity. £100 was not an inconsiderable sum in 1970, to us at least.

A week or two later, I looked out to see a ramshackle blue van pull away from the open doors of the garage and drive off down the road. My first thought was of a bomb. My wife ran out to the garden, where the children were playing, and got them under cover behind the back fence, while I went to investigate. I peered gingerly around the open door and saw two one-hundred-weight sacks leaning against the wall with the shape of what I thought were potatoes showing clearly through them. I we knew we would not get a mortgage on another one. Again no money at the end of June. It looked as if we might be forced to pull up stakes and move, but to where? No ready answer presented itself. Then Michael Connolly, my brother-in-law, came to the rescue. He gave me a loan, which was enough to keep us going until the end of the trial. We could not afford to look much further ahead at that stage.

I was now free to concentrate on preparing my defence against what I knew were false charges, which would have to be based on false and fabricated evidence. Jack Lynch was the mastermind behind the charade. Gibbons had made that clear to me on May 1. He was the man who attempted to bring me to my knees, taking the bread out of the mouth of my family by the vindictive expedient of blocking payments to which I was morally and legally entitled after years of service to the State. He was the lawyer so craven that the concept of innocent until proven guilty was not allowed to apply in my case. Vindictiveness had so overtaken him that I was to be punished in advance through my family.

Because I had refused to co-operate with him on May 1 in promoting his dastardly plan to make the proposed arms importation illegal by removing the statutory authority, Gibbons, from the frame, it was obvious that he was willing to use any means possible to break me, even to the extent of penalising my young family in the manner outlined.

Such was the lead-up to the arms trials later in the year.

CHAPTER 12

The trial opened at the Four Courts at eleven o'clock on the morning of September 22. The court was packed: so many journalists from all over the world had arrived to cover the trial that many of them had to be accommodated in a separate room. Loudspeakers relayed the proceedings but since the speakers often were not named, and to strangers one Irish accent is the same as another, the foreign journalists' confusion increased as the days went by.

The court rose to Mr O'Keeffe, glasses glinting in a round cherubic face. This was the man in charge, the reluctant arbiter of the law, and I watched him closely as he settled fussily on his dais.

I was represented by Mrs Pat Moynihan, solicitor, from the office of James Fitzpatrick & Co., Mr James D'Arcy SC, Mr Thomas Finlay SC and Mr Peter Sutherland BL.

Pat Moynihan's eye closed in a wink of encouragement recalling the long weary days of briefing, hour after hour in the hot office until we had covered the ground practically day by day from August 12, 1969 to May 1, 1970. The teamwork of my legal representation was assured and I was calm and confident when the proceedings opened.

After legal argument, the following amended version of the indictment was read to the jury:

"That on diverse dates between March 1, 1970 and April 24, 1970 in the area of the application of the law enacted by the Oireachtas they conspired together and with other persons unknown to import arms and ammunition illegally into the State."

Mr Seamus McKenna SC, leading for the State, was confident and fully aware of the drama of the occasion when he opened his address to the jury:

> "On the evening of Saturday April 18 last, shortly before 6.30 pm, the accused, Mr Haughey, who was then Minister for Finance, made a telephone call to Mr Peter Berry, who was then and still is Secretary to the Department of Justice. That call was to the plain effect that Mr Haughey asked Mr Berry if he was aware of a certain cargo that was due to arrive at Dublin Airport on the following Sunday... It will undoubtedly be established conclusively to your satisfaction that the cargo was intended by him and others to consist of five hundred pistols and approximately 180,000 rounds of ammunition."

Mr McKenna's sense of the dramatic and his confidence were to evaporate rather rapidly during the next month, but on September 22, he was on the scent, however false, of a kill, and he went surging into the attack in a not unimpressive fashion. In referring to me, having remarked that I went on holidays to Northern Ireland in August 1969 and reported back to Colonel Hefferon, he went on:

> "Some time around mid-January it became obvious to Colonel Hefferon that Captain Kelly's emotions had gone a great deal further than the perhaps natural sympathy any person would feel in relation to events in Northern Ireland at that time, because Captain Kelly told Colonel Hefferon as early as mid-January of this year that a number of defence committees in the North had asked him to help in the purchase of arms for their defence should they be subjected to a total attack from other sections of the Northern population."

It would have been logical at this stage for Mr McKenna to point out to the jury that as an intelligence officer I had taken what was correct action in reporting to my superior officer, Colonel Hefferon, Director of Intelligence. Mr McKenna, however, was not entirely his own master in the presentation of the case. He had to depend on his prosecution witnesses to substantiate his words and when the statements of evidence of two of these, Mr Gibbons the former Minister for Defence, and Colonel Delaney the new Director of Intelligence, were taken together, *suspicion and emotion* were the operative words. Colonel Delaney's statement was so verbosely inapplicable, however, that the prosecution decided against introducing it into evidence at either this or the subsequent trial. The more sophisticated Mr Gibbons, on the contrary, was allowed to develop and enlarge upon his thesis of suspicion and disloyalty to the full.

Much was to be said at the two trials – and ultimately discounted by the jury. But what concerned me most was the evidence of my former Minister.

Mr Gibbons was called to the witness-box on September 24. With shoulders high and forward, he walked up the narrow aisle between press and counsel, and as he stood to take the oath I felt an element of compassion towards him. I wondered how he was going to extricate himself from an intrigue of his own making. He did not leave me long in doubt, however, in the process effectively eliminating any hint of compassion that might have stirred in me.

The chair in the witness-box was scarcely warm beneath Mr Gibbons when, with reference to a discussion he claimed to have had with me in mid-March, he stated: "Captain Kelly informed me that it was his intention to leave the army because he, having served in the North for a considerable period as an intelligence officer, had decided to give his allegiance to the people in the North, and for that reason he proposed to leave the army."

It was a traumatic experience for me to listen to this assertion coming so smoothly from the Minister's lips, because in all my dealings with people from Northern Ireland I had insisted that any help given would have to be on the authority of the Dublin Government. I had therefore reported all my activities to the Director of Intelligence and, because I considered the matter of such importance, I had arranged a meeting with Mr Gibbons, the Minister for Defence as he then was, on March 4, and had reported to him thereafter, while I continued to report to Colonel Hefferon.

Mr Gibbons went on to say that he could not remember whether it was on that occasion or later that the question of guns arose.

> "But I asked him how did he propose to provide for himself and his family, having left the army in these circumstances. I asked him first whether he was married and how many children he had, and he told me he was married and that he had a number of children. And I deemed it the most expedient thing to say to him that he should not rush precipitately out of the army because of his expressed conviction, but that he would allow me to cast about to see if some alternative employment could be found for him. I was considering his personal position at this time and at this time I was impressed by what I considered to be an honourable declaration of change of allegiance."

"You said this to Captain Kelly?" Counsel prompted.

"I do not recall in any detail at all what I said to Captain Kelly but I think I did express appreciation of the services he had given which I recognise from official circles as having been of a high order."

"Did he say anything in response to your suggestion about a change of position?" Counsel asked.

"He appeared to be agreeable."

Skillfully intertwining truth with fiction, Mr Gibbons was walking a tightrope of plausibility with some success, but he had admitted that I had brought the question of guns to his notice and went on: "Captain Kelly said that they – meaning the people in the North with whom he was associated – proposed to import guns from the Continent and that he proposed to help them."

He agreed that there was a subsequent reference to a particular lot of guns:

> "I cannot be absolutely precise about the date but I would, from recollection, say it would be possibly the last days of March. On that occasion Captain Kelly, at the request of another member of the Government, came to my office in Leinster House and he informed me of a visit that had taken place at Dublin docks in the recent past and his story was to this effect that they, or we, meaning the people who conspired to take the guns, expected them to come into Dublin docks and when they went down to meet them, that the Irish army was there in strength taking delivery of a regular army shipment of weapons and at that stage I said to Captain Kelly, 'I presume at that stage you disappeared into the shadows?' and from my recollection again, he seemed to assent to this."

Once again, while basically telling the truth, Mr Gibbons could not resist drawing on his imagination, for instead of disappearing into the shadows on the day in question, I had actually shaken hands with and spoken to the sergeant-in-charge of the army guard, Nicholas Murphy, a man with whom I had served some years previously.

Mr Gibbons continued: "I said I presume that's the end of that anyway and Captain Kelly said 'no, it isn't', and indicated that by some means or other, it might be possible to retrieve them. I seem to have a recollection of Captain Kelly mentioning the possibility of having them shipped through a port on the Adriatic, for I suggested to him 'would that port possibly be Trieste' and his reply was rather vague and I don't recall it".

It was clear from Mr Gibbons' evidence that I briefed him on the essentials of what had taken place at Dublin docks on March 25, and that he had also been told about likely follow-up action. Apparently, it did not seem strange to Mr Gibbons that I, having, he alleged, already told him that I was giving my "allegiance to the people in the North", should inform him about a consignment of arms. If there had been any logic in Mr Gibbons' position, this consignment would have had to be smuggled North without the Government's authority. If I was not acting under the authority of the Minister for Defence, is it conceivable that I would tell him about the proposed arms importation? This, in essence, was the major weakness in Mr Gibbons' evidence as it applied to me. It made nonsense of his "change of allegiance" allegation.

Mr Séamus Sorahan, representing John Kelly, elicited from Mr Gibbons the fact that he had met a delegation from Northern Ireland in the

the Parliamentary Secretary's dining-room in Leinster House early in March. The Minister admitted that John Kelly was present at that meeting, but stated that I had only appeared at it briefly. In fact, I sat in on the meeting during the entire three or four hours it lasted, with the exception of a few minutes when I took a phone-call in a further corner of the room. As I went to the telephone, Mr Gibbons commented "there goes Ho Chi Minh", a remark which the Northern delegates found extremely amusing in the circumstances. To Mr Sorahan, Mr Gibbons denied having any recollection of the remark, stating that he could see no similarity between me and Ho Chi Minh.

"Have you ever heard of the Ho Chi Minh trail? Might you have meant this as a reference to his being in charge of the trail?" Mr Sorahan asked.

Gibbons: "No. What I have said and what I repeat is that I have not the slightest recollection of making any reference to Ho Chi Minh, the Ho Chi Minh trail or anything else of that kind."

It was a most emphatic reply despite the fact that the Ho Chi Minh reference was the type of pertinent witticism for which Mr Gibbons had something of a reputation and which, if only because of the reaction from a conversant Northern audience, he might be expected to remember.

When Mr Sorahan asked whether, at the end of the meeting, Mr Gibbons had called John Kelly and another member of the delegation aside and requested that they keep in touch with him, the Minister replied: "This arose when I mistook Mr John Kelly for Captain Kelly."

Mr Finlay returned to the alleged mistaken identity, later when he queried Mr Gibbons: "You told My Lord and the jury that, on that occasion, you mentioned to John Kelly to get in touch with you again, as a mistaken identity for Captain Kelly". Mr Gibbons agreed.

Finlay: "I think they are somewhat similar in appearance."
Gibbons: "I think I said I would like to see you soon."
Finlay: "They are somewhat similar in appearance."
Gibbons: "Yes."
Finlay: "May we take it from that that you knew the appearance of Captain Kelly as of March 3?"
Gibbons: "No, I recall clearly when Captain Kelly came into the room I was quite surprised to discover that it was not the person I was expecting."
Finlay: "And you were anxious at that time to speak to the person you

identified as Captain Kelly – one of your own officers – not John Kelly?"
Gibbons: "I was curious about him."
Finlay: "The message you gave to John Kelly to come and talk to you some time was intended for Captain Kelly."
Gibbons: "Yes."
Finlay: "So you are anxious as of March 3 to meet and talk with Captain Kelly. Is that right?"
Gibbons: "The remark was very casual."

However casual Mr Gibbons may have wished his remark to appear to the court, there was no necessity for it at all, because my appointment with him for the following morning had been made before he met the delegation. Further, even if he was speaking to someone whom he supposed to be Captain Kelly, he would hardly use the words "I would like to see you soon" in the circumstances. The fact is that he was quite emphatic in his request to John Kelly and another member of the delegation to keep in contact with him. He gave them his telephone number and impressed upon them that they should feel free to call him at any time. There was no need to go to such extremes with an army officer, who knew quite well how to get in touch with his Minister, as the Minister himself was fully aware.

In further cross-examination, Mr Finlay asked Mr Gibbons if he were aware of the meeting of Defence Committee representatives that had taken place in Bailieboro. Mr Gibbons replied that he was not aware. Yet, not only had the Taoiseach discussed this meeting with Mr Gibbons, but also when Mr Gibbons and I met during March and April, the Minister referred to the Berry/Taoiseach misinterpretation of what had happened in Bailieboro, clearly implying that the Taoiseach was *au fait* with subsequent developments and not likely to be led astray by Mr Berry again.

When questioned on army contingency plans in the early Spring of 1970, Mr Gibbons claimed privilege.

Finlay: "...this being a criminal prosecution brought by the State..."

"By the Attorney General," Mr Justice O'Keefe cut Mr Finlay short.

Finlay: "It is brought by the Attorney General as an arm of the executive."
O'Keeffe: 'No. Let us be clear on this. The Attorney General, when he brings a prosecution, brings it as representing the people and as a constitutional officer in his own right."
Mr Finlay submitted that the prosecution was brought by the State and

that having been brought as a criminal case, there was a principle prohibiting the State from claiming privilege in any matter which was, or appeared to be, relevant to the defence: that it would be unjust for a person to be put on trial and find that matters directly relevant to the charges against him were, by virtue of executive action, to be concealed from the jury.

Finally, when Mr Finlay had made various submissions in support of his reasoning, Mr McKenna stated that as far as the Attorney General was concerned, the instructions were that no defendant in the case was to be deprived of any single bit of information material to his defence, whether or not such information would normally be privileged or where it would normally be in breach of the Official Secrets Act. The Attorney General was anxious that the judge and jury should know every bit of evidence that was material to the case, Mr McKenna said. As enunciated by Mr McKenna it seemed that there was going to be no obstacle in the way of a fair trial.

The cross-examination of Mr Gibbons continued. He admitted knowledge of a Directive issued by him to the army on February 6, but he was imprecise and vague as to details.

When asked the reason why the Directive was issued, he replied:

> "The functions of the army and the directions of the Minister to the army are, in my opinion, matters of privilege and I am not at liberty to disclose in any detail at all what was in contemplation at that time. I submit, sir (to the judge), that this is a privilege matter."

Arguments for and against, and State counsel announced that it was no part of the Attorney General's intention to withhold any information from the defence, but, that in this particular case, the claim for privilege would seem to be justified. Fair play all round, but don't bet your life or your freedom on it.

Finlay: "Mr Gibbons, was there a Directive issued by you on or about February 6 in relation to the necessity to make completely conditional and contingency plans towards possible future events in Northern Ireland?"
Gibbons to Judge: "I take it, sir, that you are allowing this question now?"
Judge: "Within limits".
Gibbons: "Well, I got such instructions and passed them on to the army."
Finlay: "Was one of the decisions reached as a result of your directions that the army should acquire further arms which might, I emphasise – in

certain circumstances to be decided by the Government – be distributed to persons in Northern Ireland?"
Gibbons: "This is hardly accurate... The intention was that a sufficient stock of suitable weapons should be readily available for any emergency that might present itself. The emergencies themselves, as far as I can recall now, were not specified."

The matter of the Directive was let lie at that stage. Meanwhile, it was back to the five hundred rifles sent to Dundalk on April 2.

Sorahan (Counsel for John Kelly): "To your knowledge as Minister for Defence, was there a plan to move arms to the Border at the time of the Ballymurphy riots? To Dundalk Barracks? Have you any recollection of that?"
Gibbons: "Of what?"
Sorahan: "Late night moves in high places, and the decision by the army and perhaps by you to send 500 rifles to Dundalk Barracks as a matter of urgency to have them ready for distribution across the Border, if the need arose?... Any recollection of that?"
Gibbons to Judge: "Is this question admissible, sir?"
Judge: "I think it probably is, yes."
Gibbons: "I was on my way home to Kilkenny through Naas, and I was stopped by the police and asked to ring Mr Neil Blaney. Neil Blaney said that he had information of the direst kind, and that he'd been in touch with Mr Haughey, and that somebody was being sent to find the Taoiseach in order to acquaint him of the position, and I was requested by Neil T. Blaney to send a certain consignment of arms to Dundalk. I rang the Chief-of-Staff, and I think the words I said to him were to this effect: I spoke to him in Irish: that I had this request from Mr Blaney, and it might be better to comply with it, and to make sure that stringent security was observed at all stages. I think I recall saying something to the effect that 'if I don't do this, he may do something rash himself'."
Sorahan: "The order was given and to your knowledge was carried out properly?"
Gibbons: "Yes."
Sorahan: "And arms were moved to Dundalk?"
Gibbons: "Yes."

Mr Finlay, my counsel, was not willing to let go of the rifles. He was intent on making absolutely clear where responsibility for their movement belonged.

"On your initiative?" he queried.

Gibbons: "Yes."
Finlay: "Was it correct to say that the purpose of sending them there was that, if a decision was made subsequently by you to distribute arms to Northern Ireland, that would provide a stop convenient to the Border?"
Gibbons: "That need not necessarily be the function of sending the rifles. It could equally be said that these rifles which, at all times, were in the control of the Irish army, could be used for defensive purposes."
Finlay: "I fully appreciate that, Mr Gibbons, but am I not right in understanding, that the request with which you complied that week-end was to send up arms, one of the possible uses of which was going to be distribution into the North of Ireland."
Gibbons: "I don't think this would have happened because I… "
Finlay: "I'm not asking you whether you think it could have happened or not. What I want to get from you is whether you do not agree with me that one of the purposes for which you were asked, and did send up these arms, was the possibility that they might eventually be used in that way?"
Gibbons: "Arms would not have been used at all for any purpose without the full agreement of the Irish Government."
Finlay: "I fully understand that. And I am asking you again whether one of the possible purposes for which they might be used – if the Irish Government so decided – was distribution into the North of Ireland?"
Gibbons: "We get back to the fundamental reason why any country maintains an army, and it is for the defence of life, that is for the defence of life and property. I deemed it the most expedient thing at that particular time to send a consignment of weapons from one part of the army to another for reasons that were not directly related to their use elsewhere."
Finlay: "Were they indirectly related to the possibility of their use elsewhere?"
Gibbons: "They were related to a situation which purported to be, and, as I now believe, did not exist at all in fact."
Finlay: "I fully appreciate that but were they indirectly related to the possibility – if the situation had been as reported to you – of use in Northern Ireland by persons other than the army?"
Gibbons: "The only thing I can say about that is that on my instructions the rifles were moved to Dundalk, and I feel that as Minister for Defence, if I felt it necessary or desirable, it would be within my authority to remove any particular batches of weapons from point A to point B – provided that, at all times, they were within the keeping of the Irish army, and that their moving remained within the law."

Finlay: "Can I again ask the first question, as to whether one of the possible reasons which might have been behind the moving of the arms was that, in the event of a Government decision to that effect, they could be distributed in the North to persons other than persons in the army?"
Gibbons: "I think counsel is trying to put words in my mouth."
Finlay: "I have asked you that question five times, I think, and I only want a yes or no answer."
Gibbons: "One cannot give a yes or no answer to such a complicated question. The ultimate function of a rifle is the taking of life. A rifle is a thing for killing, and the thing we want most is to avoid killing."

Mr Gibbons was obviously not going to answer what should have been a simple question for the Minister responsible at the time of the despatch of the rifles, and although Mr Finlay pressed hard, he did not get a direct answer.

The truth of the matter is that serious rioting had taken place in Belfast's Ballymurphy on April 2. When it seemed that it might escalate, placing the overwhelmingly Nationalist community in the area in grave danger, a request was sent South to the Dublin Government for arms. Mr Gibbons's response was to order that arms stored for that very purpose in Dublin's Clancy Barracks be moved to Dundalk with all possible speed, for possible distribution in Northern Ireland. The sense of urgency was such that some of the gas masks dispatched were thrown into the trucks to lie scattered loosely on top of the arms and ammunition. For days afterwards, gas masks found on the Dublin to Dundalk road were handed in at police stations along the way.

Mr Gibbons's equivocation and avoidance of the truth was explained by his anxiety not to admit that he was putting into effect Government contingency plans to intervene in Northern Ireland as late as April 1970. It was purely incidental that the arms did not cross the Border. The simple reason was that they were no longer needed.

One of the army officers who supervised the movement of the Ballymurphy arms was a friend of the then Minister, Kevin Boland. Mr Boland, of course, had served in the army during the war years and knew many of the older officers. His officer friend was at pains to point out that the movement of the arms could not have been carried out so efficiently in the middle of the night unless it was a pre-planned, push-button affair. Mr Boland himself was adamant that "it was the Contingency Plan put into effect in the belief that the hour of catastrophe was at hand", as recorded in *Up Dev.*

Mr Gibbons told the court of a meeting he had with Mr Haughey: "It was either Friday, April 17 or Monday April 20, I am not certain, and the reason I contacted him was I had been approached by the Secretary of my Department."

McKenna (prosecuting counsel): "Was it a personal conversation or did you contact him on the telephone?"
Gibbons: "I rang Mr Haughey on the telephone and I said I had a matter of great importance to discuss, and would he kindly wait in his office for me. And he said, 'Come on over' and I went over. It was in the afternoon, incidentally rather late in the afternoon. I told him of certain phone calls that had come to the Department of Defence concerning the shipment of weapons and ammunition into the country, and I asked him if he knew this, and he said, 'The dogs in the street are barking it.' I asked him if he was in a position to stop it, and he said, 'I'll stop it for a month', or words to that effect. I said, 'For God's sake, stop it altogether'."
McCarthy (Haughey's counsel) cross-examining: "On the date, Mr Gibbons, on which you went to Mr Haughey about what you had heard?"
Gibbons: "There were several of these dates."
McCarthy: "The one on which you say that Mr Haughey said, 'The dogs in the street are barking it?' "
Gibbons: "Oh, yes."
McCarthy: "You said in your evidence yesterday, Mr Gibbons, that it may have been either Monday, the 20th or Friday, 17th?"
Gibbons: "It's general uncertainty…"
McCarthy: "Is that a characteristic of yours, Mr Gibbons?"
Gibbons: "I can't recall precisely whether it was on Monday or on Friday."
McCarthy: "No, but, generally speaking, do you tend to be uncertain, say, in regard to dates or facts?"
Gibbons: "I am not good on dates."
McCarthy: "You are not good on dates?"
Gibbons: "No, I can't remember dates."
McCarthy: "You made a statement to the Garda officers, presumably this forms the substance of your statement of evidence?"
Gibbons: "I did, yes."
McCarthy: "And you have read your statement of evidence, I rather inferred from your evidence yesterday?"
Gibbons: "Yes."
McCarthy: "You have read it recently?"
Gibbons: "In the last few days."
McCarthy: "You know that in your evidence you said 'on Monday, the 20th April' in reference to this?"

Gibbons: "Yes."
McCarthy: "You know also, I suppose, that in your statement of evidence you said, 'I spoke to Charles Haughey on the phone, and told him that a telephone call had come to the Department of Defence from Dublin Airport asking if the army expected delivery of a consignment of arms, and of other calls from the Department of Transport and Power'?"
Gibbons: "Yes, that's an inaccuracy."
McCarthy: " How did such an inaccuracy arise?"
Gibbons: "I don't know. It is through no fault of mine, sir. What happened, and I am telling the court now, was that I rang Mr Haughey on the telephone. I said I had a matter of great importance to discuss with him, and would he please wait in his office until I called round to see him."
McCarthy: "Why didn't you put that in your statement?"
Gibbons: "I am not sure that I didn't put that in my statement, but that is the fact of the matter anyway.
McCarthy: "When did you first receive the statement of evidence to read?"
Gibbons: "Possibly about three weeks ago, I should think."
McCarthy: "Did you read it then?"
Gibbons: "Yes."
McCarthy: "Why didn't you point this out then?"
Gibbons: "I didn't spot it then."
McCarthy: "But surely it was the most important meeting you had with Mr Haughey, would you agree – over this matter?"
Gibbons: "Yes."
McCarthy: "You know Mr Haughey had been charged and returned for trial concerning this matter?"
Gibbons: "Yes."
McCarthy: "How is it, Mr Gibbons, that, where not merely the date is doubtful but the manner of communication is totally wrong, that you didn't draw the attention of the Gardaí or the State Solicitor to it?"
Gibbons: " The question of the telephone call escaped my attention. I did mention to the Department of Justice my doubts about the 17th or the 20th of April as the day on which this conversation took place."
McCarthy: "Mr Gibbons, in your statement of evidence, and perhaps I will repeat to you, 'On Monday, April 20th, I spoke to Charles Haughey on the phone and told him a telephone call had come to the Department of Defence from Dublin Airport asking if the army expected delivery of a consignment of arms, and of other calls from the Department of Transport and Power. He said, 'I'll stop it for a month.' I said, 'For God's

sake, stop it altogether.' That is a summary of the conversation you gave. You are now expressing doubt as to the date and you are stating positively that the conversation took place in Mr Haughey's office."

Gibbons: "Yes."

McCarthy: "I want you to give such explanation as you can as to why this appears in your statement."

Gibbons: "As to the date, I expressed a doubt to the Department of Justice as to whether it was the 20th or the 17th. I have told the court more than once that I am not certain whether it was the one or the other. As for the rest of the – "

McCarthy: "When do you say you told the Department of Justice this?"

Gibbons: "I would think shortly after the time I got my statement."

McCarthy: "I see. Some three weeks ago?"

Gibbons: "Yes."

McCarthy: "Well, what about the phone call?"

Gibbons: "The phone call I would look upon rather as bad construction of English, ambiguous English, than making any material difference. I spoke to Charlie Haughey on the phone, that is correct, literally. And told him that a telephone call had come to the Department – but I did the telling verbally."

McCarthy: "I know – but you had to go from Parkgate Street to Merrion Street?"

Gibbons: "Yes."

McCarthy: "In order to do so?"

Gibbons: "That's right."

McCarthy: "Did you hear Counsel for the State, opening the prosecution, tell the jury – Were you in court, Mr Gibbons?"

Gibbons: "Yes, sir."

McCarthy;: "And you heard Mr McKenna opening the case to the jury?"

Gibbons: "With some difficulty. It was difficult to hear down there" (the body of the court).

McCarthy: "Well, I am going to quote to you what I believe he said: 'Mr Gibbons would say that on Monday, the 20th, he spoke to Mr Haughey on the phone and told him that a phone call had come to the Department of Defence, etcetera.' Exactly quoting from your statement of evidence?"

Gibbons: "Yes. I suggest that this is ambiguity rather than inaccuracy."

McCarthy: "I suggest that it is rather misleading to the defendants, Mr Gibbons, to have it stated in the statement of evidence, stated by leading counsel for the prosecution, and uncontradicted until you give evidence. Can you give any explanation, Mr Gibbons, as to why you didn't correct it even last Wednesday when Mr McKenna stated it?"

Gibbons: "I don't know that I heard the actual speech of Counsel."
McCarthy: "Did you read it in the paper?"
Gibbons: "Not carefully. I am not well acquainted with legal procedure, and, for the life of me, I cannot see how it affects the question materially."
McCarthy: "I would suggest to you one way, Mr Gibbons. I will ask you if you'll agree with me that having heard Mr Fegan's evidence, and my questioning of him, it became apparent to you that it would be better if the events had taken place on Friday, the 17th... Does that commend itself to you?"
Gibbons: "This appears to be a suggestion from you that –"
Judge (intervening): "It is a suggestion that you altered your evidence in order to make it fit with something that you heard in court."
Gibbons: "Yes, and this is something I deny. Absolutely."

The Mr Fegan, to whom Mr McCarthy referred, had been Mr Haughey's personal assistant in the Department of Finance. He had given evidence on the second day of the trial that he had phoned me in Vienna on the morning of April 20, with instructions to call off the operation. In view of this, it would be pointless for Mr Gibbons to have his alleged conversation with Mr Haughey on the afternoon of Monday, April 20. It did not make sense, as the operation was already called off.

With uncertainty, doubt, ambiguity, doubtful English, the mysteries of legal procedures and "not good on dates" to the forefront, it was an incredible performance by a clever, articulate man, a Minister of State with a reputation for wit, urbanity and verbal dexterity. By times he did not seem to believe himself. In this he was at one with most others in the court. As Tom McIntyre wrote in *Through the Bridewell Gate:*

> "This witness is crumbling, voice thinning, physique thinning – shuttle of the psyche, shuttle of flesh and bone – exactly as if the onslaught of the past two days has pushed him back back back into some livid trauma of adolescence."

CHAPTER 13

Albert Luykx had been appointed Irish agent for Herr Otto Schleuter on April 3 1970. A man not willing to let the grass grow under his feet, he arranged that a representative of Schleuter's would come to Ireland on May 3 to give a demonstration of military equipment to the Department of Defence. Two weapons were sent to Ireland in advance. Albert wrote to the Minister for Defence informing him of what was planned. In court, Mr Gibbons denied that he had been informed by either me or Colonel Hefferon that Schleuter was the arms supplier.

Wood (Counsel for Mr Luykx): "Mr Gibbons, cast your mind back as to whether you were told by Captain Kelly or indeed Colonel Hefferon that Schleuter was the arms supplier?"
Gibbons: "I never heard the name Schleuter until the question came into the newspapers."
Wood: "Surely, Mr Gibbons, your memory is at fault?"
Gibbons: "It is not , sir, not on this."
Woods*:* "Do you remember Mr Blaney handing you a copy of a letter from Mr Luykx to the Minister for Defence?"
Gibbons: "Yes".
Wood: "That is dated April 23rd?"
Gibbons: "Yes."
Wood: "Do you have that?"
Gibbons: "I gave it to my Private Secretary and I told him to destroy it."
Wood: "Did you?"
Gibbons: "Yes. This letter was given to me by Mr Blaney. He told me it was a copy of a letter which had been sent officially to the Minister for Defence and had gone to the Ministry rather than the Minister in the ordinary way, and I gave this letter to my Private Secretary and I said: 'Destroy that thing.' "
Wood: "Your Private Secretary sounds a little like the public hangman. Why not destroy it yourself?"
Gibbons: "I was going through various letters in my pocket, as I remember, and this document that had been handed to me by Mr Blaney was among them. Some of them would have been constituency letters, various documents of one kind or another. What the letter purported to be was –"
Wood: "No, I asked why you wouldn't destroy it yourself?"
Gibbons: "Because it is customary for my Private Secretary to deal with my correspondence."

Albert Luykx

Wood: "And did he tear up your waste paper? Tell me now, Minister, why did you want it destroyed?
Gibbons: "My attitude was that I didn't want anything to do with this particular firm."
Wood: "Why?"
Gibbons: "Because by now it was apparent to me that they were in some way involved in this affair, and the giving of the letter to me by Mr Blaney was in some way suspicious to me."
Wood: "Were you afraid of something?"
Gibbons: "I was."
Wood: "And that was that you would be associated with the obtaining of arms from Schleuter. Is that so?"
Gibbons: "I don't recall the name Schleuter."
Wood: "Mr Gibbons, would you answer the question you were asked?"
Gibbons: "What question are you asking?"
Wood: "Was there anything in the contents of the letter that made you afraid?"
Gibbons: "The letter, as far as I can recall, offered the Irish army — "
Wood: "I asked you was there anything in the contents of the letter of which you were afraid?"
Gibbons: "Yes."
Wood: "What?"
Gibbons: "I was afraid the letter for some reason or other was a plant."
Wood: "Was a plant?"
Gibbons: "Yes."
Wood: "Now this letter was destroyed, Minister, by your secretary?"
Gibbons: "I told him to destroy it."
Wood: "No copy was put on the departmental file."
Gibbons: "I don't know about that."
Wood: "You don't know. Do you know if any reply was sent?"
Gibbons: "I don't."
Wood: "Does it strike you as odd, Minister, that a letter should not be replied to by your department?"

Gibbons: "Not in these circumstances."
Wood: "May I take it that you didn't reply because you felt you had burned your fingers with Mr Blaney ? "
Gibbons: "No, on the contrary. I felt, as I have said already, that this was a plant of some kind."
Wood: "Was it a plant by Mr Blaney?"
Gibbons: "I think so. Yes."

Mr Gibbons never heard the name Schleuter until the question came into the newspapers. He was confident and cocksure, all set to put that issue to bed once and for all, but by half-time in a short bout of cross-examination, he was telling us that he didn't recall the name Schleuter. There is a big difference between "I never heard the name…" and "I don't recall the name…". The first is a very positive assertion, either true or false, while the latter might get you something of a "fool's pardon", a poor man with a bad memory, God help him, if the denial proved to be false. And, as Wood prodded and jabbed with his own special brand of subtle pomposity, It looked more and more as if the denial, however phrased, was false. In fact, it was impossible to conclude otherwise, when Schleuter's name was on the letter proposing to send a representative to Ireland to demonstrate military equipment.

When Mr Gibbons was questioned about an interview I had with him between April 5 and April 15, Mr Gibbons claimed that he had no memory of it.

Finlay: "I must put it to you, in fairness, that it will be part of Captain Kelly's evidence that he particularly pointed out to you at that time that the distribution of Irish army rifles in Northern Ireland would be a crazy operation as every Irish army rifle has a serial number on it and is entirely traceable. Do you understand?"
Gibbons: "Yes, sir."
Finlay: "Do you remember Captain Kelly saying that?"
Gibbons: "I have not the slightest recollection."
Finlay: "And I suggest that you and he discussed the urgent necessity of untraceable arms if this event were ever to recur?"
Gibbons: "No, I have no recollection of that."

There were other reasons why Mr Gibbons should have remembered that particular meeting, a meeting for part of which Mr Neil Blaney, then Minister for Agriculture, was present. One of the subjects discussed in Mr Blaney's presence was the appointment of Colonel Delaney as Director of

Intelligence. Previously, Mr Gibbons had discussed with me the possibility of Colonel Hefferon's remaining past his retirement age as Director of Intelligence, first because of his long experience in the position and, secondly, because of his intimate knowledge of Northern Ireland affairs. This would have meant finding an alternative position for Colonel Delaney. On April 9, Colonel Hefferon, the outgoing Director of Intelligence, visited Mr Gibbons in company with the incoming Colonel Delaney. Afterwards, Colonel Delaney suggested to Colonel Hefferon that his appointment had been due to Mr Gibbons' influence. I challenged Mr Gibbons about this but the Minister vehemently and categorically denied using his influence to have Colonel Delaney appointed. Later, when both Mr Gibbons and Colonel Delaney emerged as prosecution witnesses working in apparent unison and harmony, the conversation very naturally came to mind, to my mind, at any rate. In fact, Gibbons and Delaney were old friends. In the early seventies, I met Commandant Fergus Fleming, a former intelligence colleague of mine, who was working in Zambia during the arms trials. He told me that back in the early sixties, he and other officers got involved in attempting to form an Army Officers' Club in Dublin, an initiative that did not find favour with the establishment. Colonel Delaney was one of the officers supporting the formation of the Club. He claimed that his good friend, Jim Gibbons, through his political contacts, would do all he could to help bring the Club into being. There was no doubt in Commandant Fleming's mind but that Delaney and Gibbons were good friends at that time.

In continuing his cross-examination, Mr Finlay asked whether the Minister had received a query early in April about excusing Captain Kelly from regimental duties.

Gibbons: "No, not that I recall. When Captain Kelly came to see me first to indicate his intention of leaving the army, I asked him if he would take up regimental duties and what his intentions were. He said that he was leaving because of his allegiance to the people of the North."

While harking back to his "change of allegiance" allegation, Mr Gibbons, obviously briefed on the dual meaning of "regimental duties" in military circles, confused the issue by his misinterpretation of the phrase in the sense that it had been used by Mr Finlay. The latter was referring to the twenty-four hour stint as Duty Officer, Army Headquarters, for which Captains and other ranks on the headquarters staff are detailed in turn. This is known as a regimental duty or duties. The term "regimental duties" is also used to designate an appointment with a *line* unit such as an infantry battalion, as distinct from staff duties as, for example, at Army Headquarters.

Not to be diverted, Mr Finlay re-phrased his question: "Were you in fact involved in a decision to excuse Captain Kelly from regimental duties over the weekend from April 2 to 4 to permit him to go abroad?"

Gibbons: "No, I was not aware that Captain Kelly was going abroad at all. I understand that some time previously, he had applied for leave to visit his sister in Frankfurt. I took it that he had a sister there."
Finlay: "Isn't it correct to say that at that time, the official information available to you was that he was going in connection with these affairs to the Continent, to Germany, and that the ostensible reason being given out as a cover for that was that it was to visit his sister in Frankfurt?"
Gibbons: "The Director of Intelligence told me that he had applied for permission to visit his sister."
Finlay: "Didn't the Director of Intelligence say that the real reason for going out was to vet arms?"
Gibbons: "He dealt with it in a rather equivocal way. He said 'I have an idea the real reason may be to vet arms'. That was the expression used."
Finlay: "So the Director of Intelligence told you, this would have been some time around the middle of February, that Captain Kelly, he believed, was going to vet arms and that he was giving as a cover or ostensible reason for that leave that he was going to visit his sister in Frankfurt?"
Gibbons: "Yes, I asked him if he had a sister in Frankfurt and I understood him to say that he had. That was my knowledge of the situation at that stage. To me it appeared to be a somewhat unreasonable assumption."

Officers go to the Continent frequently enough to visit sisters or otherwise and it is not necessary to refer the matter to the Minister. If I had merely been visiting my sister, the Minister would not have been approached about my leave either. He was approached because I was going to vet arms and the Director of Intelligence wanted to keep him in the picture. In fact, I travelled to the Continent on February 19 without taking leave, precisely because the Minister had authorised the trip.

As the replies to Mr Finlay's questions indicate, Mr Gibbons switched from my Continental visit in the first week of April as soon as he could. This trip was made necessary by the non-arrival of the consignment of arms expected at Dublin docks on March 25 of which Mr Gibbons, as his evidence showed, was fully aware. In order to facilitate my going to the Continent on April 1, the Director of Intelligence had requested Mr

Gibbons to arrange cancellation of a regimental duty for which, it appeared, I was scheduled on April 4.

Mr Gibbons denied any knowledge of my April 1 trip and subsequently Colonel Hefferon rebutted that denial. It is ironic, therefore, that I was not detailed for regimental duty during the first week in April at all. Through an error in communication, I had been told that I was on duty on Saturday April 4, whereas in fact I was not rostered for duty until the following Saturday, April 11. Otherwise it is possible that but for the duty contretemps Colonel Hefferon might not have approached Mr Gibbons before the trip. He might, for example, have waited for a routine talk with the Minister to inform him of my visit to the Continent – such a routine talk might not have taken place because Colonel Hefferon retired shortly afterwards. This would have allowed Mr Gibbons, while in the witness-box, to deny specific authorisation without fear of contradiction by another prosecution witness, Colonel Hefferon.

When questioned on an application for retirement I submitted in mid-January in conjunction with a proposal to employ me in some other branch of Government service, Mr Gibbons, building on his "change of allegiance" allegation, attempted to convey that his primary concern was to get me out of the army because he disapproved of my activities. One of the cover jobs suggested for me was that of pig smuggling preventive officer. Mr Finlay asked whether the purpose of this was not that I should continue the work I had been doing for army intelligence under different cover.

Gibbons: "No, the real thing was that I wanted him out of the army. My real anxiety was that he would be picked up on the other side of the border by the Northern authorities. I discussed this with the Director of Intelligence and said: 'they must be blind if they are not on to him now' to which he replied, 'they must indeed be', and I spoke to another colleague in the Government about this."

It was not possible that Mr Gibbons should have had such a discussion with the Director of Intelligence after mid-January because I had not crossed the border since the previous October – on the orders of the Directors of Intelligence. During one of our discussions when the subject of a cover job was mentioned, Mr Gibbons suggested that I might go and live in the North the better to carry out my work and I explained to him that it was not necessary and that, in fact, it had not been necessary for me to cross the border since October 1969. He accepted this and from that time his attitude was that there was no real necessity for a cover job, and he indicated that the Government would take responsibility for my activities as a legitimate intelligence exercise if the question ever arose.

In the witness-box, Mr Gibbons stated that rather than having any intention of providing me with a cover job, his interest was in getting me a post in the Government service which would give me a pay structure similar to that of an army captain and that, because of this, he had suggested getting me a job in the Ordnance Survey. It was Mr Haughey, he said, who suggested the job of pig preventive smuggling officer, "who thought it was a lovely idea as he watched the soldiers marching along on parade". Again Mr Gibbons' penchant for the colourful, if perhaps trite, phrase had let him down, for the parade which Mr Haughey had reviewed was the St Patrick's Day Industrial Parade and while there was a guard-of-honour drawn up opposite the reviewing stand, there were no soldiers "marching along on parade".

In reply to further questioning by Mr Finlay, Mr Gibbons agreed he knew that, while still serving as an army intelligence officer, I intended to continue with the arms importation. Against this, he claimed, he had balanced what he hoped would be my removal from the army, as he had also balanced information he had obtained from the then Minister for Justice, Mr Ó Moráin, who had indicated that he was anxious about my activities and those of some of my colleagues – an anxiety which, Mr Ó Moráin had intimated, he proposed conveying to the Taoiseach. From that time, Mr Gibbons said, he knew that I was under Special Branch surveillance.

Mr Micheál Ó Moráin, former Minister for Justice, was called by the prosecution immediately after Mr Gibbons. A solid citizen, he sat squarely in the witness chair, eyes heavy in an apparently neutral face. He said that he had not, during his period as Minister for Justice, given a licence or authority under the Firearms Act to any of the defendants to import arms or ammunition into the State, nor had he, to his recollection, given any such licence or authority on an application made on behalf of the defendants for such importation.

Mr Sorahan, representing John Kelly, asked:

"I think you retired through ill health, was it in May or June?"

Ó Moráin: "I cannot be sure about dates. I think I may save time if I say this here and now: these events with which the court is concerned took place six months ago or more. I tried last Friday to see the documents with which I was concerned, on some of which I made notes, and I was refused permission to see them by the present Minister for Justice and the Attorney General, so on the question of dates and, indeed, any of these matters, I am under quite great disability."

This revelation brought a gasp from the body of the court and well it might, for it made a mockery of prosecuting counsel's earlier assertion that "the Attorney General was anxious that the judge and jury should know every bit of evidence that was material to the case".

The evidence that the Minister for Justice had supported the Attorney General in his refusal to allow Mr Ó Moráin to see the relevant documentation made the situation all the more sinister. It made a mockery of Mr Justice O'Keefe's categorical declaration that "the Attorney General, when he brings a prosecution, brings it as representing the people and as a constitutional officer in his own right".

Mr Ó Moráin agreed, in answer to Mr Sorahan, that John Kelly's name had been mentioned in reports or at Cabinet meetings.

Sorahan: "The name came up?"
Ó Moráin: "Yes."
McKenna (prosecuting): "From the point of view of the jury, there could be a tremendous difference whether the name came up in reports or at Cabinet meetings."
Sorahan: "Yes, it came up in reports."
Ó Moráin: "Yes."
Sorahan: "May it also have come up at Cabinet meetings?"
Ó Moráin: "As a result of reports."
Sorahan: "Did it come to your knowledge that there was something going on under the umbrella of Army Intelligence in relation to arms? Did you get some hint or whisper about that as Minister?"
Ó Moráin: "There was, I recollect, some information about Captain Kelly and arms. This would be very little. I have no knowledge at all of what..."

Asked how he would describe the relationship between Garda and Military Intelligence, Ó Moráin replied: "There was a grave lack of co-operation between the two bodies, that one crowd did not seem to know what the other was doing and I tried to do something about this."

Sorahan: "Did you ever have reason to think that Military Intelligence was reluctant to part with more than the minimum information to the police force, and particularly to the Special Branch?"
Ó Moráin: "In effect, yes, my Lord."
Sorahan: "Did you take steps then between September 1969 and April 1970 when you became ill, to remedy this situation, try to get rid of it?"
Ó Moráin: "My recollection would be that it was even this year in the few months before April, that I suggested that a Cabinet sub-committee be set

up for the purpose of coordinating these matters. Among other things, I made that suggestion to Mr Gibbons and to the Taoiseach."
Sorahan: "What was the suggestion?"
Ó Moráin: "That there be a Cabinet subcommittee to deal with Northern matters, including this intelligence."
Sorahan: "Was that suggestion adopted, can you say, by the Cabinet?"
Ó Moráin: "No. Well, it did not come before the Cabinet. I made it to Mr Gibbons and the Taoiseach. Nothing was done about it."
Mr Peter Maguire, counsel for Charles Haughey, asked Mr Ó Moráin if, as of April 18, he knew anything of the expected consignment of arms arriving at Dublin Airport on that date.

Ó Moráin: "In the days immediately before April 18 there were different conflicting reports. At one stage I remember... We were not aware of the stories being told here, and certainly at one of these stages I thought it was a case of one official implicating another. That would be a few days before April 18. Of these dates I cannot be too sure, but I know there were different reports coming in and in a general kind of way that there was a question of importation of arms."
Maguire: "In the days before April 18 you were under the impression, as far as you knew about it, that it was an official operation?"
Ó Moráin: "At a stage before this. Again, of the time, my Lord, I can't be sure..."
Maguire: "Now, were you aware, Mr Ó Moráin, of the Government's desire that the Army would prepare contingency plans to meet any developments in the North during the period we are dealing with?"
Ó Moráin: "I was."
Maguire: "And is it correct to say that the Minister for Finance, Mr Haughey, was at that time authorised to make moneys available to the army in connection with these contingency plans?"
Ó Moráin: "Yes, he was given authority, himself and Mr Gibbons, to do anything, get anything that was required."
Maguire: "And that included getting arms?"
Ó Moráin: "Oh, yes, as far as I understand it."

Mr Ó Moráin's understanding was that the importation of arms was an official operation. He had information associating me with arms and he stated that John Kelly's name had cropped up in reports and at Cabinet meetings. He felt that there was a grave lack of co-operation between the police and Army Intelligence in the matter, even thinking at one stage that officials were trying to implicate one another. The reason for this was hinted at when Mr Sorahan asked:

"Do you know is there a section of the Special Branch which is responsible to and reports directly to Mr Peter Berry and not to the Commissioner or the higher echelons at Garda Headquarters?"

Ó Moráin: "I do not think I should answer that."

In further cross-examination Mr Ó Moráin said that long reports on the operations of the Special Branch in the North came to him personally through the usual channels. He was not aware, he said, where they were actually prepared, but they were brought to him by Mr Berry.

Asked whether he was aware that these reports were made direct to Mr Berry rather than to Commissioner Weymes of the Garda Síochána, Mr Ó Moráin agreed that that could be so.

Mr Ó Moráin had suggested to Mr Gibbons and the Taoiseach that a Cabinet sub-committee be set up to co-ordinate State security services. The suggestion was ignored and it must be wondered why. Presumably Mr Ó Moráin gave Mr Gibbons and the Taoiseach his interpretation of events in at least as great detail as he submitted in evidence, which would mean that the Taoiseach was informed by his Minister for Justice some time "in the few months before April", of the possible importation of arms under the auspices of Army Intelligence. As his evidence showed, Mr Gibbons was aware of this possibility from February, a possibility that became a probability when, on his own admission, I told him of the Dublin docks incident on March 25 and the future plans for the retrieval of the arms and ammunition. And yet Mr Gibbons stood up in the Dáil on May 8, and in reference to a suggestion that any attempt I had made to smuggle arms was done with his knowledge and consent stated: "I wish emphatically to deny any such knowledge or consent…"

On the following day, May 9, also in the Dáil, Mr O'Higgins, a Fine Gael deputy, declared: "It was established yesterday that the facts of this attempted gun-running, this conspiracy to subvert the security of the State, had been in operation since last November." This was in support of a previous statement that "it was not merely on April 21 that an astonished Taoiseach came to learn that his Ministers were behaving suspiciously, if not disloyally." Shortly afterwards, the Taoiseach interrupted to say: "Would the deputy give way for one second? The first indication I got was on Monday, April 20. So I do not know what the deputy is relying on for asserting otherwise."

O'Higgins: "The Taoiseach says the first indication he got was on April 21."

Chapter 13

The Taoiseach: "Monday, April 20."

Gibbons knew of an attempted importation, Ó Moráin knew there was a question of an importation and Ó Moráin had informed the Taoiseach of his knowledge prior to April, yet on May 9, the Taoiseach told Deputy O'Higgins and Dáil Éireann that the first indication he got was on April 20.

CHAPTER 14

On the morning of September 28 I met Mrs Moynihan, my solicitor.

"Colonel Hefferon may be called today," she said.

"Don't worry," I told her. "He'll tell the truth."

Of all the people concerned with the case Colonel Hefferon was the one I knew best and over the longest period. He had been Director of Intelligence from October 1962 until his retirement the previous April. I had worked with him as a personal staff officer during all of that time, except for two years when I served with the United Nations, and a further period, from October 1968 to July 1969, when I had attended a Command and Staff course at the Military College.

"Colonel Hefferon is stern, forthright: the jut of jaw under moustache and spectacles, the parade of the shoulders say, 'This is how I am, how I have disciplined myself to be: take or leave —' and the jury take to him at once. A good witness", Tom MacIntyre stated in *Through the Bridewell Gate*.

In reply to Mr McKenna, Colonel Hefferon stated that I had been on holidays during August 1969 and that when I returned I told him I had been in Derry and Belfast and had given him a detailed account of what had taken place in both cities. He went on to say that he was glad to get such a report from a trained observer and that he had instructed me to develop the contacts made and to report directly to him. The fact that I was told to report directly to him placed me in a different position from other intelligence officers, Colonel Hefferon said.

He also told the court that after about two months, in September or October, he had given me specific instructions that I should no longer go into Northern Ireland; apart from that I was allowed a wide discretion. He described how I reported to him several times a week from September onwards, either by telephone or in person. If I had anything of particular interest or of a confidential nature I came to the office, he said, and on occasions he had instructed me to report matters of general interest to the general intelligence staff. On the question of arms, Mr McKenna asked: "From what Captain Kelly told you, who were these arms to be for?"

Hefferon: "They were to be for the Defence Committee, in the event that it would become necessary, in the event of the Government agreeing to them going to them."
Mr Justice O'Keeffe: "You said that the arms were to be for the Northern

Colonel Hefferon

Defence Committees in the event of a Government decision that that was where they were to go?"
Hefferon: "Yes."
O'Keeffe: "What was to happen to them in the meantime?"
Hefferon: "I gathered that they were to be put in a safe place pending a decision. It was not clear to me who was going to give the decision, but I understood, it would be a Government decision."
O'Keeffe: "Did he mention where the safe place was?"
Hefferon: "I'm afraid I will have to ask for privilege on that."

Mr McKenna then made the point that the Attorney General was not claiming privilege. Colonel Hefferon said that it was something that should not be published in the newspapers, that he would prefer to write the name down and give it to his Lordship. The judge objected to this, stating that he did not see why evidence should be given to him and not to the jury. Mr McKenna suggested that Colonel Hefferon should write the answer for the judge and that the latter could then decide whether or not the question of privilege arose.

O'Keeffe to Hefferon: "Am I to understand that this was a proposal by certain people in the Northern Defence Committee that arms should be imported into Dublin with the assistance of Captain Kelly, that they would be bought by the Northern Defence Committee group and put into a place of safety somewhere in Dublin?"
Hefferon: "I did not say Dublin."
O'Keeffe: "Somewhere in the State? They would remain the property of the Northern Defence Committee, or the group that brought them in?"
Hefferon: "The group that brought them in."

In the sense that John Kelly and I comprised the group, Colonel Hefferon's answer was correct, but the choice of terminology was rather unhappy. In fact it seemed to me that the judge was suggesting, contrary to the facts, that the arms would be under the control of some nebulous group, possibly outside my control, and thereby outside Government or official control. Mr McCarthy, for Charles Haughey, seemed to have a similar thought because he intervened to say that the judge should not put words into the mouth of a witness in a vital matter of this kind, claiming that the Northern Defence Committees were being put into a paramount position which, perhaps, they did not occupy. He said that his Lordship was telling the witness something and asking him to agree and that it was undesirable that any words should be put into the witness's mouth in this way. Mr Justice O'Keeffe chose to ignore what seemed to be a legitimate protest and went on to ask Colonel Hefferon: "Did Captain Kelly tell you who was going to pay for the arms?"

Hefferon: "He did."
O'Keeffe: "Who?"
Hefferon: "The Northern Defence Committee. The money was to come from those funds, the funds under the control of the Northern Defence Committee."
O'Keeffe: "Captain Kelly was to assist in selecting or purchasing the arms?"
Hefferon: "Yes."
O'Keeffe: "He was to assist in some way with the importation?"
Hefferon: "Yes."

O'Keeffe: "During that time where were they to be stored?"
Hefferon: "This is where I must claim privilege. I am quite willing to write down the answer."

Mr Justice O'Keeffe went on to explain that this was not a matter of public policy in respect of which a claim of privilege would arise, but rather that a group of individuals was going to import arms and that until a certain decision was taken the arms would be under my control as a member of the group. Perhaps Mr O'Keeffe was trying to get at the truth in some roundabout way, but it seemed to me that he was suggesting that I was in some way associated with a group which was operating without due authority. Once again, Mr McCarthy protested that he was putting words into the mouth of the witness, to which Mr O'Keeffe replied "You can protest as much as you like."

Colonel Hefferon told Mr O'Keeffe that the arms would be under my control for some time after coming into the country.

O'Keeffe: "Under Captain Kelly's control as an army officer or as a person assisting them?"
Hefferon: "As an army officer?"

This seemed to satisfy Mr O'Keeffe that the arms would be officially under my control, but his next question was "would you say where they were to be kept?"

Hefferon: "In a monastery."
O'Keeffe: "Where?"
Hefferon: "In Cavan."
O'Keeffe: "What monastery?"

For me this was one of the most dramatic moments of the trial. If Colonel Hefferon had attempted to answer the question I was prepared to jump to my feet and protest most vehemently, but Mr Sorahan was already standing. He objected strongly to the question and said that he was amazed and horrified that, given the situation that existed in Ireland, the judge should ask such a question.

"I am horrified and protest even if I do it alone," he declared.

O'Keeffe: "Does counsel want the truth or not?"

Apparently it did not occur to Mr O'Keeffe that truth or lack of it was not at issue. Counsel for myself and the other accused joined with Mr Sorahan in protesting against the judge's attitude; Mr Wood, for Albert Luykx, stated that he resented his Lordship's remarks as to whether counsel wanted the truth or not.

O'Keeffe: "I do not see how, consistent with the public administration of justice, we are going to have evidence in open court by writing it down and handing it to the jury and allowing nobody else to see it. I am not ready to adopt that course."

There were very few in court who missed the point which seemed to evade the judge – a point made by Mr McCarthy when he stated that if the place were discovered it might lead to reprisals from people in the North against individuals in the Southern jurisdiction, leading perhaps to injury and even death. Finally, prompted by Mr Sorahan, Mr McKenna, to the relief of the court in general, came to the rescue by suggesting that he should be allowed to pass from the question and that if the justice of the case, from any side required an explanation later, a direction could be given that they return to it.

Concerning my Continental trip in the first week of April, Colonel Hefferon told Mr McKenna that he ordered my return.

Hefferon: "... a direction was received from the Chief-of-Staff to move rifles to Dundalk. On that evening, knowing that Captain Kelly was abroad, and being very worried about the situation should it be necessary to distribute the arms, I rang his wife and asked her to get in touch with him and have him return immediately."

Mr McKenna then established that Colonel Hefferon had been telephoned at home on April 18 by Mr Anthony Fagan, Mr Haughey's secretary: that he had called briefly at Mr Fagan's office on April 20 and that he had heard from me on April 23. How had he heard from me?

Hefferon: "By phone. He told me that he was meeting Mr Blaney in his office at Government Buildings and that he was anxious that I should come along too. I went along to the office and I met Mr Blaney for the first time there. We chatted for some time. Then he called Mr Gibbons who came to the office. My memory of the general conversation was that a number of civil servants and the Revenue Commissioners and so on were being questioned by the Special Branch and as Mr Haughey had been seriously injured the day before, no one was too sure why."

McKenna: "Was there any conversation about arms or intended importation of arms at that meeting?"

Hefferon: "Yes, I recall Mr Gibbons saying to Captain Kelly that "you are in the hot seat now." He said it rather smilingly, jokingly. And Captain Kelly replied, "I am not in the hot seat", or words to that effect. And I think Mr Gibbons said, "you are a brazen bastard." It was all said in a jocose way. They had some conversation at that time that I did not follow because I was on the far side."

Later, Colonel Hefferon told Mr McKenna that he had visited me at my home after my retirement.

In cross-examination, Mr Wood asked:

"At that interview when Mr Gibbons said to Captain Kelly that he was in the hot seat, am I right that the atmosphere of that meeting was that the Minister was trying to pass responsibility for what happened on to Captain Kelly?"

Hefferon: "It could be interpreted in that way, but I thought he spoke in a rather jocose manner to Captain Kelly."
Wood: "But it sounds like somebody, using the expression, of somebody trying to pass the buck; wasn't the Minister trying to pass the buck to Captain Kelly?"
Hefferon: "Yes. Captain Kelly took it that way, anyway."

Questioned by Mr Finlay on the Bailieboro meeting in early October, when I met members of the Defence Committees, Colonel Hefferon said that I had reported that meeting in some detail – what was said, what the intentions were and the requests that were made.
Finlay: "In general, or in broad terms, these people were apprehensive of being left defenceless in certain areas of Northern Ireland?"
Hefferon: "That's right, arms and training facilities."
Finlay: "Did you make a full report to Mr Gibbons shortly afterwards?"
Hefferon: "I did. The Minister would have known about the meeting and what went on about the middle or more towards the end of October…"

Colonel Hefferon said that in January 1970 he had a series of discussions with me about the possibility of my resigning from the army and he later discussed the matter with the Minister for Defence.

Finlay: "And did he then communicate to you a decision that Captain Kelly should not then resign from the army?'
Hefferon: "He did."
Finlay: "In your conversation with Mr Gibbons as a result of which he

made his decision that Captain Kelly should not then retire from the army, did you tell him that Captain Kelly had been asked for assistance by the Northern Defence Committees in connection with the purchase of arms?"
Hefferon: "I did."
Finlay: "There was nothing concrete at that stage whether arms would come into the State?"
Hefferon: "That is right."
Finlay: "A general directive was given to the army, I think on February 6, by the Minister for Defence, Mr Gibbons?"
Hefferon: "Yes."
Finlay: "In general terms did it request the army to make plans or provide for contingencies arising out of the possible situation in Northern Ireland?"
Hefferon: "It did."
Finlay: "Was one of the contingency plans then made by the staff of the army that surplus arms should be made available?"
Hefferon: "I don't think I would put it that way. The Directive was to the Chief-of-Staff. The general terms were that surplus arms and ammunition should be set aside and made available for such contingencies."
Finlay: "Did you discuss that Directive with Captain Kelly?"
Hefferon: "I did, about a week after the Directive was issued."

In reply to Mr O'Keeffe, Colonel Hefferon explained that the Directive instructed the army to prepare for incursions into Northern Ireland and to set aside surplus arms and ammunition for this purpose, and also to provide gas masks. He assured Mr O'Keeffe that he had discussed the Directive with me.

Finlay: "Did that discussion include a discussion on the possible contingency of having to distribute arms to the civilian population?"
Hefferon: "Yes, that arises from the Directive."
Finlay: "Did you discuss this with Captain Kelly?"
Hefferon: "In a general way."
Finlay: "Was one of the matters you discussed that if such a contingency did arise that it would be very desirable if the arms were untraceable?"
Hefferon: "I don't recall discussing it with him at this time; but way back in September or October we had gone into this question in some detail."

In further reply to Mr Finlay, Colonel Hefferon said that he had told the Minister for Defence that my first Continental trip in February had been to vet arms and that in the first or second week of March I had told him, Colonel Hefferon, about an expected shipment of arms.

Finlay: "Did he discuss with you the way in which it could or should be met?"
Hefferon: "I recollect his coming to see me some time and telling me that he had made arrangements for arms to come in, I think on *The City of Dublin*, and that he was arranging and trying to make arrangements to get them through Customs. I advised him that the proper way to do this was to have the Minister responsible give the instructions."
Finlay: "Before that course was decided on, would I be correct in saying that Captain Kelly had suggested to you that the arms should be met by ordinary army personnel and stored in Cathal Brugha Barracks?"
Hefferon: "He mentioned it to me at one stage and I said I thought it would be impossible. It would attract tremendous attention and once the arms were got into army custody it might be difficult to get them out again..."
Finlay: "Was it only when you advised against that method of meeting them that discussion arose about methods of getting Customs clearance if they were to come in any other way?"
Hefferon: "Yes."

Colonel Hefferon said I had informed him that the arms had not left Antwerp or Belgium because the Captain of the ship would not take them without certain documentation.
Finlay: "Did he also tell you that some alternative method of bringing them in was to be found?"
Hefferon: "Yes."
Finlay: "Did he tell you personally of any interview he had had with Mr Gibbons, the Minister for Defence, during that period?'
Hefferon: "Yes."

I had to return to the Continent because of the difficulties that arose in Belgium. This was the occasion on which, mistakenly, I assumed that I was on regimental duty on April 4. I informed Colonel Hefferon of my dilemma, and in reply to Mr Finlay he related how he had told the Minister that I was going abroad in connection with the inspection or importation of arms, and had requested that the Minister should therefore use his good offices to have me excused regimental duties.

When I was away the rifles were dispatched to Dundalk and Colonel Hefferon said he rang my wife, to get in touch with me because he was worried that it might become necessary to distribute the rifles. He explained that the rifles had been very quickly dispatched because of the decision that if it became necessary to have them distributed to civilians in Northern Ireland it would be better to have them nearer the border than Dublin.

Finlay: "Did you say that the purpose for which you might require him was to assist in the distribution of those arms, the five hundred rifles, because he knew the people in Northern Ireland?"
Hefferon: "That is right."

Colonel Hefferon said that he was satisfied that the imported arms would be under my effective control as an army officer.

Mr Finlay went on to ask whether Colonel Hefferon had communicated to his successor, Colonel Delaney, the detailed information he had about my activities up to the time of his retirement. The Colonel said he had not, and explained:

"I felt that the project of importing the arms was one of very great secrecy in which some Government Ministers, to my mind acting for the Government, were involved. I felt it should more properly be communicated by the Minister for Defence."

Finlay: "Were you satisfied that at all times the Minister for Defence had full knowledge of the activities of Captain Kelly?"
Hefferon: "Yes."

Mr Finlay established from Colonel Hefferon that my first visit to the Continent had taken place on February 19.
Finlay: "Am I right in understanding that from that time up to the date of your retirement you never directed or ordered Captain Kelly to cease the activities which he was carrying out in connection with the importation of arms?"
Hefferon: "I did not."
Finlay: "Am I right in understanding that, during the period, neither did you ever convey to him in any way that what he was doing was without the authority of the Minister for Defence?"
Hefferon: "No, I did not."
Finlay: "Did you ever receive any order from the Minister for Defence to stop or direct the stopping of these activities by Captain Kelly?"
Hefferon: "No."
Finlay: "Did you ever receive any communication from the Minister for

Defence indicating that what Captain Kelly was doing was without his authority?"
Hefferon: "No."

In fact, Colonel Hefferon, in his original statement to the Gardaí, had stated that anything "Captain Kelly had done he had done with the authorisation of the Minister for Defence". That vital sentence by my superior officer did not appear in the alleged copy of the Colonel's statement in the Book of Evidence.

In itself, that one statement would have meant that there was absolutely no case against me; it would have meant that there was absolutely no case against the other defendants either. This scandalous and most reprehensible manipulation of the evidence of a prosecution witness, to make possible the prosecution of a false case, was one of the most heinous crimes perpetrated under the guise of justice, since the foundation of the State.

Fortunately, Colonel Hefferon, whom the State had dragooned into acting as a prosecution witness, conveyed to the court that I was acting under authority, which was never queried by either himself or the Minister.

Mr McCarthy, for Charles Haughey, asked Colonel Hefferon about training provided for citizens of Northern Ireland. Colonel Hefferon said he thought it took place during the last week of September 1969. He stated that citizens of Derry were involved and that the training was undertaken in an army post, Dunree in Donegal. Under further questioning, he added:

"On the Friday of the week in which the training was finishing, I became aware that the fact that the training was going on in Dunree might become known to the press. On the following day, a further course was due to report there, on the Saturday."

Stating that he had got in touch with an Intelligence Officer in the Donegal area, Colonel Hefferon continued:

"I gave instructions for him to contact the leadership in Derry and have the coming course cancelled. I did this on my own responsibility."

McCarthy: "Was that the end of that?"
Hefferon: "The course was cancelled. Nobody reported for training."

Had Colonel Hefferon informed Mr Gibbons?

Hefferon: "I informed the Chief-of-Staff at the earliest possible stage."

McCarthy: "Did you personally inform Mr Gibbons?"
Hefferon: "No, I informed the Chief-of-Staff."
McCarthy: "Both of your knowledge and of your action?"
Hefferon: "Yes."

In re-examination, Mr McKenna referred Colonel Hefferon to the Directive of February 6, asking if he had seen it.

Hefferon: "I was present when the Directive was given."
McKenna: "By whom and to whom?"
Hefferon: "By the Minister for Defence to the Chief-of-Staff."
McKenna: "I take it then it was an oral Directive?"
Hefferon: "Yes, it was."

Colonel Hefferon said that he had made a note of the Directive in his notebook which he still had and explained that the military interpretation of the original Directive had been committed to writing in the Chief-of-Staff's Branch in the Plans and Operations Section.

McKenna: "Did you or the Chief-of-Staff, at the time it was given to you, make any note as to the terms of it?"
Hefferon: "Not at the time but shortly afterwards... The Chief-of-Staff made the record. I understand that he returned to the Minister for clarification of some aspect of it."
Judge: "Did you see it at all after it was reduced to writing?"
Hefferon: "My Lord, I still don't know whether a written record of it existed, but I believe that in the Chief-of-Staff's Branch the staff did make a record of the Chief-of-Staff's recollection of the Directive given, and that the Chief-of-Staff returned to the Minister at some later stage for clarification."
Judge: "Counsel was asking had you got that written document into your possession and you said, 'No', and I wondered if perhaps it had been shown to you by the Chief-of-Staff or any member of his own staff?"
Hefferon: "I made a note myself of the Directive the following day, and at some later stage, it was quite recently, I checked on my recollection of it against the record that existed in GHQ, and they were substantially the same."
McCarthy (for Mr Haughey): "If the Directive exists it is the best evidence, no other evidence should be permitted."
Judge: "That's true."
McCarthy: "And, as I gather from Colonel Hefferon's evidence it was sub-

sequently – in some form of note – sent for clarification and exists in a clarified form."
McKenna: "If the witness saw this, I want to know where."
Judge: "You don't know where it is?"
McKenna: "Quite a detailed search has been made already, and no such record can be discovered so far."

Colonel Hefferon said that he had made a note of the Directive in a notebook which he still had and explained that the clarification of the original Directive had been committed to writing and existed in the Chief-of-Staff's Branch in the Plans and Operations Section.

Mr Justice O'Keeffe: "You said quite recently that you checked against the record in GHQ."
Hefferon: "I sent a message to the Chief-of-Staff's Branch that I wished to see it, as I wanted to check my recollection. I was told the terms of it – and I did not see it – the terms, which, in my understanding, had been extracted from the Directive."
O'Keeffe: 'Whom did you contact?'
Hefferon: 'Colonel O'Donovan was the officer I contacted.'

To me as an army officer accustomed to the acceptance of authority and to operating within a chain of command, it seemed that Colonel Hefferon had fully established that I had at all times operated with due authority. Further, his evidence followed a clear, logical pattern and where it differed from that of the Minister for Defence it was unequivocal.

Colonel Hefferon directly contradicted Mr Gibbons on four specific points: the Bailieboro meeting; the reason for sending the rifles to Dundalk; the approach to Mr Gibbons concerning my regimental duties; Mr Gibbons's knowledge of my Continental trip in the first week of April.

Colonel Hefferon was very definite that he had briefed Mr Gibbons on the Bailieboro meeting. On the question of rifles, when Mr Finlay had asked Mr Gibbons... *if in the event of a Government decision to that effect, they could be distributed in the North to persons other than members of the army* Mr Gibbons had replied, "I think counsel is trying to put words into my mouth." On the contrary, Colonel Hefferon was quite positive that, in certain circumstances, the possibility was that the rifles would be distributed to civilians in Northern Ireland, and he quoted the Directive of February 6 to back up his statement. When asked if he had been involved in a decision to excuse me from regimental duties in early April, to permit me to go abroad, Mr Gibbons had answered:

whereas Colonel Hefferon had stated that he had told Mr Gibbons I was going to the Continent in connection with arms, and he wished to have me excused regimental duties because of this.

Colonel Hefferon's description of how and why he stopped the Donegal training went unchallenged at the first trial. Mr Gibbons's particular version of how it was brought to an end was not given until the second trial. The Directive, and more especially the manner in which Colonel Hefferon had verified its contents through official channels, was not challenged, but despite the best efforts of the defence, the prosecution refused to produce the official record. It was a most bizarre situation, with Colonel Hefferon able to have his recollection and notation of it confirmed by the senior staff officer in Plans and Operations at GHQ, while the Counsel for the State was forced to get up in court and declare that no such record could be found.

At one stage, Mr McKenna spoke of "certain steps which had been taken overnight". One wondered if the destruction of the record was one of the "certain steps". Whatever happened, no blame could be attributed to Mr McKenna for misleading the court. The question was who was misleading Mr McKenna? The Attorney General mounted the prosecution on "behalf of the people" and must be assumed to have briefed Mr McKenna. Who misled him? Was it the Minister for Defence? Was it the Minister for Justice? Was it the Taoiseach himself? Gibbons had told me that it was a Taoiseach's investigation. Was that still the case?

The questions may never be answered, but the fact is that the interpretation of the Directive, confirmed by Colonel O'Donovan to Colonel Hefferon, floated off into the *unknown*, never to be seen again in its original form.

CHAPTER 15

Colonel Patrick Delaney was the next prosecution witness. He had been appointed Director of Intelligence on April 10, 1970, having been understudy to Colonel Michael Hefferon from the previous February 9. He had been Officer-in-Charge of the Command and Staff School during 1968/1969, when I attended my course there. I found him pleasant and affable, and in fact in February 1969 I asked his advice as to whether I should retire from the army at that stage.

A London publishing house had expressed an interest in some of my work on politico-military affairs, and in connection with this I was negotiating a lecture series with an English university. Both ventures offered interesting prospects, but if I were to do justice to them and myself, I felt that they would require my full attention. For a family man, leaving the security of the army, for what could be a less secure future, was a major step and I decided to consult Colonel Delaney.

His advice to me was thoughtful and restrained. While he would generally advise army officers not even to consider leaving the army in such circumstances, knowing something of my background and capabilities he did not feel that I should reject a challenging, if possibly uncertain, career out of hand. He recommended that I should not make a decision until I had completed my Command and Staff Course. I accepted Colonel Delaney's advice and I had not reached a final decision when the events of August 1969 in Belfast and Derry intervened.

Colonel Delaney said in evidence that on September 29, he had seen me once, but had not spoken to me during his period as understudy. It was only a small point, but in fact I had a clear recollection of meeting and welcoming Colonel Delaney to his new appointment shortly after he took up his understudy duties. This meeting may have slipped his mind, but his statement of evidence, a copy of which had been submitted to the defence, could not be excused as a slip of the mind. This was such a remarkable document that prosecuting counsel chose to ignore major portions of it in both trials. I quote from it:

> "On 8 April 1970 I visited the Minister for Defence, Mr Gibbons, in his office, accompanied by Colonel Hefferon. It was normal practice for the incoming Director to be introduced to the Minister. At this time, I had come to the conclusion that Captain Kelly should be transferred from the Intelligence Section. My reasons were as follows:

1. Captain Kelly operated openly as an intelligence officer; he did not provide suitable cover, which fact could seriously compromise legitimate intelligence activities as he became so well known.
2. He openly consorted with subversive groups.
3. Captain Kelly was well informed of the activities of the Intelligence security sub-section and knew exactly how it worked and all its liaison contacts. The seriousness of his position *vis-á-vis 1* and 2 above could not be overemphasised.
4. His emotional reactions to events in Northern Ireland pointed to his having lost that cool behaviour so necessary to an intelligence officer."

Colonel Delaney apparently saw no inconsistency in listing his opinions about me having already stated that "Captain Kelly did not report to me or make my acquaintance or give any account of his activities, past or present", following this with the declaration that "I did not receive any brief on Captain Kelly's activities from Colonel Hefferon at any time." The only other people associated with Intelligence Section over the period were Commandant O'Sullivan and Captain O'Shea, members of security sub-section, but Colonel Delaney invalidated even them as a possible source of information, when in his statement, he declared:

> "During late August, September and October 1969, Captain Kelly reported in from time to time. Most of his reports went direct to Colonel Hefferon but occasionally, some little information was given to security sub-section. During November 1969 he had no contact with security sub-section except for one incident in mid-November, but visited Colonel Hefferon occasionally in his office. He visited Colonel Hefferon on an average once a week, but irregularly, during the period November 1969 to the end of February 1970. He was on annual leave from 30 January 1970 to 15 February 1970. As far as is known, he did not report at all during the month of March 1970. From 10 April 1970 to 27 April 1970 he did not report at all."

It would be interesting to analyse the litany of non-reporting. It reminded me of a definition of an officer given by "Ginger" O'Connell, a former Director of Intelligence and the man who sparked off the Civil War, when he was held prisoner by Rory O'Connor in the Four Courts in 1922. In one of his more cynical moments, O'Connell defined an officer as "one who works in an office".

Colonel Delaney, on his own admission, had no direct knowledge of my activities. How then could he depose as he did? I could scarcely avoid recalling that, apart from Colonel Hefferon, the only person *au fait* with my activities was the Minister for Defence, but as the evidence in court showed, he was not willing to reveal his knowledge of these activities, but was intent on putting across an interpretation based on an alleged "change of allegiance".

It is possible that the prosecution ignored Colonel Delaney's statement because it was so obviously hearsay, but it could also have been ignored because of its inherent weakness as a discrediting weapon. Its focal point was the four stated reasons why Colonel Delaney wished my removal from the Intelligence Section and they do not stand up to analysis.

An intelligence officer is not some kind of super spy who must always operate under cover, as Colonel Delaney seemed to suggest. In fact, the necessity for cover had been rejected in my case and, indeed, in the circumstances in which I operated, the fact that I was known as an Army Intelligence officer was my greatest strength. It was only when my identity was firmly established as a person working for the Government that people, North and South, came to trust me. To suggest that because I was well known, I "could seriously compromise legitimate intelligence activities" was merely making use of pejorative phraseology to suggest disloyalty. It was an attempt to cast suspicion on a par with the second reason, which was so inane as to be ridiculous. If I "openly consorted with subversive groups", the Taoiseach, Mr Gibbons and several other Ministers could have had the same charge made against them. Very few of the people with whom I had openly associated had not been received by a member of Government at one time or another. The third reason collapsed because of the collapse of the first two. The charge of emotionalism was on the same level as the "under suspicion" of Mr Gibbons. As to "that cool behaviour so necessary", lack of coolness is not one of my characteristics.

It is interesting to compare Colonel Delaney's statement with an answer given in evidence by Mr Gibbons to Mr McCarthy:

> "Yes, my concern was this. I got the idea that if Captain Kelly, who had worked in the North for the previous nine or twelve months, had become emotionally involved and if he was unceremoniously kicked out of the army, or if his resignation was grabbed gratefully, he might go out of the army with a grievance. He was not an ordinary army officer. He was the special personal assistant to the Director of Intelligence and as such had access to a great deal of

highly confidential information. I deemed it the most discreet thing to do to try to ensure that he went out of the army without any sense of grievance which might endanger the security of the State."

By implying that I had become emotionally involved through working in the North for nine or twelve months, Mr Gibbons conveyed the essence of Colonel Delaney's statement. This was part of the background to the appearance of Colonel Delaney on the stand in the Four Courts.

In reply to prosecuting counsel, Colonel Delaney stated that although I was a member of the Intelligence Section I was not working as an intelligence officer from the time of his appointment on 10 April.

"I took steps to see that he was not," he said with emphasis.

Cross-examining on my behalf, Mr D'Arcy asked Colonel Delaney whether he had issued an order to be conveyed to me through Captain Dan O'Shea on April 11.

Delaney: "I did."
D'Arcy: "That Captain Kelly was to continue his present duties?"
Delaney: "No, certainly not."

To the observant, Colonel Delaney was too aggressively decisive when he denied that I was given an order to continue my present duties.

D'Arcy: "But you did communicate an order through Captain Dan O'Shea?"
Delaney: "Yes."
D'Arcy: "Was the order to the effect that he was to be excused regimental duties?"
Delaney: 'Yes, that's correct."

When Captain O'Shea rang my home on April 10 – not April 11 – my wife answered the phone and when she asked if he wished to speak to me, he said no, that she could take the message. I was upstairs at the time and as soon as she had put down the phone my wife shouted up the message to me.

"That was Dan O'Shea. He said you are excused duty on the 11th and that you are to carry on with what you are doing."

I came to the top of the stairs and asked her to repeat the message. I then said:

"That's great. Delaney must be briefed."

Commandant Dan Tracey, officer in charge of Officers' Records at Army Headquarters, had no trouble in getting through to me by phone around the same period. Called as a prosecution witness, Commandant Tracey produced a document, dated April 13, 1970, from his records. It read: "I agree to secondment to the Department of Agriculture as requested," and was signed by me.

Having explained that secondment meant that the officer concerned was posted to the Army General List and, while remaining on army strength, was assigned to another Department of State on loan, Commandment Tracey told the court that he had requested my agreement to the secondment by telephone and that, having agreed verbally, I commented that secondment was a matter for higher authority.

When examined on this matter by my counsel, James D'Arcy, I stated that during his telephone conversation with me, Commandment Tracey "specifically mentioned Colonel Delaney, the new Director of Intelligence, as pressing the matter".

Colonel Delaney's initiative to have my secondment arranged, which presumably took place between April 10, the date on which he assumed his new position, and April 13 the date of my written agreement to secondment, was a further indication that he had been briefed about my activities, especially when it is associated with a remark he made to Colonel Hefferon a few days before April 10. In reference to me and his intention to have me replaced in Intelligence Section, he suggested to Colonel Hefferon that *I might compromise him with the British,* and implied that Mr Gibbons was responsible for his appointment as Director of Intelligence. Because Mr Gibbons denied playing any part in Colonel Delaney's appointment, it is difficult to reach a firm conclusion about Colonel Delaney's position *vis-á-vis* Mr Gibbons before April 10, but Captain O'Shea's message of April 10 was a reality, as also was Commandant Tracey's request (under pressure from Colonel Delaney) for my agreement to secondment. It can therefore only be assumed that Colonel Delaney was fully briefed some time in the early days of April if not before. In any event, neither Colonel Delaney nor any of his staff attempted to contact me again until April 28. The only conceivable reason why the Colonel should not attempt to contact me was because he knew what was going on. Consequently, he first told me to carry on and, second, interested himself in receiving my secondment because, as he had suggested to Colonel Hefferon, he might be compromised with the British. It is interesting that when I mentioned Colonel Delaney's fears of being compromised with the British to Mr Gibbons, the latter's reaction was *Who did the Colonel think he was working for?*

On April 17, the situation must have changed dramatically for Colonel Delaney, as is obvious from his own statement of evidence: "On April 17,

1970 Captain Kelly was under notice as being concerned in an attempt to import arms from the Continent and a military and Garda investigation into his activities began."

Having received this momentous news, momentous even though Colonel Delaney did not see fit to class the attempted importation as illegal (if he was briefed as the evidence suggests he would not, of course, have regarded the importation as illegal) the question may well be asked why he still did not attempt to contact me. As my Commanding Officer it would have been the obvious action for him to take, especially if he had been unaware of the operation until then. His failure to do so could only be explained if he was *au fait* with the situation and did not take any action until he had consulted the Minister for Defence, who was in a position of having to work out a strategy whereby he could deny ever having approved or authorised the arms importation. This would explain Colonel Delaney's lack of action over a period of eleven days, from April 17 to April 28, as it would also explain his later denial of his order of April 10.

Colonel Delaney described in evidence how on April 28 after a discussion with the Minister for Defence he had sent two officers to my house to tell me I was required in his office. The Colonel apparently wanted the court to believe that it was necessary to send two officers to my house to convey a simple message. Why did he not tell the whole truth?

It was about half-past nine and I was still in bed on the morning of the 28th when the doorbell rang. I went down to be greeted by a worried-looking and somewhat hesitant Captain Dan O'Shea. Commandant O'Sullivan sat in his car across the road. The demeanour of the two officers, with both of whom I had worked closely for several years, suggested anything other than that they had come to deliver a message. I invited the trench-coated O'Shea in. He hesitated, glancing back at the grim-faced O'Sullivan, who, as though on a prearranged signal, jumped out of his car and came striding purposefully across the road. They entered the house, O'Sullivan declaring that they were there to bring me to Colonel Delaney. In a most officious manner, O'Sullivan told me that I had ten minutes to get into uniform.

When I appeared in uniform, O'Sullivan issued orders for the big move. I was allowed to bring my car, but O'Shea was to drive in front, while O'Sullivan was to bring up the rear. As we manoeuvred into our allotted stations, I waved, casually I hoped, to a neighbour standing at her front window and we were off, in convoy, down the deserted road. All the way to Army Headquarters, O'Sullivan stuck to my rear bumper. Having reached there, officiousness had so overtaken him that he rudely commented on some detail of my dress before opening the office door.

In Delaney's office, the atmosphere was coldly formal. I suppose the intention was to create an impression of extreme official displeasure, but it was pure farce, with Delaney, a grim-faced automaton, reading from a sheet of paper and O'Sullivan, an equally grim-faced, if less important automaton, standing by with notebook and pencil poised. Delaney's orders were to the effect that I was to discontinue my present duties; that I was to break all contacts I had established in the course of those duties; that I was to concentrate on legal soldierly duties in future and that I was to be transferred to the Eastern Command Training Depot in Cathal Brugha Barracks.

Delaney made some mistake in designating my new unit and O'Sullivan immediately corrected him. It was obviously a very special document that Delaney held in his hand. Probably through the use of the magic word, "legal", it was intended to convert my previous duties into illegalities. It was a good trick if it could be pulled off, but by definition, it was difficult to see how duties could be illegal. Delaney asked me if I wished to have the document read again and I told him that there was no need. I was then ordered to report to Cathal Brugha Barracks without delay. I made no comment. I felt none was called for, but it was sobering to see one's comrades converted into machines without a trace of humanity, at the whim, presumably, of their political masters.

If Commandant Joe Fitzpatrick, the officer commanding the training depot, was bemused by my sudden arrival, he restrained himself admirably. He was quite agreeable to my taking some leave and I went home shortly before lunch. In the afternoon, I got a phone message to say that my leave was cancelled and that I was to report for duty on the following morning. There was no longer any doubt but that I was under some form of restraint.

Shortly after noon the same day – the sixth day of the first trial – the incident which was to bring the first trial to its abortive conclusion occurred. Mr Peter Berry, the Secretary of the Department of Justice, was in the witness-box. Counsel for the State was first into action.

McKenna: "Mr Berry, do you recollect the evening of Saturday, April 18 last?'
Berry: "Yes."
McKenna: "On that evening did you get a telephone call to your house?"
Berry: "Yes."
McKenna: "Can you recall whether you answered the phone personally in the first instance or whether somebody else answered it?"

Berry: "I answered the phone personally in the first instance."
McKenna: "Who was making the call?"
Berry: "The voice was familiar to me. It was Mr Haughey's."
McKenna: "Will you take it slowly? I don't wish to complicate you in any way but tell us how the conversation went?"
Berry (having got the Judge's permission to use notes): "Going carefully through what was said, Mr Haughey said, 'You know about the cargo that is coming into Dublin Airport on Sunday?' I said, 'Yes Minister.' He said, 'Can it be let through on a guarantee that it will go direct to the North?' I said, 'No'. Mr Haughey then said, 'I think that it is a bad decision.' I made no comment. He then said, ' Does the man from Mayo know?' I said, 'Yes.' He then said, 'What will happen it when it arrives?' and I said, 'It will be grabbed.' He then said, 'I had better have it called off.'

"My Lord, I think I should say here that in Counsel's opening to the jury – in describing my conversation as of paramount importance – he used the expression, 'I had better call it off'. The expression used by Mr Haughey was, 'I had better have it called off.'"

Judge: "It is very important that that should be rectified."
Berry: "I made notes there and then in my personal diary as to what Mr Haughey said. Furthermore, on going to the Department of Justice on Monday morning I made similar notes."

Mr Berry told the court that he knew what was meant by "the cargo, and that the "man from Mayo", referred to his Minister at the relevant time, Mr Ó Moráin.

Once his direct evidence had concluded, Mr Wood, on behalf of Albert Luykx began to cross-examine.

In reply to Mr Wood, Mr Berry stated that on February 7 1969 he had given Albert Luykx a letter of clearance as a person who had not come in contact with the criminal law or who had not been in touch with any subversive groups in Ireland. Mr McKenna asked if the letter was being put in evidence and Mr Wood, rather casually, it seemed, replied:

"If you wish."

The letter was read and then Mr Berry, uninvited, went on to explain that on February 7, Albert Luykx handed him a letter which he allowed him, Berry, to photostat.

"I then handed both the original and the photostat copy back to Mr Luykx," Mr Berry said.

"I asked him if I could have a copy for the record. Mr Luykx replied that I could and I have a copy of it here in court. Mr Luykx then told me that he required the certificate of character in order to refute allegations made in the letter I had photostated. Mr Luykx told me that he had been excluded, now that he was an Irishman and no longer a Belgian, by the Minister for Justice in Belgium, from entering that country, as he had been suspected of certain neo-Nazi activities."

Mr Berry went on to say that the letter which Mr Luykx produced was in English. It was a translation of a letter from a man in Antwerp dated December 13, 1968, and addressed to Mr Albert Luykx, Sutton House, Sutton, Dublin. As Mr Berry started to read the letter, Mr Wood objected on the grounds that it contained personal matters.

Mr Justice O'Keeffe: "Of course it does. This is what you asked for."
Mr Wood said that he had asked for the certificate which showed that Mr Luykx was not involved in any subversive activities in this country nor had he come under any unfavourable notice from the police, and said that he did not think that Mr Luykx's personal affairs should be trotted around the court more than was necessary. Mr O'Keeffe refused to accept this, saying that as Mr Wood had asked for the certificate and put it into evidence, the jury was entitled to know how it came to be given. Mr Wood objected, saying:

"Why Mr Luykx's affairs should be bandied around the court I don't know. I don't know what they are, but I strongly suspect that your Lordship thinks they might hurt Mr Luykx in some way." He paused and then continued:

"It is only illustrative of the rather unfair tone in which your Lordship sometimes has conducted this trial."

Silence descended on the court, as the judge glared down from his bench, announcing after a considerable period:

"I will rise now until 2 pm."

When the court resumed, Mr O'Keeffe said that he felt that the stage had been reached where he would have to discharge the jury and arrange to have the trial begun again before a new judge.

The pleas of the various counsel had no effect and when Mr McCarthy commented:

"Such an attack could be made on any judge at any time."

Mr O'Keeffe replied:

"This is true and then you would have to start all over again. There are six other judges, and it could happen to them, but then it would be some time before you would be back to me again."

The jury was discharged and Albert Luykx was directed by the judge to pay the costs of all parties. While counsel for the other accused declined to apply for costs against him, the Attorney General was granted costs against Albert Luykx.

As Mr O'Keeffe retired towards his sanctum behind the bench, the usually inscrutable Haughey, the hooded eyes flashing, normally inexpressive face flushed with rage, jumped to his feet and shouted: "Get off the bench, O'Keeffe, you're a disgrace."

I could not but applaud. Haughey was right. I knew that in a previous major case, Mr Wood had referred to Mr O'Keeffe, then Attorney General, as a "Forensic Teddy Boy". While not suggesting that old spite had anything to do with the O'Keeffe decision to withdraw from the trial, it was a travesty of justice at that advanced stage as far as the defendants were concerned.

This was emphasised outside the Four Courts when a man, whose face was vaguely familiar, caught my arm. He was a juryman.

"You had the case won," he said. "I came into the court with no preconceived ideas. I was ready to convict, but at this stage I know you are all innocent."

"Why?" I asked.

"I took notes when Gibbons was giving evidence," he said, "and I took notes when Hefferon was giving evidence, and there was no doubt about who was telling the truth. It was not a guilty verdict, even at this stage."

I thanked him and hurried away.

"The best of luck," he shouted after me, "I'll be here the day they finally find you not guilty."

Next morning the bread man greeted me.

"Your man, Hefferon, fairly put the kybosh on Gibbons. A pity someone didn't put it on O'Keeffe," he said.

He was succinct, if not much more so than *Private Eye* on October 9, 1970, which carried a feature entitled "Kelly's Heroes". "As the trial went on," it said, "it became clear that if Mr Haughey and his co-defendants were guilty of importing arms into Ireland, so was the entire Irish Cabinet."

CHAPTER 16

The second trial, or re-trial, opened on Tuesday, October 7, before Mr Justice Seamus Henchy. As I stood in the domed foyer of the Four Courts waiting for proceedings to begin, a legal friend of mine said:

"You know, it's the conventional wisdom that a re-trial gives a marginal advantage to the prosecution." He was emphasising what had been indicated the previous evening when the defence was told that Colonel Hefferon had been dropped as a prosecution witness.

As soon as the jury had been sworn, the defence lodged its objection to the dropping of Colonel Hefferon, Mr D'Arcy stating that in the previous trial there had been no suggestion by the State that he should be treated as a hostile witness. At this point, the judge intervened to say that if they were going to discuss what happened at the previous trial they should do so in the absence of the jury. The jury then retired and the submissions continued.

Mr McKenna, in defending the decision to drop Colonel Hefferon, said:

"My instructions in this regard are mandatory. This step was only taken by the Attorney General with the greatest reluctance and fully conscious of precisely what was involved in not tendering this witness as evidence to the jury." He continued:

> "In at least one vital matter of relevance the witness gave an answer which was totally at variance with his original statement to the police, and that was in cross-examination by counsel for Captain Kelly. Secondly, I have been instructed only since the last trial that investigations reveal a true and definite and frequent association between this witness and one of the accused. It was an association between this witness and Captain Kelly... Thirdly, the prosecution was unaware until the witness was giving evidence of a call by the witness on another of the accused, Mr Haughey, during an obviously very critical period in this case, April 20. Fourthly, the prosecution was unaware that... Captain Kelly was asked by his then superior officer, Colonel Hefferon's successor as Director of Army Intelligence, Colonel Delaney, to report to him on April 20 and for that purpose had sent two officers to ask him to come in. No sooner had this happened than Colonel Hefferon interested himself on behalf of Captain Kelly and got in contact with Colonel Delaney."

Mr McKenna went on:

"In no circumstances will I tender Colonel Hefferon as a witness and if ultimately your Lordship feels the trial cannot proceed fairly without him, then I regret without discourtesy to any, your Lordship is at liberty to call him yourself, but only in the circumstances which I state will I cross-examine."

The judge replied that, while he did not accept Mr McKenna's point of view as necessarily correct, the prosecution had put forward *prima facie* reasons for considering the witness unreliable. The defence, he said, would have to suggest "an oblique reason" behind the reasons offered. If it seemed that the witness was being excluded because of this "oblique reason", then there would be a case for calling him.

Earlier, Mr McCarthy had in fact attempted to show an oblique motive...

"Colonel Hefferon said that he kept Mr Gibbons informed all the time of Captain Kelly's operations and, in fact, engaged his co-operation in securing permission for Captain Kelly to go to Europe."

Judge: "If your submission is correct, Mr McCarthy, that this is being done for an oblique motive and if that emerges in the course of the trial to my satisfaction, I shall call the witness."

The last word, practically, fell to Mr McKenna, when he said:

> "I do not wish to be, perhaps, unintentionally misrepresented by Mr McCarthy as justifying the non-calling of Colonel Hefferon, because of a conflict of evidence with Mr Gibbons. That is something the Attorney General did not consider and I reject it on his behalf. Secondly, my Lord, I want to completely repudiate the suggestion that in conducting the prosecution, the Attorney General is doing anything other than what is his constitutional duty of representing the Irish people and to reject, for the benefit of those in court only, any suggestion that pressures were brought to bear on him from a higher quarter or any quarter whatever."

I do not know why Mr McKenna should have wanted to reject any suggestion of pressure *for the benefit of those in court only*, but he may have been aware of the story discussed by everyone in the precincts of the court that morning. A meeting was reported to have taken place in a named south-eastern hotel during the previous weekend at which the Minister for Justice (Mr Desmond O'Malley), Mr Gibbons and the Attorney General (Mr Colm Condon) arranged the dropping of Colonel Hefferon as a prosecution witness. As Mr McKenna rejected the report, Shakespeare's line: *Methinks the lady doth protest too much*, sprang forcefully to mind.

Whatever about the validity of Mr McKenna's disclaimer, most of those in court who had attended the first trial believed that the prosecution was seeking an opportunist advantage by dropping Colonel Hefferon. Because legal technicalities barred the judge from referring to the first trial, he was forced to accept as *prima facie* the grounds on which the prosecution impugned Colonel Hefferon's reliability. For the same reason, he could neither accept nor reject Mr McCarthy's interpretation of an oblique motive. If it had been possible to refer to the first trial, it is doubtful whether the four reasons put up by the prosecution would have stood up to the most cursory of examinations.

In the first place, Colonel Hefferon did not call on Mr Haughey on April 20. He called on Mr Fagan, another prosecution witness, and not only had he stated this in his evidence to the police, but Mr McKenna had elicited the same information from him in the first trial. In fact Colonel Hefferon had not seen Mr Haughey since the previous October. This meant that one of Mr McKenna's reasons was an error of fact. As regards the claim that Colonel Hefferon had deviated from his statement in one vital matter of relevance, it was not true. In his evidence, Colonel Hefferon had stated that I was acting with the authority of the Minister for Defence. This was fully in accord with his original statement to the gardaí. It must be assumed that Mr McKenna, as an innocent functionary acting on instructions, was referring to the doctored Book of Evidence, with my superior officer's assertion exculpating me, expunged.

The alleged deviation was later shown not to be a deviation at all, eliminating a second reason for the dropping of Colonel Hefferon.

The two remaining grounds concerned me directly. The suggestion that Colonel Hefferon should not associate with me could only merit contempt. I had worked closely with him over a period of eight years and we had become good friends. To suggest that because I was on a criminal charge he should break all contact with me was not only inhumane but could he classified as unjust, running counter, as it did to a central and much quoted concept in Irish law, that an accused is innocent until proven guilty. Further, at the first trial, Colonel Hefferon had told Mr McKenna that he had visited my home after my retirement.

Colonel Hefferon had contacted Colonel Delaney on my behalf on April 28 as a concerned, responsible person, who knew an injustice was being perpetrated. Further, immediately after my "arrest" by my former colleagues, my wife, naturally concerned, rang Colonel Hefferon and requested him to make enquiries why I had been taken from my home in such peculiar circumstances. Therefore, when Colonel Hefferon rang Colonel Delaney, he was aware of what had actually taken place that morning. Colonel Delaney assured him that I was not under any form of restraint, but that I was simply being transferred to the Eastern Command, from where I would probably ring my wife. Mr McKenna's use of a phone call by Colonel Hefferon to Colonel Delaney in such circumstances as a ground for invalidating Hefferon as a prosecution witness was incredible. Certainly if the judge had been able to consider Mr McKenna's reasons in the context of the first trial, he would have seen that Colonel Delaney had not told the full story of his activities on the 28th.

The judge's inability to refer to the first trial was a major anomaly because all the stated grounds for excluding Colonel Hefferon had some reference to the first trial; as one of the spectators, who had attended the first trial also, put it:

"Hefferon couldn't have been barred if there hadn't been a first trial."

This same anomaly prevented Mr McCarthy from proving an oblique motive and to paraphrase one of the defending counsel, the case went forward to the jury with Colonel Hefferon categorised as a liar on specious arguments.

A great part of Colonel Hefferon's evidence was very relevant to the trial, as Mr McKenna admitted and as became evident when Mr Justice Henchy later called him as a witness.

Mr Justice Henchy acknowledged the reality of the situation when he told the jury:

"It would be idle to pretend that this trial does not have political undertones and implications." The question they would have to answer, he continued, was a question of fact: had the accused come to an agreement to import arms and ammunition into the State without the authority of the Minister for Defence?

Mr McKenna repeated this in an opening address which, in general, followed the same lines as in the previous trial, but with a noticeable difference in emphasis and order of presentation. The dramatic introduction based on Mr Haughey's telephone call to Mr Berry was relegated to the end of the speech which was delivered in a lower key and in a more pedestrian manner than on the first occasion.

The charge was based on an alleged contravention of Section 17 of the Firearms Act. In the witness-box, Mr Thomas O'Grady, a principal officer of the Department of Defence, said he kept and supervised a register in which were entered particulars of authorisations given on behalf of the

Minister for Defence for the importation of firearms and ammunition. He produced the register and said that in the past two years there was no record of any authorisation having been issued to any of the accused or to Welux Ltd, the consignee for the projected shipment of arms. Mr O'Grady told Mr Walsh, prosecuting counsel, that the Minister did not sign the authorisations – they were signed by himself or one of his deputies.

Mr Finlay SC asked Mr O'Grady if he had a copy of the Firearms Act and Judge Henchy said he was sure that he had one "properly annotated and up-to-date", which drew its predictable laugh from the court. Unsmiling, Mr O'Grady took his copy of the Act from his briefcase and opened it as instructed at Sub-section 8 of Section 17. Sub-section 8 exempted from the entire provisions of Section 17 firearms and/or ammunition imported into the State on the authority of the Minister for Defence for the use of the Defence Forces, or on the authority of the Minister for Justice for the use of the police force.

When Mr O'Grady had read the sub-section, Mr Finlay asked him if there was any necessity for a formal authorisation or licence in the case of arms for the use of the Defence Forces. In apparent surprise, Mr O'Grady responded with a muted "no".

It was perfectly clear from this evidence that no form of written authorisation was necessary, but the prosecution and others chose to misrepresent the issue by references to pieces of paper and necessary signatures. For example, when putting the case for the prosecution to the jury on October 23, Mr Walsh said that Mr Gibbons was the man who could have legalised the whole operation by writing his name on a piece of paper. If he had done so, Mr Walsh continued, they might think this was a deplorable decision, but if he had done it, he would have put all the defendants outside the reach of the law. This was scarcely in accord with the evidence of Mr Walsh's own, expert witness on the subject. Actually, it was intolerable, unacceptable and outrageous that a Senior Counsel should use the courts in this way to promote a grave misrepresentation of the facts. After Mr O'Grady's evidence, it should have been obvious to the most obtuse person, legal or otherwise, that Ministers for Defence did not sign authorisations for the importation of arms. But it was to be wrongfully used by ill-disposed persons as a version of what the law required.

On November 4, Mr Colley, Minister for Finance, speaking on the motion of confidence in the Taoiseach and his Government, stated in defence of Mr Gibbons:

"I also wanted to say that if the then Minister for Defence had been involved in this matter, as has been suggested, he would, of course, have signed a certificate under the Firearms Act. There would have been no problem with customs, no problem with anybody else. But he did not."

On the same day, the Taoiseach, also feeling constrained to defend Mr Gibbons, took a leaf from Mr Colley's book and told the House:

"Evidence has since been adduced that Deputy Gibbons, on learning of the attempted importation of arms, not only took steps to try to stop it, but refused specifically to sign a certificate that would have facilitated the importation of these arms."

At that stage, both the Taoiseach and Mr Colley should have known that the Minister did not sign authorisations for the import of arms; that in fact no formal authorisation was necessary. Mr Finlay, for the benefit of the jury, explained the exact meaning of the Minister for Defence's authority by relating an allegorical example. It should also have explained it to the satisfaction of the Taoiseach and Mr Colley.

"If you had in your home a gardener," Mr Finlay told the jury,

> "and he came to you in the morning and he said to you, 'I'm thinking of cutting the hedge in the front' and you said nothing and maybe you asked him was it the right or the left of the hedge he was going to cut and he told you that information too. You went away for the day and he came back to you at the end of that day and said, 'I didn't get the hedge cut because the hedge cutter wouldn't start.' You received that information and you asked him, 'Well, I suppose you'll mend the hedge cutter so' and he said 'yes' and you went away and you paid him for that day's work and he went off and he cut the hedge the next day and you paid him for that day's work too. Do you think that any man, in his common sane senses, could possibly describe that hedge as having been cut except under your authority? Just look at it as a problem. Supposing you, for some reason or other tried afterwards to dispute the authority of your gardener to cut the hedge on those set of facts, wouldn't it be nonsense? *That's the meaning of authority in this case.*"

Mr Finlay's analogical explanation of the actual authority exercised by the Minister left little room for much legalism or misinterpretation.

Mr Ó Moráin was called on the third day of the trial.

Under cross-examination by Mr McCarthy, he said that on his direction there were several officers of the Special Branch operating in Northern Ireland in the autumn of 1969. He could not be certain about dates, but he got reports relating to their operations and the information they had obtained. Asked if the Special Branch officers would have been involved in ascertaining the ability of people to defend themselves, Mr Ó Moráin, who, as in the previous trial, had explained that he was at a disadvantage because the Minister for Justice and the Attorney General had denied him access to documentation, replied:

"I cannot recollect. I have given it in a general way. There were several discussions in that period of time about conditions in the North and one of the big matters involved was the matter you mentioned. There was a grave fear down here that a lot of people would be decimated and that there would be a repeat of the pogroms."

McCarthy: "Could you say where these discussions took place and with whom they took place?"
Ó Moráin: "When I speak of discussions in this context, I mean discussions at the Cabinet."
McCarthy: "Can you recall any specific matters that were gone into with regard to what these contingency plans might involve?"
Ó Moráin: "There were different plans, including what I think they called limited incursions by the army into the North, and there was some discussion on these, and we did not know at that time what might transpire, what might happen. There were discussions on different alternatives depending on events which were rapidly changing and expected to rapidly change from day to day."
McCarthy: "Can you recall discussions around the end of January or beginning of February that this matter should be put in hand immediately?"
Ó Moráin: "Yes, there was. I remember a discussion at which the Minister for Defence complained about lack of equipment, unpreparedness, as far as the army was concerned, some time around January."

On re-examination, the prosecution asked Mr Ó Moráin "Who was the Minister who would have had at that time particular responsibility for carrying out the Government's intentions in relation to the army?"

Ó Moráin: "It was Mr Gibbons and he was coming back with some of these plans, having consulted with the army about them."

Many people in court thought that Mr McKenna sat down rather suddenly at that stage.

In his evidence Mr Gibbons told Mr Sorahan that he had never heard of any contact with the Special Branch. Later he said:

"What is discussed at Cabinet meetings, my Lord, I would prefer to claim privilege upon, but in this period of time at any rate I can recall no reference to Special Branch reports, so it is therefore in my opinion of no relevance to this."

Mr Sorahan also cross-examined Mr Berry, Secretary of the Department of Justice, on Special Branch activities.

Sorahan: "So I take it as a result of that, were Special Branch officers sent to the North?"
Berry: "No."
Sorahan: "It was for some other reason they were sent?"
Berry: "No, there were no Special Branch officers sent to the North, if you are speaking of 1969."
Sorahan: "Yes, from August 1969 to the spring of this year."
Berry: "I state categorically there were no Special Branch officers sent to the North in 1969."

He stated further that no Special Branch officers were sent to the North in the spring or early part of 1970.

Sorahan: "If Special Branch officers went up there, you know nothing about it?"
Berry: "I know that no Special Branch officer went to the North."

Chief Superintendent Fleming told Mr Sorahan that he was in charge of the Special Detective Unit, which he agreed had been known as the Special Branch.

Sorahan: "Is it correct to say that several members of the Special Detective Unit had to go there (to the North) on the instruction of Mr Ó Moráin?"
Fleming: "No, that is not correct."
Sorahan: "And if anybody said that it would be quite wrong?"
Fleming: "I am positive about that."
Sorahan: "Are you quite sure about this?"
Fleming: "Absolutely positive."

Here was a major divergence of evidence, with the former Minister for Justice, Mr Ó Moráin, being out-gunned by the Secretary of the Department of Justice, Mr Berry, and the head of the Special Branch, Mr Fleming.

Mr McKenna threw some light on the question, when he explained:

"There is no mystery about the matter. It can be very easily clarified as to what is accurate and I am quite happy if your Lordship will consider it relevant to have it clarified..."

Judge: "Clarified in what way?"
McKenna: "Clarified in the way that the jury will know the truth as to what Garda officers operated in the North of Ireland."
Judge: "Who is to give that evidence?"
McKenna "Either Chief Superintendent Fleming may give it or Mr Berry may give it."
Judge: "That is my point, if Mr Ó Moráin is recalled you will want to recall these two witnesses and there will be no end to the matter."
McCarthy: "It seems to me, my Lord, I infer from what my friend is saying, that it is just another half-truth – the Special Branch were not, but some officers of the Garda were. Perhaps that is the truth. That Mr Berry's evidence was strictly accurate, although incomplete."

The problem was solved when Mr John Lincoln, Garda Síochána Assistant Commissioner, was called to the stand.

He said that on August 8, 1969 in the absence of the Commissioner, he was called to the office of Mr Ó Moráin, Minister for Justice, where he got instructions to send experienced, mature officers into the Six Counties to make on the spot observations and to report back. Where possible, he said, these men were to have a Northern background, but there was no question of it being a Special Branch operation and no Special Branch men were sent.

Mr Lincoln told Mr McCarthy that the Special Branch had no particular statutory function, but was set up to deal with subversive elements in society. Its members were ordinary Garda officers, he explained, except that they did not wear uniforms.

Mr Berry was present when he received his instructions from the Minister, Mr Lincoln said; the reports which came back were transmitted through Mr Berry to Mr Ó Moráin and where eventually to go to the Government.

Mr Lincoln claimed privilege when asked how many officers were involved and how many reports were sent back.

Stating that he was the one who raised the matter, Mr Sorahan asked:

"Were any of the officers you sent former members of the Special Branch?"

Lincoln: "My Lord, I also claim privilege on that."

There was a spontaneous burst of cynical laughter from the court and Mr Sorahan commented:

"Well, I think it would be useless for me to ask the forty or fifty questions I had intended, if this is going to be the answer. It would waste your Lordship's time and the jury's time."

Judge: "And your time."

In his closing speech to the jury on behalf of Mr Haughey, Mr McCarthy referred to the Special Branch conundrum:

> "Mr Berry was asked a series of questions by Mr Sorahan about the operation of the Special Branch in Northern Ireland and quite correctly, in respect of each question, he was categorical and clear that the Special Branch had never operated in Northern Ireland. It would appear... that the Gardaí or special Gardaí who, particularly chosen for their connection with Northern Ireland, were sent in to get reports, call them intelligence reports or whatever you like, but they were sent in and the reports were brought eventually to the Government. This was a decision of the Minister for Justice, passed through Mr Berry to Commissioner Lincoln. I would have thought that a public servant, not a public master, but a public servant, would when asked about one branch of the force which is part of his department, the Garda Síochána, when asked if one branch of it had gone to the North and made reports, and knowing that another had gone to the North and made reports, would not have confined his answer to saying, 'No, the Special Branch did not go', but that he would have been forthcoming with the information which obviously was being sought. It didn't matter whether it was the Special Branch or not, what mattered most was that reports were being got about conditions in the North."

Mr Lincoln had defined Special Branch officers as ordinary Garda officers who did not wear uniforms and who were specially organised to deal with subversion. He claimed privilege when pressed by Mr Sorahan as to the exact status of the officers sent North, but it was clear that the distinction between the specially selected officers sent North not wearing uniform and the Special Branch as defined by Mr Lincoln was hairsbreadth, if such a distinction existed at all.

On the day Mr Berry gave his evidence, there was present in court a man from Northern Ireland (not John Kelly) who told me about a meeting he had in County Fermanagh with one of the Garda officers sent North.

It seems that the officer – whose name and home station my informant knew – had let it be known that he had ammunition to offer in return for information. He claimed that the ammunition was part of the stock captured by the Special Branch during the IRA campaign of 1956/1962. My informant, upon hearing this, went to meet the officer and as he wryly put it:

"I gave my information and got my fifty rounds."

The veracity of information obtained in this way can be left to the imagination, but it was frightening to think that such dubious information probably formed the basis of reports to the Government. Being aware of the version of the Bailieboro meeting that Mr Berry had given to the Taoiseach, I was not altogether surprised at what my Northern Ireland friend told me.

The privilege in Dáil Éireann was again abused by such luminaries as An Taoiseach and George Colley, Minister for Finance, by suggesting that the signing of a certificate by the Minister for Defence was necessary to authorise the importation of the arms. Not to put too fine a point on it, it was absolutely disgraceful and a gross abuse of democracy and of the integrity of parliament by both Lynch and Colley, two alleged defenders of truth and justice in Irish political life.

CHAPTER 17

In the second trial, Mr Gibbons' evidence generally tallied with what he had given previously, with certain changes of emphasis. There was a greater air of uncertainty about him than at the start of his evidence in the first trial. He seemed more like the Mr Gibbons of May 1 on whose nervousness Chief Superintendent Fleming had commented. In describing the Dublin docks incident, while he still had me disappearing into the shadows, he added that he remembered using that particular expression and he thought I shrugged in an affirmative kind of way. He reminded the court that he was speaking from recollection, but he thought I had said that a couple of the boys or a couple of us went down to the docks the other night and were expecting some stuff to come in. He might have sounded less like a Robert Service poem if he had taken note of the evidence of Dermot O'Riordan, another prosecution witness, on the previous day.

Mr O'Riordan was the Surveyor of Customs and Excise whom John Kelly and I had met when we went to Dublin docks on Wednesday, March 25. Mr McKenna asked him:

"Did you go on your ordinary duties on that day?"

O'Riordan: "Yes."
McKenna: "At what time and where did you report?"
O'Riordan: "Well, I went to Alexandra Quay or I went to Ocean Pier at about nine o'clock on that morning."
McKenna: "Did you meet any of the accused there?"
O'Riordan: "Yes, I met Captain Kelly and Mr John Kelly."
McKenna: "Where?"
O'Riordan: "At Ocean Pier."

This should have convinced Mr Gibbons that there was little point in trying to suggest that our visit to the docks was carried out surreptitiously by the light of the moon.

Mr Gibbons persisted in his story that he wanted me out of the army and described how he had explained to Mr Haughey that I had to be got rid of as quickly, but as discreetly, as possible. The reason, he told Mr Haughey, was the fact that I was an Intelligence Officer and not just any army officer who wished to retire. My going from the army, therefore, should be as easy and as painless as possible and should be effected without angering me or giving me any sense of grievance. He remembered describing me as *hot*, in the sense that I was a man who could be potentially dangerous.

When questioned on contingency plans, Mr Gibbons was more forthcoming than in the first trial, admitting that among the possibilities was one which came to be described as the Doomsday situation, an absolutely extreme situation in which incursions might be considered for the specific purpose of protecting life and property, particularly life. Colonel Hefferon, it should be remembered, had appeared once and Mr Ó Moráin twice in the witness-box since the last appearance of Mr Gibbons and incursions were mentioned by both men. Mr Gibbons went on indirectly to refer to the Directive of February 6 when he said that he thought there were minutes in the Department of Defence resulting from his conversation with the Chief-of-Staff.

Admitting that there existed a written record of the Directive or of his conversation with the Chief-of-Staff, as he called it, Mr Gibbons highlighted a curious aspect of the discussion involving the Directive. In the first trial Mr Justice O'Keeffe had suggested during Colonel Hefferon's evidence that if the Directive existed, it was the best evidence and no other should be allowed. Mr McKenna said that he did not know where to get it.

This seemed surprising, especially when, in the first trial, Colonel Hefferon, a retired officer, could, by making a simple phone-call, obtain the terms of it from Army Headquarters. What was more surprising still was that Mr Gibbons, in the second trial, could confirm, essentially if not precisely, that a written record of the Directive existed in the Department of Defence. Was it possible that the prosecution, with all the resources of the State behind it, having made *quite a detailed search*, could not find a record available in such an official place as Army Headquarters? It was not possible. That was the short answer. The jury's inability to consider what happened at the earlier trial inhibited the defence in pursuing this important question.

In cross-examination, Mr McCarthy asked Mr Gibbons:

"On the February 6 did you issue a Directive to the Chief-of-Staff to prepare contingency plans to deal with the worsening of the situation in the North?"

Gibbons: "Yes."
McCarthy: "And did you instruct him to obtain surplus arms?"
Gibbons: "I instructed him that surplus arms be concentrated in certain areas."

McCarthy: "Obtain, I suggest?"
Gibbons: "Obtain."
McCarthy: "Yes."
Gibbons: "Does counsel mean to purchase new arms?"
McCarthy: "However one obtains them?"
Gibbons: "This was a matter that had to be discussed. Mr H got instructions from the Government to discuss together th further supplies of arms."
McCarthy: "Well, surplus arms! I emphasise the word surplu
Gibbons: "This would hardly be an accurate definition of. text."
McCarthy: "Was there any written… was yours a written Dir
Gibbons: "Mine was not a written Directive."
McCarthy,: "Spoken Directive?"
Gibbons: "Yes."
McCarthy: "To whom?"
Gibbons: "A conversation with the Chief-of-Staff."

Actually, the conversation was with the Chief-of-Staff and t Military Intelligence, both there at the Minister's behest, l suit the Minister to admit that Colonel Hefferon was party tive on the day it was given.

McCarthy: "Was there any record made of it?"
Gibbons: "I understand that the minutes were made of it afte army."
McCarthy: "Have you ever seen them?"
Gibbons: "Yes."
McCarthy: "You have seen them?"
Gibbons: "I have seen a copy of them."
McCarthy: "Have you seen them lately?"
Gibbons: "Yes."
McCarthy: "I don't mean in court. Have you seen them sir trial?"
Gibbons: "Yes."
McCarthy: "Are they then, I take it, in GHQ?"
Gibbons: "Presumably."
McCarthy: "Where did you see them?"
Gibbons: "I got them from official sources."
McCarthy: "Does that mean the army?"
Judge: "You don't have to answer, Mr Gibbons."
Gibbons: "Official sources."

The judge allowed Mr Gibbons to claim privilege on the source from which he had obtained the document. Mr McCarthy then proposed to ask the witness about discussions he had had concerning Colonel Hefferon's evidence but his request was disallowed on the grounds of irrelevance. When Mr McCarthy insisted further, the jury was instructed to leave the courtroom and there followed a prolonged argument about the validity of discovering to what extent Mr Gibbons had discussed the previous trial with his colleagues. However, the judge continued to disallow questioning on this subject, emphasising that it would involve reference back to the first trial which he had forbidden in his initial ruling.

Mr McCarthy stated:

> "I also want to bring out the fact that Mr Ó Moráin, on the last occasion, gave his evidence after Mr Gibbons and yet the State was absolutely determined, in respect of a witness whose direct evidence was purely technical, was adamant, that he should not give evidence after Mr Gibbons. I want to bring these things out, my Lord, because in my submission, they are indicative of a prosecution that is being conducted to the unfair prejudice of the accused."

Judge: "Well, I have ruled out already and I rule out again, any interpretation to the jury of what happened at the last trial."

After further discussion Mr McCarthy continued:

> "Mr Ó Moráin did say that he was called out of order. He said it himself, but it is more than that, my Lord, it is a matter of far greater importance that I bring out the fact that Colonel Hefferon's evidence contradicted that of Mr Gibbons and that I am suggesting that is why he is not being called. I must question the witness to that effect."

Judge: "I must disallow that, Mr McCarthy."

Once again, the ruling that the last trial could not be discussed was working to the disadvantage of the defence. Without the previous trial, there would have been no question of dropping Colonel Hefferon and the prosecution would not have felt it necessary to call Mr Ó Moráin before Mr Gibbons. This question could not be discussed in the presence of the jury. The case of the missing Directive was not to be resolved either, it seemed, but was to remain a mystery, surrounded by claims of privilege.

At a later stage, Mr McCarthy referred to the Directive again. The judge asked him to state his question:

McCarthy: "Did Mr Gibbons read the minutes of the Directive since the last trial in company with anybody else, and if he says yes, I was going to ask him, who?"

Once again Mr Gibbons claimed privilege, this time on the grounds that the source from which he obtained the minutes was "an official source" and that he thought it essential to State security not to disclose the names of those present when he read the document. The judge allowed the claim to privilege.

In contrast to Mr Ó Moráin's experience, Mr Gibbons had full access to official documents, but the information he obtained was obviously not for the benefit of the court. To me, it was incomprehensible that Mr Henchy should have allowed the Minister's claim of privilege. The contingency plans were one of the bulwarks, if not the bulwark, of my defence. They evolved from a direction to the Chief-of-Staff from the Minister, which began with the solemn words: "The Government have instructed..." and authorised planning for the provision of surplus arms for distribution to civilians in certain circumstances. They dealt with a matter of State security, but security in regard to them had already been broken. Why, then, did Mr Gibbons not want to disclose them? He was baiting a trap for the Defence, was the short answer.

This became clear when Mr McKenna was called upon by the judge. He said that he was not concerned with the matters in which Mr Gibbons had claimed privilege, but that if Mr McCarthy in fact wanted to have the contents of the Directive made available to the court, he would consult the present Minister for Defence to find out whether this was possible.

It was obvious at this stage that there was a major shift in prosecution strategy regarding the Directive. Mr Gibbons seemed to be more forthcoming about it second time round and, now, Mr McKenna, who said it could not be found despite an extensive search at the first trial, was actually challenging the defence to ask the new Minister for Defence to produce it.

The defence did not take the bait, for the very good reason it knew that the original record of the Directive had been replaced at GHQ by a forged document.

I got an inkling that something like this had taken place, a week or so after the first trial. An Intelligence Officer friend of mine attached to GHQ, whom I had known for many years, rang me saying that it was a matter of extreme urgency that he speak to me. He suggested that we meet in a supermarket car park in Dublin's southside.

In the car park, he was at the door of my car before I could open it.

"Sit where you are," he told me. "Listen carefully, I'll be fast".

It seemed that he had overheard or had been party to a conversation in the Director of Intelligence's office in GHQ, which indicated that I would be discredited in the second arms trial. My claim of authorisation would be counteracted in a most positive fashion, as would Colonel Hefferon's evidence. There was talk of an amended document or record. My defence of authorisation, supported by the Colonel, would crumble when it was produced, was the belief.

"They're out to get you, Jim", he said, walking away.

When my friend left, I sat in my car pondering and, then, I drove to the home of James D'Arcy, SC, one of my legal team. I told him the story, suggesting it might be the Directive that was at issue.

"You could be right", he said. "Go through the story again and I'll take notes".

The plain fact of the matter, incredible as it seems, was that the terms of the Directive, confirmed by the senior officer in Plans and Operations at Army HQ to exist in the first trial, and quoted by Colonel Hefferon, no longer existed at that august institution. They had been substituted.

In his book, *Up Dev*, Kevin Boland throws light on the matter:

> "I have not dealt with the mysterious matter of the 'lost and found' transcript of the verbal Directive about possible incursions into the Six Counties, which was given by Mr Gibbons to the Army on the direct instructions of the Government… There are just two aspects I think I should mention. It was stated in the abortive trial that the transcript, which the Defence wanted to be produced, could not be located. I think few people could have believed such an important document could have been mislaid in Army HQ. During the second trial, Mr Gibbons himself volunteered the information that it had now turned up. For a time it appeared as if the Defence were now being challenged to repeat their request for it to be produced. In fact, it had been rewritten in the meantime in the office of Mr Gibbons' successor with the assistance of phone calls to the Taoiseach. Apparently, it was felt that this 'reproduction' could safely be produced in court, but when the matter was further considered, wiser counsels prevailed.
>
> The Chief-of-Staff, to whom the verbal Directive had been given, and who dictated the original transcript, and whose evidence would have been necessary to authenticate the (forged) document was Lieut. General Sean Mac Eoin, who had served with distinction as United Nations Commander in the Congo and who was known to be a man of absolute integrity.

After the existence of this document had been made known in court, I received information and was able to make one of the defence counsel aware of the rewriting of the document, of the people present when it was done, of the name of the army officer who actually wrote it down and of the phone calls to the Taoiseach. Whether this became generally known or not, there were other rumours of other meetings in connection with the rewriting of the document...

The document was not produced in court: Lieut. General Mac Eoin did not appear on the witness stand; instead he went to visit the troops serving in Cyprus and, when his term of office as Chief-of-Staff expired, he was not reappointed. He was succeeded by Colonel Delaney who had also succeeded Colonel Hefferon."

The army officer to whom Mr Boland referred was present in court for the second trial. The assumption was that he was there to swear to the authenticity of the substituted interpretation of the Directive. This was the same GHQ staff officer, who was party to interpreting the first and genuine Directive, describing it at the time as "the most important document since the foundation of the State".

The ministerial Directive was an oral one issued in general terms, which was the responsibility of the General Staff to interpret. Thus, the interpretation became the operational document, clarifying how the Directive should be put into effect. As such, it assumed a major significance, superseding the Directive, in that it dictated how the army should act in response to the parent document.

This interpretation was referred back to the Minister for Defence by the Chief-of-Staff in the days after February 6. At this stage, the Minister expressed himself as not totally satisfied, especially with the issue of surplus arms which, as he put it, were "to be made immediately available".

The end result was the interpretation to which Colonel Hefferon testified and which, as he also testified, he discussed with me.

The GHQ Staff Officer was not called to the witness box to authenticate the substituted forged interpretation. The absence of General Mac Eoin as a prosecution witness stymied the effort to introduce it in court. The prosecution was well aware that the defence was prepared to have the Chief-of-Staff brought back from Cyprus and the word was that he would tell the truth if put to the test. As Kevin Boland has indicated, his reputation was such that the forged Directive, unless authenticated by him, was worse than useless as a prosecution weapon.

Kevin Boland and Tom Barry, the Cork guerrilla chief (Old IRA) at Crossbarry, 1973

The person who told Kevin Boland about the forgery was Mr Patrick Murphy, Assistant Secretary and later, Secretary, of the Department of Defence. He was at the meeting and was horrified by what took place. He found it incredible that an Irish Government would act in such a manner and he found it impossible to accept that Department of Defence colleagues, both civilian and, more especially, military, should be party to a subterfuge designed to discredit both Colonel Hefferon and me. Mr Murphy, faced with a major moral dilemma, consulted an old friend and former Minister for Defence, Kevin Boland, giving him full details of what had taken place. In turn, Mr Boland felt it was incumbent on him to prevent what was a clear Government attempt to subvert the course of justice by suborning servants of the State. Consequently he put his information in the hands of counsel for the defence.

The meeting, at Army HQ, was chaired by the new Minister for Defence, Mr Cronin. Present were senior ranks of the army, including the Chief-of-Staff, General Sean Mac Eoin, and senior members of the Secretariat. Twice, Mr Cronin rang the Taoiseach, Mr Lynch, to verify the acceptability of the new verbiage.

Years later, I met Defence Minister Cronin in Dáil Éireann. He greeted me warmly. In the course of our conversation, I mentioned the changing

Office of the Chief o
Defence Forces Head
Parkgate,
Dublin 8
Phone: 01 - 804260
Fax: 01 - 83678

06 August 1998

Dockrell Farrell Solicitors,
51/52 Fitzwilliam Square,
Dublin 2.

Dear Sir,

I refer to your letter of 03 July 1998 in which you state that your client James Kelly, (Captain, Rtd.) wishes to receive a copy of the directive, and any notes interpreting it, issued on behalf of the Government to the Minister for Defence on February 6th 1970. Having regard to the nature of such relevant documents as may be held at this Headquarters I must, with regret, refuse to accede to your clients wish.

G. J. McMAHON

LIEUTENANT GENERAL

CHIEF OF STAFF

Negative response of Chief of Staff to request for a copy of the Directive of February 6th, 1970 and its interpretation.

of the Directive and his part in it. Far from denying it, he accepted what happened and excused his part in the affair on the basis that he was new to the office; and that he accepted the good faith of the Taoiseach, Jack Lynch, in the matter.

"Jack was the boss. I trusted him, " he explained.

Mr Cronin was still Minister for Defence in 1971, when the Dáil Committee of Public Accounts Inquiry into the money that paid for the arms requested a copy of the Directive from the Chief-of Staff, General Sean Mac Eoin. The essential part of the General's reply was quoted to me by one of the Inquiry members, Justin Keating:

> "I should inform you that I have been directed by the Minister for Defence to claim privilege in regard to the Directive of February 6, 1970...
>
> For the information of the Committee I should also say that none of the matters covered by the Directive is in any way relevant to the expenditure of the Grant-in-Aid or any funds the subject matter of the Inquiry...
>
> The Directive gave no authority, whatever, direct or indirect, to the Department of Defence or any other body, officer or person to purchase, procure or acquire arms or equipment."

The reply was very explicit and detailed in its denial of authority, but it had nothing whatsoever to do with the February 6 Directive, as originally interpreted by Plans and Operations Section at the Chief-of-Staff's Branch at Army Headquarters. It was clearly based on an interpretation of the Directive, rewritten, as already described, in the interval between the two trials. Obviously, the substituted document had become the official record at GHQ in 1971. It had become the false document of record for historians and future generations to peruse and wrongly conclude that it was the genuine article. Thus the perniciously invidious and criminal sleight-of-hand practised by Government in 1970 in an attempt to falsely convict four people was promulgated as truth. In an effort to clarify and, if necessary, remedy the matter, I, in 1998, through my solicitor, wrote to the then current Chief-of-Staff, Lieut. General Gerry McMahon, for a copy of the February 6, 1970 Directive and its interpretation. I got a negative response *(see opposite page)*:

That the forged document was on record at GHQ in 1980 emerged in an article in *Magill* magazine by Vincent Browne in May of that year, entitled 'The Arms Crisis 1970'. Mr Browne, who stands by his sources twenty years later, published a copy of the Government Directive issued to the army by Mr Gibbons on February 6, 1970 and a claimed copy of the interpretation as follows:

> 'The Government have instructed me to convey to the Army a Directive that plans be immediately put in train for operating in

> Northern Ireland, in the event of the situation (in the opinion of the Government) warrants interference. The Government further directs that training and planning programmes be directed to cater for such an eventuality.
>
> The Directive was delivered verbally by Mr Gibbons to the Chief-of-Staff of the Army, General Sean Mac Eoin, in the presence of Colonel Hefferon. Subsequently, the Directive was written down by the Plans and Operations Officer at the direction of the Chief-of-Staff.
>
> Later on, the Chief-of-Staff interpreted the Directive and the interpretation was cleared by Mr Gibbons. The interpretation reads: *'The Government directs that the Army (1) prepare to train the forces for incursions into Northern Ireland, (2) make weapons and ammunition available and (3) make gas masks available'.*"

It is exceedingly odd that a copy of the Directive and its interpretation should come into the hands of a magazine ten years after the event, when such documentation could not be found in Army HQ during the first trial. It was also interesting to note that the actual Directive, published by Mr Browne, was precisely correct, word for word as recorded at GHQ immediately after it was issued on February 6, 1970. It also tallied with Colonel Hefferon's record of it, but it was not the wording of the Directive that was at issue; it was the interpretation of it that was of vital importance and the interpretation that was published by Mr Browne differed from the recorded version at GHQ, confirmed by Colonel John O'Donovan to Colonel Hefferon prior to the latter giving evidence to the court.

In evidence, unchallenged and uncontradicted in the two trials, Colonel Hefferon told the court that he had made a note of the interpretation of the actual Directive, which he had in a notebook still in his possession. He gave the terms of that interpretation as: "*The Government directs that the Army (1) prepare for incursions into Northern Ireland, (2) set aside surplus arms and ammunition for this purpose and (3) provide gas masks.*"

In replies to the Judge, he confirmed that he had checked his recollection of it "against the record that existed in GHQ and they were substantially the same... the terms which, in my understanding, had been extracted from the Directive".

The Hefferon Papers, donated to Military Archives by Mrs Peggy Hefferon after her husband's death, contain two pages of a manuscript in the handwriting of the late Colonel. The incomplete manuscript is obviously part of an *aide memoire* hurriedly written around the time the Directive was issued. This contemporaneous document gives an invaluable insight into what the Directive was really about and the events surrounding its issue. It is quoted in full and exactly as written:

6 Febr.
CS (Chief-of-Staff) held a meeting
Informed him of an ap I had with the Minister at 3. 45 & asked his permission to leave at that time
Did so and went directly to Ministers office
Sit down Col. I have an important communication from the Government for the Chief. He will be along any moment now
At that moment the Chief came in
I arose to leave but the Minister waved me down with the words -
What I have to tell the Chief affects you too Colonel. Stay.
Then turning to General Mac Eoin he said
"General I have a Directive from the Government for you. You will prepare the Army for Incursions into NI should the situation in the opinion of the Government warrant it. You will arrange to make Surplus arms available for these operations and also Gas Masks.
By the way General what plans have you for a contingency like this.
The Chief when he got his breath back mentioned certain documents which he had discussed with the Minister relating to the procurement of armaments for the Army in view a such a possible contingency amongst others
Mr G. appeared to be dissatisfied and pushed further -
Yes I know all about that he said a trifle impatiently - "but what about plans for operations in NI based on what you have?
Do you have any such in fact.
The pace of events at this stage…

The extant portion of the MS ends at that point, but there is another document in the Hefferon Papers that continues the story. Entitled "Notes On The Directive", it was obviously written much later than the arms trials. Clearly based on the *aide memoire*, it reiterates what the two pages of the manuscripts state, before continuing:

> "The Minister said: 'Yes. Yes, I know, but what I want to find out is what the Army, from its studies of the situation, plans to do should they be faced immediately with a breakdown of order in the Six Counties?'
>
> General Mac Eoin, who was a bit taken aback by the task now

being thrust upon him, replied: 'Well, yes, you will remember, Minister,that we presented you with a brief on the Army's requirements some time ago.'

The Minister said: 'Yes, yes, I know, but what I want to find out is what the Army, from its studies of the situation, plans to do should they be faced immediately with a breakdown of order in the Six Counties?'

To this, General Mac Eoin replied: 'We sent you a report of a study made by a Board of Officers dealing with the capabilities of the Army in such a situation.'

I have not received it then. Please see that it is on my table on Monday morning."

The two officers went back to the conference which they had both left. The Chief quickly brought it to an end, instructing 'the Defence Council Officers and the Plans and Operations representative to remain behind'. He briefed them on the Directive, instructing them 'to let him have up-to-date figures on the numbers of gas masks serviceable, as well as figures on the surplus arms…'"

Towards the end of his narrative, the Colonel stated that on the next day he wrote down in a personal notebook "my own recollection of the Government Directive". Later, as the date for the arms trials approached, he wrote in reference to the Directive:

> "Whilst I was reasonably certain that the note I had made at the time represented the exact message given by the Minister, it was my understanding that the Chief went back to Mr Gibbons for clarification on certain points and I felt it would be helpful to have permission to view the final form… I was careful to suggest to Colonel O'Donovan (Plans and Operations) that he should seek the Chief-of-Staff's personal permission for me to get this facility as, for his sake, I did not want a situation arising where I got sight of the document in any other than a regular way.
>
> About a week later, I met Colonel O'Donovan, who read out to me from notes compiled from the original; the exact terms of the Directive. These did not differ in any material way from the note (interpretation) I had made on the day following the issue of the Directive."

This was the final agreed, official interpretation of the Directive as recorded in the Chief-of-Staff's Branch at Army Headquarters and as given in evidence by Colonel Hefferon in the High Court. It remained as such, as Colonel O'Donovan had confirmed to Colonel Hefferon, until the Government fabricated a substitute Directive between the two trials.

Undoubtedly, the interpretation of the Directive given to Vincent Browne was a fake. It was the substitute forged document, concocted at GHQ between the two trials, with the purpose of undermining Colonel Hefferon's evidence as a prosecution witness, in conjunction with undermining my case, which was based solely on the key issue of authorisation. If I went down, John Kelly and Albert Luyxk would go down also. Charlie Haughey was another matter. He had an ace in the hole, an each-way bet, with denial of knowledge of any arms as the saver. He was likely to go free, whether or which.

To appreciate the distinction between the Hefferon interpretation and what we will call the forgery, it is necessary to do a comparative analysis of the two interpretations, which, of course were formalised as orders.

Hefferon Interpretation – 1: Prepare for incursions into Northern Ireland.
The Forgery – 1: Prepare to train the Forces for incursions into Northern Ireland.

The Hefferon Order 1 was definite. It could not be misunderstood. Part of such preparation inevitably included pinpointing and developing whatever indigenous support was available in the area.

The Army, in its usual methodical fashion took this on board and appointed two senior GHQ officers to formulate plans for what was a proposed invasion of Northern Ireland.

I was ordered to contribute a paper on the likely indigenous support in the area and how it might be developed and used. I did so.

In such a situation, it is obvious that the people on the ground in Northern Ireland, most of them civilians without military training, would need some training, with the availability of arms a major factor, as Order 2 indicated.

The Forged Order 1 merely ordered the Forces to prepare to train for incursions into Northern Ireland. It could be argued with a major degree of credibility that this did not envisage any action other than making plans for training. Certainly, there was a big difference between preparing for training for incursions and actually preparing for incursions. The lawyers could make hay of this, to the detriment of Colonel Hefferon and me, if the forgery was accepted as genuine by the court, precisely what its framers, advised by Mr Lynch, had in mind.

Hefferon Interpretation – 2: Set aside surplus arms and ammunition for this purpose.
The Forgery – 2: Make weapons and ammunition available.

The Hefferon Order 2 was again definite. It was also self-explanatory. Get the extra arms and ammunition, surplus to normal requirements, and store them where they would be available for distribution to the indigenous support groups in Northern Ireland as preparation for the proposed invasion. In the context of invasion, it might even have been considered necessary to store the weaponry in areas of Northern Ireland in advance. Taken in conjunction with Order 1, it would be difficult to argue against such an interpretation, a view which Mr Gibbons substantiated when in a cross-examination by Mr McCarthy (already quoted), he stated that had instructed the Chief-of-Staff that "surplus arms be concentrated in certain areas".
The Forged Order 2 might well be interpreted as providing sufficient arms for the Forces of the State only, to prepare for training for incursions. When taken in conjunction with GHQ Order 1, it would be difficult to argue otherwise.

The Hefferon Interpretation – 3: Provide gas masks.
The Forgery – 3: Make gas masks available.

Both orders were irrelevant in the context of the arms trial.

It is obvious that if the prosecution could have introduced the GHQ forgery at the second trial, with all the weight of GHQ and the Department of Defence behind it, the defence case of authorisation at best would have been seriously undermined, or, more likely, completely scuppered.

CHAPTER 18

Mr Gibbons, when questioned further by Mr Finlay on my behalf, said it was common knowledge that in the early Autumn of 1969, Citizens' Defence Committees had been set up in Belfast, Derry and other parts of Northern Ireland to provide for the defence of isolated communities that might come under attack, but he denied that he was aware that in October, 1969, representatives of these Committees met in Bailieboro, Co. Cavan.

When Mr Finlay suggested that he had been informed in detail of the Bailieboro meeting, Mr Gibbons said he did not remember receiving any report of that meeting.

Finlay: "Did you know in October 1969 that representatives of these committees were seeking the assistance of the Government here for the provision of arms, if they could get them?"
Gibbons: "No. The only information conveyed to me in the matter of the procurement of arms was that it appeared to be a rather regular occurrence for individual householders to present themselves at various army posts asking the officers in charge if they could be given some type of weapon to defend themselves and their families."
Finlay: "Where were the army posts?"
Gibbons: "It appeared to occur all along the border."
Finlay: "Are you suggesting that you were unaware of any request or requests by representatives of these Committees in the North for arms to be supplied to them by the Irish Government?"
Gibbons: "I have no recollection of the remotest kind. I disbelieve its truth."

Mr Gibbons had no recollection, but I had submitted a written report to the Director of Intelligence of the Bailieboro meeting. It was probably the only meeting where representatives from so many areas in Northern Ireland put forward the case for arms for defence and for training in the use of those arms. My brief was to ascertain (a) the purpose for which the arms would be used, whether defensively or offensively; (b) levels of training, if any, and what further training and type of training was considered necessary.

It was accepted that Defence Committee people with experience in the use of arms would likely be associated with the IRA and most of those attending the meeting were either past or current members. There were also ex-servicemen, both British and Irish, associated with the Defence Committees.

Colonel Hefferon told the court that he had reported the Bailieboro meeting to Mr Gibbons. Later, at the subsequent Committee of Public Accounts, the Inquiry into the funds used to purchase the arms, he and I testified that Mr Gibbons got my report of the Bailieboro meeting and that it was brought to the notice of the Taoiseach. At the same Inquiry, Peter Berry, Secretary of the Department of Justice, revealed that he had informed Mr Lynch of my activities, inclusive of the Bailieboro meeting, on October 17, 1969, when Mr Lynch called to see him in Dublin's Mount Carmel Hospital. Taoiseach Lynch admitted that the meeting with Berry took place, attempting to play down its significance by suggesting that Mr Berry was too ill to be fully coherent. He accepted, however, that Berry made him aware of the meeting.

The most significant revelation, however, concerning the Government's state of knowledge of the Bailieboro meeting was made by Kevin Boland, when he described how Mr Gibbons had brought the meeting to the notice of the Cabinet, stating in *Up Dev:*

> "I have disclosed that the Minister for Defence was aware from the beginning of Captain Kelly's activities in relation to the Six Counties and, in particular, that he, I and every other member of Government was aware of the Bailieboro meeting."

Mr Boland also disclosed:

> "During the period from August 1969 to May 1970, the activities of Captain James Kelly, as an army intelligence officer in relation to the Six Counties, were discussed several times at Government meetings and they were answered for by the Minister for Defence. My recollection is that he was first mentioned in the early stages, probably as early as August, when background information in relation to what we read in the papers came mainly from Neil Blaney. The Minister for Defence, Mr Gibbons, gave a generally similar picture based on Captain Kelly's reports."

Mr Boland went on to state that the Gibbons introduction of my report on the Bailieboro meeting was in response to the meeting being brought up by the Minister for Justice, Mr Ó Moráin, on the basis of Mr Berry's report.

I knew that Gibbons knew about the Bailieboro meeting. So did Colonel Hefferon. It now emerged that Mr Berry, Secretary of the Department of Justice, knew about it; Mr Lynch, the Taoiseach, knew about it; members of the Cabinet knew about it; and Mr Boland has confirmed that Mr Gibbons not only knew about it, but brought my report on it to the notice of the Cabinet. By denying knowledge of it at the two trials, Mr Gibbons committed perjury twice in relation to it.

Mr Gibbons told Mr Finlay that he had heard of a demand by the representatives of those Committees for training by the Irish army and said that this demand was met to some extent by enrolling citizens of Derry in the FCA, and giving them a week's training at a fort in Donegal. As far as he could remember, Mr Gibbons stated, the number who received the training was nine; they were immediately enrolled in the FCA, received the training and then went back to Derry.

Asked if the training was stopped because of newspaper publicity, Mr Gibbons replied:

"The Taoiseach was on leave. I sanctioned it on my own initiative. On his return, I acquainted him of the fact. The Taoiseach considered the matter and advised that it be discontinued, and it was."

Mr Gibbons explained that the FCA was a local defence force whose purpose was to provide opportunities for persons in each area of the country to be trained in the use of arms so that they might be available as a reserve force.

Finlay: "It is not intended for the purpose of training people living outside the Republic?"
Gibbons: "Not strictly speaking."
Finlay: "Do you agree that the enrolment of the people of Derry on your order into the FCA was an unorthodox method of achieving what you thought a proper objective?"
Gibbons: "Yes."
Finlay: "It was making use of the Defence Forces to assist the minority in Derry to be in a position to defend themselves ?"
Gibbons: "Yes."
Finlay: "You thought that a proper action to be taken at that time?"
Gibbons: "Yes, at that time of serious stress and strain."

Mr Gibbons added that the nature of the training would have been determined by the army, but that he would imagine that it would have application to the conditions in which the Bogsiders might find themselves and he presumed that it would be elementary training in the use of weapons.

Finlay: "Did you make any enquiries as to what guns they had when they went back to Derry?"
Gibbons: "I am quite certain they had no weapons that were properly Irish army weapons or, for that matter, any weapons."

After further questions, Mr Finlay asked whether Mr Gibbons would not agree that it was pointless to train the men in the use of guns unless they were going to get guns.

Gibbons: "I would not agree."
Finlay: "What was the point of training them in the use of guns if they were not going to get guns?"
Gibbons "My chief motivation in this gesture would be to convey to them that their dire straits were perceived by us and were sympathised with by me."
Finlay: "May I take it that your purpose or idea in permitting the enrolment of a number of citizens from Derry in the FCA was simply to make a gesture of sympathy to the people in the Bogside?"
Gibbons: "I think that would be accurate."

When Mr Gibbons again referred to the Taoiseach's decision to end the training, Mr Finlay said:

"I must suggest to you that it was stopped by Colonel Hefferon on his own initiative because of publicity in the newspapers and that you were subsequently informed?"

Gibbons: "What I have told the court and the jury is my recollection of the events as they took place."

Mr Gibbons' memory was faulty. Colonel Hefferon had stopped the training in the manner and in the circumstances I have already outlined.

When Mr McCarthy asked Mr Gibbons about an oath of loyalty to the Taoiseach on taking office as Minister, Mr Gibbons said that the acceptance of the Seal from the President meant that one undertook to carry out the duties of one's office to the best of one's ability.

As Minister he had the duty in Parliament to give information requested of him as fully and as fairly as possible within the limits of national security.

McCarthy: "Did you at any time deny that civilians were being trained by the army in Co. Donegal?"

Gibbons: "I don't recall having done so."

Mr McCarthy then quoted an extract from a speech by Deputy Ryan of Fine Gael during the marathon Dáil debate of May 8 in which Deputy Ryan said:

"It is quite clear that evidence has been given to the Taoiseach which links certain names with such activities not related alone to the attempted importation of arms from Vienna but related also to training, which was given in at least one army camp to civilians in the use of arms."

Mr Gibbons, according to Mr McCarthy, interrupted Deputy Ryan to say, "That is not true." In court Mr Gibbons resisted the clear implication.

McCarthy: "They were not civilians?"
Gibbons: "They were fully attested members of the FCA."
McCarthy: "You intervened expressly because of allegations of your own implication?"
Gibbons: "Yes."
McCarthy: "And in the course of that did you say that there was some reference to the training of civilians in Donegal?"
Gibbons: "I wanted to point out that the Defence Forces trained only members of their own ranks."
McCarthy: "Was that telling the whole truth, Mr Gibbons?"
Gibbons: "This was a declaration that the people who were trained in Dunree were members of the FCA and were duly attested as such."
McCarthy: "Do you think that it was perhaps not telling the whole truth, that civilians from Derry, citizens of another State, were enrolled in the second line of the Defence Forces, the FCA, for the express purpose of training themselves to go back to Derry to defend themselves?"
Gibbons: "A great many of the members of our Defence Forces come, in fact, from the Six Counties."
McCarthy: "Do any members of the FCA come from the Six Counties?"
Gibbons: "I was given to understand that people living in the Six Counties do."
McCarthy: "Can you turn up an instance of it?"
Gibbons: "When I spoke to Colonel Hefferon about this at the time, his view was that army recruits, and we were recruiting at that time, were not unduly quizzed as to where their origins were."

Mr Gibbons said that it was quite a normal thing for six-county people to join the Permanent Defence Force. But he might have added, anomalous as it may sound, that regulations specifically forbade the acceptance of six-county people into the FCA.

McCarthy: "Does not that mean that this was a device to enable the army to train them for the defence of the Bogside ?"
Gibbons: "I admit that this was a device to enable Derrymen to join the FCA and obtain training."
McCarthy: "Do you think then that your reply to Deputy Ryan was not something of a half-truth?"
Gibbons: "I am suggesting that what Deputy Ryan said was inaccurate."
McCarthy: "Would you accept that in this instance you had not told the truth but only half the truth?"
Gibbons: "This was a Dáil debate."
McCarthy: "Is that your answer, Mr Gibbons, that one is not bound to tell the truth in a Dáil debate?"
Gibbons: "This is a Dáil debate in which Deputy Ryan and his colleagues are seeking to demolish the Government and the Government party."

During the absence of the jury on the morning of October 13, Mr D'Arcy, representing me, introduced the case for the calling of Colonel Hefferon. He agreed that the defence could call him, but in that case the defence could not cross-examine the witness.

Judge: "Counsel for the other accused can cross-examine."
D'Arcy: "Well, they can, my Lord, but of course whoever has to call him as a witness will not be the person who will cross-examine him. And it is as clear as A follows B, my Lord, that whoever wants to call him, which there is no secret about… it would be in the interest of Captain Kelly and his evidence will be most relevant. It might not be relevant at all as far as any of the other defendants are concerned."

When the judge suggested that one of Mr D'Arcy's colleagues might call Colonel Hefferon – although there was no onus on either them or Mr D'Arcy to do so – Mr D'Arcy replied:

> "No, my Lord, but there is this link pin in the case. In the chain of command between the Minister and Captain Kelly, is Colonel Hefferon. He is after all a deposition witness and a witness on whom the charges were made. I would respectfully submit, my Lord, that in view of the evidence which has been given in the trial, it is essential that Colonel Hefferon's evidence be put before the jury and there is no onus on me, if the presumption of innocence still exists and that the onus of proof still remains on the State… I strongly urge your Lordship, firstly, to direct the prosecution to call Colonel Hefferon, and if your Lordship won't adopt that course, your Lordship at this stage should call Colonel Hefferon…"

Later Mr Wood protested:

> "In all my thirty-eight years (at the bar) I have never heard of a case in which the prosecution declined to tender for cross-examination a witness whose evidence, let's face up to it, does not suit the prosecution's case. The grounds on which it is suggested that he is unreliable are so doubtful as to be ridiculous. Because this witness associated with Captain Kelly, that is the only concrete proposal to suggest that he is unreliable. Is a man because he is accused to be treated by witnesses as a sort of social pariah to whom people can't speak? This is outrageous. It is a contradiction of the principle of the innocence of an accused. It is a kind of presumption that this prisoner is guilty... Why cannot the witness be tendered unless this trial has descended to the level where it is being conducted upon the basis of political gamesmanship?"

Mr McCarthy objected that if the judge should call Colonel Hefferon the prosecution would be the last to cross examine:

"I think that there is one very self-evident reason for this. Mr McKenna has a statement from the witness, at least one, He may have more, but, presumably, he has a signed statement from the witness which he can produce out of the hat at the end in order, presumably, to try to undermine the cross-examination that I imagine will be largely that of Mr D'Arcy or Mr Finlay, who are acting for Captain Kelly..."

After all this, Mr Justice Henchy called Colonel Hefferon as a witness, but gave a major advantage to the prosecution by allowing counsel for the Attorney General to cross-examine him if necessary.

In reply to Mr Finlay, Colonel Hefferon confirmed the evidence he had given in the first trial. He said he had reported the Bailieboro meeting to Mr Gibbons at the end of October or in early November, at which time he became aware that certain complaints had come from the Department of Justice. He said that my name had been mentioned specifically in relation to the meeting; this might seem a small point, except that Mr Gibbons had claimed in evidence that Colonel Hefferon referred to me as "my young man". As Colonel Hefferon himself put it:

"I did not refer to you that way if only because you were the oldest intelligence officer in the field."

Colonel Hefferon confirmed that he had cancelled or postponed the Fort Dunree training on his own initiative; that he had so reported to the Chief-of-Staff on the following Monday morning; that he told Mr Gibbons that the purpose of my February trip to the Continent was to vet arms and that the visit to my sister was a cover story. He confirmed the terms of the Directive of February 6 and that he had told me of its existence and its contents.

Asked had he made me aware of the General Staff's appreciation of what might be necessary as a result of the Directive, Colonel Hefferon replied:

"No, I don't think we had an appreciation at that time of what might be necessary."

Finlay: "Did you have a discussion at that time with Captain Kelly that one of the things that might be necessary as a result of this Directive was the provision of surplus arms, which might have to, in certain events, be made available to people in Northern Ireland?"
Hefferon: "Oh, yes, yes, this came out, surplus army arms."
Finlay: "And was that your understanding at that time, Colonel Hefferon, of one of the consequences of the Directive ?"
Hefferon: "Yes, I think the Directive said so."

Colonel Hefferon told Mr Finlay that he had approached Mr Gibbons concerning my trip to the Continent in the first week in April, explaining that I found it necessary to go abroad again in connection with this arms deal, but that I was slated for duty on that weekend.

Finlay: "And did you ask the Minister to do anything about that ?"
Hefferon: "I explained to him that on my own authority I had no function in having him relieved from his duty. I had no authority to do so. That if I started interfering, it might indeed attract unwelcome publicity. However, I said that I may be asking you to use your good offices in this matter."
Finlay: "And did the Minister agree to do that?"
Hefferon: "Mr Gibbons said what would that involve? I said I think you might have to discuss it with the Chief-of-Staff and he nodded and said alright. In the event, it was not, necessary to take any action, because I think the date had been a wrong one."

Colonel Hefferon said that when Mr Gibbons ordered the movement of the five hundred rifles to Dundalk during my absence on the Continent, he had asked my wife to tell me to return home immediately.
Finlay: "Did you tell him what the purpose of the message, which you had sent him, was?"
Hefferon: "Yes, I said that, at the time I sent the message, I was very worried about this shipment of rifles and ammunition, and that the meaning I took out of this sudden order to send rifles and ammunition and gas

masks, I think, to Dundalk was that a very bad situation was about to break out in the North and that the possibility that these rifles, or some part of them, might require to be distributed in this event could not be ruled out. It was on that basis that I asked Mrs Kelly, that when she was in touch with her husband, to tell him that it was my wish that he should return – in regard to a situation much more important than anything he would be doing abroad."

Finlay: "Did you tell Captain Kelly at that conversation that had the possibility or had the event of distribution of some or all of those rifles to people in the North of Ireland taken place, he was the man who would have had to supervise it, as he was the man who knew the right people to whom to give them?"

Hefferon: "Well, I would have looked on him in that light."

Finlay: "Did you tell Captain Kelly at that time that if the distribution had been required, what you wanted him back for was to supervise that distribution since he knew the personalities involved in the Northern Defence Committees?"

Hefferon: "Yes, in general terms, I told him. I would not say that those were the exact words, but that would be the sense of it."

Concerning the meeting in Mr Blaney's office on April 23, Colonel Hefferon repeated what he had said in the first trial and in general his evidence completely contradicted that of Mr Gibbons. Apart from the direct contradictions, the sophistry of Mr Gibbons' evidence is probably best illustrated by his explanation as to why he sent the rifles to Dundalk.

Finlay: "What was the purpose of sending five hundred rifles without men attached, even against the dire situation which you really did not believe would break out, what were they going to be used for?"

Gibbons: "Rifles! Certainly the function of rifles in our Defence Forces is for defensive purposes."

Finlay: "Ah, Mr Gibbons, you understand my question. On April 2 1970, to meet a dire situation which might break out, what was the purpose of moving five hundred rifles without men to Dundalk? What were they going to be used for?"

Gibbons: "If the Doomsday situation of which we are all afraid…"

Finlay: "What would you do with the rifles?"

Gibbons: "… broke upon us, it would be much more logical to have the rifles in Dundalk rather than elsewhere."

Finlay: "What were you going to do with them?"

Gibbons: "We had no immediate plans for their distribution."

Finlay: "Why not move blankets or anything else, why move rifles ?"
Gibbons: "Because blankets are a rather inefficient method of defending one's life."
Finlay: "Isn't the truth of the matter, Mr Gibbons, that you moved the rifles to Dundalk, while you did not think it was going to arise, against the outside possibility that you would have to distribute arms to the people in Northern Ireland?"
Gibbons: "The eventual reason probably was... we were dealing with a hypothetical situation which could take many, many forms. It could take the form of assault on the Nationalist, Catholic areas. It could take the form of total breakdown of law and order. It could take the form of the full occupation of the British security forces in other areas, with outside areas totally unprotected."
Finlay: "Yes?"
Gibbons: "There were a great many conceivable forms which this situation might give rise to, anything in the matter of the protection of life."
Finlay: "Is it not correct to say that the only way five hundred rifles without five hundred men fitted into that picture was that they were to be distributed to civilians in Northern Ireland?"
Gibbons: "No, this is not a reasonable deduction at all."

Accepting the hypothesis of a breakdown in law and order in Northern Ireland outlined by Mr Gibbons, it was a very reasonable deduction, especially when the terms of the February Directive given to the army by Mr Gibbons on behalf of the Government were taken into consideration. The Minister must have realised this, because when pressed to elucidate further, he drifted off into the realm of fantasy, as it applied to the situation in the first week of April.

Finlay: "What other use, in what you describe as a Doomsday situation, could have been made of five hundred rifles in Dundalk?"
Gibbons: "This is a very hypothetical question and many hypothetical answers can be given to it, but let us assume one as an example of the hypothetical nature of counsel's question.

If, for instance, the boot was on the other foot, if the attack was from the other side of the border as it might well be. And, in fact, incursions had been made in the recent past: there were many men such as myself, with rudimentary military training, who could, in a state of national emergency, be called upon to take those weapons in their hands and do what they could in the matter of the defence of this particular area. We are talking about a hypothetical situation."
Finlay: "You moved those rifles by a telephone call from Fianna Fáil head-

quarters in Naas?"
Gibbons: "Yes. I think they were moved that night."
Finlay: "Are you seriously telling my Lord and jury that the reason you moved these by a telephone call from a private premises in Naas was the possibility of people like yourself being brought into a situation where you might use them?"
Gibbons: "I'm talking about a hypothetical situation. Counsel is using all his endeavours to force me to say what I know is not correct and that is this: that it was a firm intention of mine or anybody else to distribute those five hundred rifles to civilians of Northern Ireland, which is not correct."
Finlay: "I never suggested it to you."
Gibbons: "You have been working around it."
Finlay: "What I asked you time and time again was the question whether one of the possibilities envisaged in the moving of those rifles was their ultimate distribution, if necessary, to people in Northern Ireland. Is that not the truth?"
Gibbons: "The short answer to your question is no."
Finlay: "And apart from the idea of yourself and like persons using the rifles, can you give us any other explanation?"
Gibbons: "I want to add to the short answer I already made. I made it several times before, that the situation in which we found ourselves at that time was totally unpredictable and that no plan of any kind could be formulated only in the light of events as they stood at that particular time. What you are really seeking to make me say is what the Government would decide in the light of events which had not yet taken place. Now I cannot, give an answer for the Government in the light of present events not to speak of events which have not yet occurred."

Mr Gibbons was saying that the Government could not make plans in relation to the Northern Ireland situation; despite the fact that ample evidence was presented to the court that contingency plans did exist, and that they ran completely counter to his thesis *that no plan of any kind could be formulated.* In fact, the movement of the rifles was merely carrying into effect the stated contingency plans of the Government. There was no way to get around this fact; perhaps that was why, with the question unresolved, Mr Justice Henchy suggested to Mr Finlay that he might pass on to another topic.

The prosecution took full advantage of Colonel Hefferon's changed status as a witness and subjected him to a rigorous cross-examination. However this did little to forward the prosecution's case. Among other things, Mr McKenna pressed hard on the storage and control of the arms.

McKenna: "To come back to the question of Captain Kelly, after the arms were imported retaining them under his sole control, I think a number of places were discussed?"
Hefferon: "One place certainly, other than Cathal Brugha Barracks."
McKenna: "There was no question of the guns and ammunition when they arrived being handed into army control?"
Hefferon: "No."
McKenna: "They were to be kept, I suggest Captain Kelly told you, in a completely non-military establishment?"
Hefferon: "Yes."
McKenna: "And that he and he alone of army personnel would either know of their whereabouts or have any control over them. Did he tell you that and make that clear?"
Hefferon: "Yes, this is true."
McKenna: "Am I correct that this is a state of affairs that you did not report to either the Minister for Defence, the Chief-of-Staff or your intended successor, Colonel Delaney?"
Mr Justice Henchy: "Colonel, you are not obliged to answer anything that would involve you in any criminal proceedings."

Having been told that he could claim privilege, Colonel Hefferon asked for the question to be repeated. Mr McKenna having done so, Colonel Hefferon replied that he had reported on the control of the arms neither to the Chief-of-Staff nor to Colonel Delaney, but that he had reported it to the Minister for Defence.

McKenna: "I put it to you that you have never told it to Mr Gibbons in any form good, bad or indifferent, that they would be stored in a non-military establishment?"
Hefferon: "I well remember telling it to him, but I do not want to elaborate on the nature of the place."
McKenna: "When do you say you told Mr Gibbons?"
Hefferon: "Some time before I retired."
McKenna: "Can you be more precise than that?"
Hefferon: "I remember quite clearly telling it to the Minister for Defence."

The court then adjourned until eleven o'clock the following morning, when Colonel Hefferon stated that he clearly remembered giving the Minister this specific information because of the circumstances and particularly because, when told where the arms were to be stored, the Minister quoted a well-known line of poetry. When Mr McKenna asked for the quotation, Mr Justice Henchy intervened to ask if the witness thought the line would disclose information that should not be revealed. Colonel Hefferon thought so.

Asked by Mr McKenna to recount his conversation with Mr Gibbons, Colonel Hefferon said:

"He asked me where were the arms to be stored when they came in on the *City of Dublin.* I told him the location and he smiled and quoted the line of poetry."

Rumour had it that it was the first two lines of "In a Monastery Garden".

McKenna: "I want to put it to you that your recollection of this is entirely wrong?"
Hefferon: "No, my recollection is very clear."
McKenna: "Did you speak to him in such specific terms that there could be no misunderstanding in the Minister's mind as to what would happen to the arms?"
Hefferon: "I did."

It was a vital piece of evidence, because it showed that Mr Gibbons was briefed to the extent that he was told where the arms were to be stored when they entered the country. At one of our meetings I had also informed Mr Gibbons of the location, but for an independent witness, to tell the court that the Minister, because of his knowledge, would have effective control over the arms, was much more significant. Unless both Colonel Hefferon and myself were fully convinced that the Minister had given his unequivocal authorisation to the arms importation, why should we give him this vital piece of information?

Colonel Hefferon told Mr McKenna that Colonel Delaney, while acting as his understudy, questioned my status in Intelligence, but that while he had no clear recollection of telling Colonel Delaney that I was a good officer with good contacts in the North, that is what he would have said about me. Colonel Hefferon also said that he had told Mr Gibbons of my report on the Bailieboro meeting.

McKenna: "Did that report arise as a result of any discussion with you of a complaint he, Mr Gibbons, had about Captain Kelly?"
Hefferon: "Yes, from the Department of Justice, from Mr Berry specifically."
McKenna: "Did you tell Mr Gibbons, in relation to the associations and

contacts he had with the North, that he, Captain Kelly, was keeping these with your approval and authority?"
Hefferon: "Yes."
McKenna: "I suggest that was all you told Mr Gibbons about the meeting of the Defence Committees, that he need not worry about Captain Kelly or anyone else, that Captain Kelly was merely carrying out orders?"
Hefferon: "No."
McKenna: "Did it go much beyond that?"
Hefferon: "It did, because the Taoiseach had asked..."

The judge intervened here and said that Colonel Hefferon should not give hearsay evidence, so Colonel Hefferon was not allowed to tell the court that not only was Mr Gibbons aware of the Bailieboro meeting, but so also were the Taoiseach and Mr Berry, and presumably Mr Berry's informant or informants.

On the question of my regimental duty in April, Mr McKenna put it to Colonel Hefferon that Mr Gibbons never said that he would intervene directly to have me released from regimental duties. Very firmly, Colonel Hefferon replied:

"He did."

McKenna: "In the course of all your association with Captain Kelly, in particular with reference to Northern matters, did Captain Kelly ever report to you or tell you of anything that you did not accept as true?"
Hefferon: "I do not have any recollection of such a thing happening."
McKenna: "Did you accept all the information furnished by him as accurate?"
Hefferon: "I did."
McKenna: "Did that form the basis of the view you had of the whole situation?"
Hefferon: "No. I was getting intelligence from many sources. He was only one of them. He was working with the Defence Committees, but I was getting intelligence and information from many sources."

This concluded Colonel Hefferon's evidence and as he left the witness-box, there was applause from the public gallery. As one of the accused I could not very well join in the applause, but I shared the feeling of the gallery.

CHAPTER 19

It was now the turn of the defence. A direction to acquit Albert Luykx was refused; no evidence was called on his behalf.

The next witness, John Kelly, elected to make an unsworn statement. Stocky and determined, he removed the chair from the witness-box and stood, shoulders back, in the "at ease" position. Looking straight at the jury, he began to speak:

"It has been my decision that I should make an unsworn statement and I came to that decision for these reasons: were I to be subjected to a cross-examination, I would have to, in my answers, expose people who reside north of the Border and I would, in effect, be a felon-setter. And it has been my experience in the three weeks that I have been present in this court..."

Judge: "You can only give your experience in this present hearing."
Kelly: "It has been my experience over the past three weeks that sufficient felon-setting has been engaged in in the course of these proceedings. And my priorities are, my Lord, that the safety of those people who have reposed their trust in me takes precedence over the requirements of my own defence. Those again are my reasons for electing to give an unsworn statement. In making this decision, my Lord, I should like to begin at the beginning. When I say that, I mean back to my family background and my education and..."
Judge: "I think, Mr Kelly, we are concerned only with the compass of the charge."
Sorahan: "My Lord, I have for seventeen years been defending criminals in criminal cases, and many innocent people in criminal cases, and on many occasions unsworn statements have been made. I have never known a person making an unsworn statement to be stopped unless he was saying something absolutely outrageous, and something to have absolutely no bearing on the defence."

As the Judge hesitated in a silent court, Ernest Wood cut in:

"I only intervene, My Lord, because this is not a matter which concerns Mr Luykx, but something which is a fundamental right in law to be preserved, and that is that the Trial Judge should not inhibit a prisoner making a speech in the dock as long as it does not amount to contempt of court..."

The silence was palpable as Mr Wood, squaring his robust frame, took a deep breath:

John Kelly

"If the law were not otherwise, one memorable speech would never have been made."

There was a burst of applause from the public gallery. This reference was to Robert Emmet, "the Darling of Ireland," who, in 1803, had gone to his death on the scaffold outside the church in Thomas Street, across the river from the court, because he had defied the British invader. There were people in Ireland still who could quote his Speech from the Dock word for word.

Judge: "This is not a Speech from the Dock. Mr Kelly, proceed now. As far as is convenient, keep within the compass of the trial. I leave it to your own discretion."

Calmly, John Kelly continued from where he had been cut off, describing his Belfast origins, his republican background, his involvement in the 1956 IRA campaign in the North, and the prison sentence it earned him.

"I was released in 1963. On my release, I endeavoured to re-establish myself again in the life of the community and, given my circumstances or the circumstances of all Republicans in the Six Counties, this was not an easy matter. However, we did eventually establish ourselves... I was working at a very good occupation. I had a very good salary and one could say I was a happily married man. But then we came to the events of August 1969 and I am sure I do not need to recall to the court what happened in the middle and latter part of August in Derry and in Belfast, but had there not been an August in Belfast of that particular nature and those events not occurred in Belfast in August, I should not be standing here today. So, I think they are of some consequence.

It began in Derry, as most people know, on August 12. On August 13, trouble and riots..."

Judge: "I think, as you have said, we are all familiar."
Kelly: "I would just like, if I may, very briefly to summarise and refresh, if you like, by a summary of those events.
Sorahan: "Surely, my Lord, that is a very reasonable request put in a very courteous tone by my client."

Apparently unperturbed, John Kelly continued his narrative:

"They spread to Coalisland on August 13, to Strabane, Newry, Lurgan, Enniskillen, Dungannon and Wednesday night saw their beginning in Belfast.

It seemed to us at this time that the Unionist Government had decided that the people of the Falls Road and Ardoyne areas of Belfast had to be taught a lesson and that the Croppies had to be brought to their knees and lie down, by tradition, to the so-called forces of law and order.

The RUC and B Specials, supported by an armed mob, were let loose against those areas. They sprayed our streets with bullets and poured heavy machine-gun fire into blocks of flats and, meanwhile, the loyalist mob came surging through the streets and several hundred homes went up in flames. In a period of some forty-eight hours, nine people were dead, including a nine-year-old boy, a fifteen-year-old boy and a thirty-one-year-old man, John Gallagher, who died when a volley of shots was fired into a crowd of Civil Rights demonstrators by a squad of B Specials. 'And one thing is definite,' said the coroner at the inquest, 'the firing which killed John Gallagher was not lawful firing.'

It was in this period that an organisation which has been mentioned very freely in this court, the Citizens' Defence Committees, were formed. And I think it is only fair to those people, since they have been mentioned here so frequently, sometimes dubiously, sometimes to create, I felt, a suspicion about their integrity or their character or their motives.

The Citizens' Defence Committees, for example, contained people of all shades of opinion, of all shades of minority opinion, within the Six Counties. They contained people like myself, who were Republicans, but they also contained people of no particular political point of view.

They were people who were drawn together because of the circumstances, because of the situation in which we found ourselves; who were drawn together to organise the defence of the minority areas in what we felt then was a Doomsday situation. They provided first-aid posts; they engaged in fire fighting, prevention of looting, and liaison with the British army. But their primary function was to organise the defence of the minority community. They were concerned with obtaining arms, they were concerned with vigilante duties; they were concerned with the manning of the barricades and the enforcing of discipline. They were, in effect, the administration of a very large part of Derry's Bogside and of a very large part of Belfast, and I cannot stress that too much since there are many people in the Six Counties still active in these organisations, people who, as I said, are of some substance and standing in the community, people with varying shades of political opinion.

I think it very sad that an Irish court should expose those people to political harassment and, indeed, to possible loss of their lives. I might say here that during those difficult days, the local Citizens' Defence Committees worked day and night to defuse the situation and this is the place to recall that during that long winter and spring and early summer of this year, the CDC, the Citizens' Defence Committees, laboured unceasingly, to co-ordinate the operations of the local vigilantes, who enjoyed such an enviable record in averting major conflict.

And I would not like to think, gentlemen, that this court would try to impute to the Citizens' Defence Committees, a word which first became known from the mouths of the Stormont Government, that this court should impute to them the tag, 'subversive', or that they would be smeared in an Irish court with this tag. It would be more than injustice, it would be a travesty of truth and something that could only be engaged in for political expediency. But I might recall that this was the situation in Belfast on the 14, 15 and 16 August and thereafter, and Dr Hillery, the Minister for External Affairs, had gone to the United Nations and asserted there that the breakdown of law and order in Northern Ireland and the plight of the minority community was due to the partition of Ireland, brought about by an Act of the British Parliament, in which not a single Irish vote had been cast, and I quote what he said next: 'The claim of Ireland, the claim of the Irish nation to control the totality of Ireland has been asserted over the centuries by successive generations of Irishmen and women and it is one which no spokesman for the Irish nation could ever renounce'.

"And Taoiseach Lynch, in what has become known as his '*We Will Not Stand Idly By*' speech, said ..."

Judge: "I am afraid, Mr Kelly, we cannot have extracts from speeches. You are entitled to say anything you wish to say to the jury which bears on your own defence, within reason."
Kelly: "My Lord, this would bear on my own attitude. This is part of the reason why I stand in this court today; these are the reasons why I stand here."
Wood: "Let me remind your Lordship, the prisoner is not giving evidence."
Judge: "It is not normal for people making statements, sworn or unsworn, to quote from political speeches."
Kelly: "Specifically, this was the situation in Belfast and what I am coming to is that it was in exactly this situation and in these circumstances that I first met Captain Kelly."
Judge: "If you would kindly pass on to that."
Kelly: "Well, I reluctantly pass on, my Lord, because I think what Taoiseach Lynch said is very, very significant as far as I am concerned, but I will pass on reluctantly."
Judge: "Please do."

"It was in this situation," John Kelly continued, "in these circumstances, and against this background of speeches by people, political figures of authority, in this part of Ireland, speeches which had led the six-county minority to believe sincerely that a new era was dawning in Irish political life.

And so it was in these circumstances, in the latter end of August, that I first met Captain Kelly. At a time when I was charged with the duty of organising Citizens' Defence Committees in Belfast and throughout the six-county area that I met Captain Kelly at his request. I met him in the home of a prominent figure in the Six Counties. Captain Kelly told me that he was an Irish army officer attached to the Intelligence Section and that his function was to find out from those who were engaged in Defence Committee activities the number of men who would be available to bear arms in a given situation and the number of arms, weapons, guns that we had in our possession.

We had a long discussion, and when I say we had a long discussion I don't mean that Captain Kelly and I had a long discussion. I mean the people who were there and, again, these were people not necessarily of a particular point of view. We had a long discussion and we adjourned to meet him the following day.

We met the following day and continued our discussion, negotiations, call it what you will, and we ended on the understanding that there had begun a liaison between the Irish Government and the Defence Committees in the Six Counties.

We kept up our contacts, our meetings, over a period of time in the Six Counties and then in mid-October, Captain Kelly informed us that any future meetings would have to take place south of the border. In other words, Captain Kelly was no longer operating in the Six Counties.

Running parallel at this stage, running parallel to our meetings with Captain Kelly, there were various delegations which came south to meet Government Ministers, sometimes at Captain Kelly's request, sometimes at the request of the Government Ministers and, again, I should like to point out in relation to these delegations that these were people from the Six Counties area, a collection of people of varying shades of minority political opinion and not made up of any particular section of the minority community.

I myself accompanied the delegation which met the Taoiseach and Mr Blaney, delegations which met Dr Hillery and Mr Haughey, delegations which met Mr Gibbons and Mr Lenihan, and if I could say at this stage in relation to one of the people who stands accused with me today, namely Mr Haughey, that I met Mr Haughey once in October, mid-October. I met him as part of a delegation. I met him again in February of 1970, and I never met Mr Haughey again until I met him in the dock at the Bridewell.

And if I could come back to the reason for these delegations. It has been said in this court on one occasion that they were courtesy calls, that they were just people that one particular Minister felt he had to entertain. I want to be very emphatic here, that we were coming from all parts of the Six Counties not to indulge in tea parties, not to be entertained, but to elicit in so far as we could what was the opinion of this Government in relation to the Six Counties.

We did not ask for blankets or feeding bottles. We asked for guns and no one from Taoiseach Lynch down refused that request or told us that this was contrary to Government policy and, if I might labour a little on the meeting that has been the subject of so much discussion in this court, that is the one with Mr Gibbons, the one I was present at on March 3 in the Parliamentary dining-room; there were other people present at this meeting.

It was not a meeting for entertainment, or for somebody to play host. It was a serious discussion on matters considered to be of vital importance in the Six Counties and the necessity for arms being provided against any breakdown in the society there.

I find it hard to understand that whereas Mr Gibbons remembers that I sat at the end of the table where I did sit, he could have mistaken me for Captain Kelly, because when that discussion ended, Mr Gibbons called me and another member of the delegation aside and he told me in very express terms that he wanted me to keep in touch with him and to keep him abreast of the situation.

These were only, if you like, parts of the background to my involvement and as I say the involvement and what I felt was the purpose of my involvement. That was to obtain arms and if I might attempt to bear this out in some way by referring to some of the evidence that has been given here. I would ask you to recall that when we went to the docks on the March 25 to await the arrival of The City of Dublin, I went in the company of Captain Kelly. We there met Mr O'Riordan, who was the Customs Surveyor for that particular stretch of dock, and having met Mr O'Riordan and having eventually told him that whereas he thought we were expecting mild steel plates, we were in fact expecting a consignment of arms and ammunition. This was the position then, that Mr O'Riordan, who was a Surveyor, the Customs Surveyor for that area, knew at some time that day that we were expecting a consignment of arms and ammunition.

He confirmed, as he told the court, from his own higher authority, that it was in order to let this through and I returned to Mr O'Riordan some four or five days later and asked him if the arms had arrived yet.

I would ask the court to consider whether, if I felt there was anything illegal about what I was doing, I would return to an official, a customs official, a ranking customs official, and ask him had the guns come in yet.

I would refer to the evidence of Mr Desmond and Mr Ryan, Mr Desmond, a Customs Surveyor at Dublin airport, and Mr Ryan, Cargo Superintendent of Aer Lingus. There was no attempt on my part to conceal from Mr Desmond or Mr Ryan the purpose of my visit. I say no attempt to conceal beyond that which is limited by the bounds of discretion and, in fact, you will recall that both Mr Desmond and Mr Ryan confirmed in court that they had checked back and that this was official and you will recall that my only concern was that the British authorities should not know about this consignment. I did not tell them that they should not tell the Garda Síochána or the Irish Army. No, my only concern was that the British authorities should not know and I ask you to judge whether or not in these circumstances I was attempting to conceal from any authority here the nature of what we were expecting. I think it is, as far as I am concerned, only right that I should point out that throughout the period from August of last year until the first time that I was arrested in Dublin, everything that happened within that time leaves me in no doubt whatsoever but that what was being done was being done with the full knowledge and consent not only of Mr Gibbons, but of the Government as a whole. And it is my conviction, whether I be right or whether I be wrong, I am only speaking from knowledge that I have, it is my conviction that what Mr McKenna said at the beginning, that this trial is an exercise in democracy or a case of the people of Ireland versus the accused, and many things have been done in the name of the people of Ireland, it is my conviction that I stand here and those who stand with me, that we are here as a matter of political expediency, and not from any desire that the course of justice be impartially administered.

My Lord, I find it a very sad occasion indeed, that these institutions for which so much was sacrificed, which had been gained by such nobility, should be abused in this manner. There is no victory for anyone in these proceedings, my Lord. There is only an echo of sadness from the graves of the dead generations. I thank you, gentlemen, I thank you my Lord."

John Kelly's speech, delivered without reference to a note, held the court enthralled. There was an awed silence as he finished, and then, as he left the witness-box, he was greeted by a loud and prolonged burst of applause. It might not have been a speech from the dock, as the judge was quick to point out, but it was noted that at least one member of the jury involuntarily applauded.

The judge announced a break after John Kelly's spell-binding speech. In the emotional atmosphere gripping the crowded lobby, many believed that the defence should rest its case then. I half hoped this would happen because I was to be the next witness.

CHAPTER 20

In the lobby of the court, friends gripped my hand and rushed away to gain admittance to the courtroom. The break was over and Peter Sutherland, my junior counsel, whispered:

"Don't worry, Jim. When you're batting from the truth, you can't go wrong." The judge entered and I was called to the stand. I took the oath and turned to face a courtroom packed to the rafters. The waves of suppressed excitement subsided and the smiling faces of the front row in the gallery signalled encouragement. Perhaps I should not have been, but I was confident as I acknowledged the grins of my two young daughters. My senior counsel, James D'Arcy, with his glasses and grey hair, was a familiar friendly figure, crouched over his book-strewn bench.

During his cross-examination Mr McKenna asked me:

"Did you hear Colonel Hefferon say that it was mid-January before you indicated to him for the first time that you were going to give assistance to the Northern Defence Committees by way of helping them in the purchase of arms?"

Kelly: "Yes."
McKenna: "Was that accurate?"
Kelly: "It was, I think."

I went on to say that there was no question of my giving active assistance until January. As an Intelligence Officer, I explained, one came across many things, knew of many things but one did not take action on them straight away; one waited to see what developed. In January people came to me and asked for assistance.

McKenna: "You made it perfectly clear to Colonel Hefferon at your first meeting in January, when this matter was raised, that you intended to bring guns into the South of Ireland at the request, or at the instance, of your Northern contacts?"
Kelly: "It was rather vague at this stage. I had been requested to assist and I had explained to my Northern contacts that they would have to operate in conjunction with the Government here and what I said to these people was that these guns would be brought in, if brought in at all, under the control of the Department of Defence and that they would be distributed at the discretion of the authorities here, on foot of which I advised some

of my Northern contacts that they should come down and see the Government about it."
McKenna: "Was Colonel Hefferon wrong when he said in his evidence that it would be necessary for you to leave the army if you intended to pursue this matter but, if not, he did not see any necessity for you to leave?"
Kelly: "You are putting the wrong emphasis on this thing and the emphasis is very important here. The context of my leaving the army or otherwise was that I was under no obligation to carry on with my work, if it involved my leaving the army. Colonel Hefferon was not putting me on a spot where I would have to leave the army."
McKenna: "Did Colonel Hefferon tell you that?"
Kelly: "I don't believe he told me that in so many words. I am trying to explain my feelings on the thing. I had been approached by citizens of Northern Ireland to assist them in bringing in arms. I went and reported this to my superior officer and we had quite a long discussion about it, going into the pros and cons of what it could involve. I consider what Colonel Hefferon came up with was very reasonable. If it became public knowledge, the secrecy of the thing would be undermined and furthermore, he said that I would not have the necessary freedom of action. In that context he said I would have to resign, but, however, he would refer it to the Minister of Defence. In the meantime, he told me to make out the forms."
McKenna: "Undoubtedly, the question of your resignation was discussed at this first meeting in January, when you indicated to Colonel Hefferon that you had been asked to assist in a practical way?"
Kelly: "That is correct."
McKenna: "Whether you agreed or disagreed with what Colonel Hefferon said to you, did you give in your resignation that day ?"
Kelly: "I cannot say."
McKenna: "You know very well ?"
Kelly: "I do not."
McKenna: "Did you come back a few days later and discuss this matter with him again ?"
Kelly: "I was not particularly worried about the thing because I knew it had been brought to the notice of the Minister for Defence and I was quite satisfied to sit back and await his decision."

Later Mr McKenna asked:

"Did you discuss with Mr Blaney the question of your resignation or transfer to another Government service because of the fact that you were about to carry out this important mission ?"

Kelly: " I discussed it with Mr Blaney at some stage, but I cannot say that I discussed it between the first and second meeting with Colonel Hefferon as you are trying to pin me down."
McKenna: "Have you any recollection of going to Mr Blaney and discussing your retirement because you were about to embark on a top secret Government mission?"
Kelly: "I have no precise recollection of going to Mr Blaney at that particular time, but I knew that at one stage Mr Blaney said that he did not see any necessity for my leaving the army."
McKenna: "When did he say that to you?"
Kelly: "That was his general attitude in the early months of the year... This whole thing of being transferred from one Government department to another did not cause me any great worry, and in fact I met people and discussed with them and I am not sure what was said or what was not said. As a matter of fact, when the Minister for Defence said there was no necessity to retire from the army, I was quite happy and forgot all about it."

As I suggested to the court, the question of my retirement, transfer, resignation or secondment had assumed an importance out of all proportion to its relevance. It only did so because it was the peg on which Mr Gibbons hung his "change of allegiance" allegation. Initially, Colonel Hefferon had suggested in good faith that if I were in some undemanding job in another branch of the Government service, it would facilitate my proposed work by giving me more freedom of movement, and if I were exposed, it would be less likely to cause embarrassment to the Government and, incidently, to Army Intelligence, which continued to have official contacts with British security elements in 1969/1970.

It is now no secret, having been exposed by a British release of State Papers at the end of 1998, that Britain and Ireland have had a unique Intelligence relationship on matters of mutual concern internationally since early in World War 2, which Military Intelligence was charged with putting into effect on the Irish side. To my knowledge, meetings between the two sides continued until I retired from the Army on May 1, 1970.

The Hefferon Papers in Military Archives document several such meetings between Colonel Hefferon and British Intelligence during 1969/1970. These documents have been given a top security rating under the Official Secrets Act and are not available for publication.

The co-operation came about as part of what could be described as a dual mandate given to the Director of Intelligence by the Government on Intelligence matters. As a result, Colonel Hefferon found himself with the

DON AIRE COSANTA,
(The Minister for Defence)
A DHUINE UASAIL,
(Sir)

De bhun ailt 47 (6) den Acht Cosanta, 1954, agus míre 19 de na
(Pursuant to section 47 (6) of the Defence Act, 1954, and paragraph 19 of

Rialacháin Fórsaí Cosanta A.15, is mian liom dul ar scor as na Buan-Oglaigh agus
Defence Force Regulations A.15, I desire to retire from the Permanent Defence Force and

iarraim ort leis seo a cheadú dhom sin do dhéanamh.
I herewith apply for your consent to my so doing.)

Is mise, le mór-urraim,
(I have the honour to be, Sir)

Do Sheirbhíseach Umhal,
(Your Obedient Servant)

S Ó Ceallaigh Capt
(0.7483)

Finné..........
(Witness)

Céim nó cáilíocht an Fhinné..........
(Rank or qualification of Witness)

Dáta 29. 1. 70
(Date)

A.F. 608.

Unwitnessed, conditional and ineffective retirement application of January 1970.

responsibility of dealing with Britain on Intelligence matters in the context of the Cold War on an international level, while, on the home front in 1969/1970, he was called upon to undertake the Intelligence aspect of preparing for a possible invasion of Northern Ireland, reporting directly to the Government through the Minister for Defence in both cases.

It is evident that the two missions were far from compatible, while it is equally evident that any Director of Intelligence charged with putting both into effect was forced to tread a very thin discretionary line between the national interest and his international responsibilities. In the circumstances, it is easy to appreciate why Colonel Hefferon might feel that it would be better if the national mission was not under, or not seen to be under, his direct control.

As a longtime Intelligence Officer with top security clearance, I was fully alive to the Colonel's dilemma and understood why he sought to compartmentalise my work outside his sphere, if possibly only technically, by having me transferred to another Government job. Nevertheless, I was somewhat upset about such an approach and expressed my reservations in a fairly trenchant manner, stating that I did not want to be involved in a James Bond type of operation, with "some po-faced character like Bond's boss denying responsibility for my actions." I insisted that, in the last analysis, the Government would have to accept full responsibility for the operation. Again adverting to the Bond analogy, I said I did not want to be the victim of any "deniability rubbish", and that I wanted that conveyed to the Minister.

On that basis, I submitted my conditional application for retirement. It was rejected out of hand by the Minister on the grounds that I was engaged on vital national work, which he was more than willing to stand over. He dismissed the co-operation with Britain as of little significance. I was relieved when I was informed that I had not to go through the charade of retirement and I got the distinct impression that Colonel Hefferon was equally relieved. At that stage, January 1970, the arms operation was at the crucial point of no return, where it was either full steam ahead or abort it. The Minister made it crystal clear that it was *full steam ahead.*

In April, over two months later, when Colonel Delaney took over as Director, he, as already mentioned, suggested that I might compromise him with the British, Mr Gibbon's rejoinder was curt and to the point: "Who does he think he's working for?"

It was still *full steam ahead*.

Mr McKenna went on to enquire how the arms importation was financed.

McKenna: "Will you tell me where did the money come from for the purchase of these guns and ammunition?"
Kelly: "Well, if you want to go into that, you had better go up to Northern Ireland and ask people up there. I am not going to divulge their names."
McKenna: "Do you know where the money came from for the purchase of these guns?"
Kelly: "I do."
McKenna: "You told Colonel Hefferon?"
Kelly: "I did."
McKenna: "Was he correct when he said that money came from the Northern Defence Committees?"
Kelly: "He was correct."
McKenna: "Directly from the Northern Defence Committees?"
Kelly: "The account was controlled by the Northern Defence Committees, under the control of people who live in the Six Counties and I am going no further with it. I don't think I should."

McKenna persisted, however, while the gallery tut-tutted, until finally after one burst of applause the judge warned that if there were any further interruptions and the Gardaí could not identify the interrupters, he would order the gallery to be cleared. This stern warning had its effect and the gallery held its emotions in check from then until the end of the trial.

McKenna: "How much did this cargo of arms and ammunition cost?"
Kelly: "Have I to answer that question?"
McKenna: "Yes."
Kelly: "I cannot give you an exact figure, but I can give you an estimate. It was over twenty thousand pounds, between twenty and thirty thousand."

Monies were in one main account and two subsidiary accounts, and I agreed with Mr McKenna that I knew that three thousand pounds had been drawn out of those funds before Christmas. I also agreed that I knew that the Northern Defence Committees and others were anxious to purchase arms and that I believed that the three thousand pounds were used as a down payment on a possible purchase of arms.

Kelly: "But I would point out to you, Mr McKenna, that as late as February 1970 I did not even know if there were any arms in existence, as a result of my visit to the continent then."
McKenna: "Did you on the 14th February tell Mr Haughey that it was intended to bring in guns to the country at the insistence of his Northern contacts?"
Kelly: "I told him what I knew at that stage... I told him the essentials. I was satisfied that he knew what I was talking about."

Mr McKenna went into some detail about the March 3 meeting between Mr Gibbons and the Northern delegation.

McKenna: "Did they make it clear whether they wanted guns there and then, or to be made available to them as soon as possible, or whether what they really wanted was a guarantee that the Irish Government would do what it could to protect them if the situation ever got completely out of hand again?"
Kelly: "They wanted a guarantee that the Irish Government would do what it could to protect them if the situation ever got out of hand again... it was put very forcibly by one of the representatives, from a rather exposed area in Northern Ireland, that if a pogrom started again, there would be no point in having guns not readily available and that arrangements should be made to have these guns readily available for distribution to these people in the event of such a pogrom arising.

This was put quite clearly to Mr Gibbons and Mr Gibbons accepted it and, as I explained to you earlier, he went to the extent of explaining how he had made arrangements to retain what one might call obsolete weapons, but still very effective weapons, under his control for this very purpose."

The Irish Army put a considerable amount of weaponry and ammunition up for sale at Christmas 1969 but Mr Gibbons blocked the sale and it was this equipment to which the *surplus arms* portion of the Directive of February 6 referred. These arms were still traceable, however, and one idea Mr Gibbons had to overcome this was the formation of a fictitious company which would purchase the arms and hold them against contingencies in Northern Ireland. In this way, the arms could not be traced back to the Irish Government. I learned later that he put this suggestion to one of the people at the March 3 meeting. This did not surprise me in the least, because he put exactly the same proposal to me at one stage.

McKenna: "Does it come to this, Captain Kelly, that whatever sympathies Mr Gibbons may have expressed for them, he made it completely clear to the delegation that there was no question of giving them guns, either then or in the immediate future, and that the only circumstances in which they would be given guns was in a Doomsday situation and after a Government decision?"

Kelly: "I never remember Mr Gibbons using the term "Doomsday" until I heard it here in the court and I don't believe he used it on that night, and certainly this question of Government decision was always there. It was there in my mind, it was there in the minds of the delegation. This is why the meeting, why the group was down there, but Mr Gibbons on his part made it clear to the delegation he was going to give them the support they sought, and, actually, the delegation was highly delighted, when Mr Gibbons left, at the reception they had received and that their requests had been so well entertained. Furthermore, I would point out to you what was pointed out in the court here yesterday, that one member of the delegation said to Mr Gibbons, 'I hope your words are not all empty promises, like promises that have been made in the past and that what you have said here tonight will be put into effect,' and he was talking about guns at this stage. There was no question or doubt about it, and Mr Gibbons, apparently insulted – he had his coat on him at this stage ready to go home – came back to the table and got very serious and said words to the effect, 'I am not that type of man, what I say I mean,' and this was in connection with the giving of guns to this delegation from Northern Ireland."

Mr McKenna went on to discuss my meeting with Mr Gibbons on the following day, March 4, when Mr Gibbons was fully briefed on happenings to date and when, as I had told Mr D'Arcy in direct evidence, I had apologised on behalf of the man who had questioned Mr Gibbons' integrity on the previous night. Queried on the originator of the plan to import the arms, I explained that it was Mr Gibbons, because he, as the competent authority, was aware of the plan from its birth in January and had given his approval to it.

Mr McKenna seemed to find it difficult to understand why I had used the name Weluks Ltd as the consignee for the projected shipment of arms on March 25 without informing Mr Luykx, one of the principals of the firm, in advance. The fact was that Albert Luykx was on holiday on the Continent for most of March.

I told Mr McKenna about my trip to the Continent on March 10, when arrangements were made for shipment on March 25, and how when the goods did not arrive on that occasion, I went again to the Continent on April 1, this time accompanied by Albert Luykx as interpreter. In reply to Mr McKenna, I said that I got a phone call from my wife on April 2 telling me to come home.

McKenna: "And your wife told you that it concerned the possible distribution of arms?"

Kelly: "She conveyed to me not in so many words and she explained how she knew, because the Northern people had come down on that date and had made an attempt to contact me and it was they who told her."

McKenna: "You said yesterday that your wife knew what it was all about?"

Kelly: "She did. Those words did not cause me one iota of concern and I said that with due deliberation yesterday. I knew at that stage, exactly, the complete background and I even discussed the matter with my wife when I came back from the Continent."

McKenna: "Did you ascertain before you came back that the arms were, so to speak, ripe for shipment?"

Kelly: "Perhaps in the interest of truth I should carry on to explain a second phone call I had on that night related to the first call of which you speak…

When I was speaking to my wife, I asked was she certain that I should go home and she said Colonel Hefferon had given this specific order. I said that I should check it out and Mr Gibbons' name was mentioned and my wife said to me that as far as she knew he was not around, but she knew Mr Blaney was available and I could ring him. I rang him and it evolved when I did that the heat had gone out of the situation. I asked him then was it necessary that I should rush home as ordered by Colonel Hefferon and he said he did not think so and that it would not be likely to he necessary to distribute these arms at that stage. I suggested that perhaps I should stay on and finish the work I was at."

McKenna: "You accepted the advice of Mr Blaney, the advice of a Minister who had no control over you as countermanding a direct order from your superior officer?"
Kelly: "I told him to try to contact my superior officer and put him in the picture as to why I was not returning immediately and as far as I know, my superior officer was so informed the next morning."

I reiterated to Mr McKenna that I knew why I had been ordered home and when I found out two hours later that the situation had changed, my return was no longer urgent. I felt it was more sensible, therefore, to continue with my job. Asked by Mr McKenna if I had kept Mr Blaney as fully informed of my reason for being on the Continent as I did my own Minister, I replied:

"I kept my Minister informed to any extent my Minister required and I was always available when my Minister sought me. On any occasion when I sought the Minister, he had no hesitation in seeing me. He was fully informed."

McKenna: "And was enthusiastic, indeed?"
Kelly: "I told you so before."
McKenna: "You kept him advised, step-by-step, of the progress of the plan and he was encouraging you to bring it to a successful conclusion as soon as possible?"
Kelly: "The Minister was briefed by me on this plan whenever it was necessary, whenever the Minister required. I told him in my conversations with him about what I knew and what I was doing. At any stage on which he asked me questions, I answered the questions and made every effort to explain to him fully."
McKenna: "You told him fully what you were doing?"
Kelly: "Of course I told him what I was doing and Colonel Hefferon told him what I was doing."
McKenna: "Not only did Mr Gibbons know what you were doing, but he approved of it and was enthusiastic about it and authorised your doing it?"
Kelly: "Whatever about the use of words, as far as I am concerned, I

briefed and fully informed the Minister. The Minister knew and fully approved."
McKenna: "And authorised you in your course of action?"
Kelly: "Of course."
McKenna: "To such an extent that you felt justified this morning in naming him as the originator and instigator of this plan?"
Kelly: "We went through all this this morning already. I explained to you in detail how it was brought to the Minister's notice in January and February as a proposal. The Minister fully accepted this and as he was the duly authorised person, I would say that he was the originator."
McKenna: "In so far as you were concerned, being an officer in Military Intelligence, he was the man in control of the plan which you and others were operating."
Kelly: "Of course. The man was the Minister for Defence. I was a serving officer and a serving army officer is under the control of the Minister for Defence."
McKenna: "You were under his control in the execution of this plan?"
Kelly: "Yes, because I kept him fully informed."

At this stage, it seemed that Mr McKenna, having lost some of his initial fire, had accepted that the attempted importation was in fact authorised. He was still an efficient prosecutor, but his case was collapsing before his eyes.

McKenna: "The abandonment of the plan to bring them in by sea and the change to bringing them in by air was a direct action on your own initiative because the circumstances had changed?"
Kelly: "I had found out the situation back in Dublin and I used my own discretion."
McKenna: "This was a change brought about on your own initiative?"
Kelly: "On my own initiative, but not out of the blue."
McKenna: "When you came back, did you report to Colonel Hefferon at any stage that you had changed your plan and that they were to be brought in by air?"
Kelly: "I did."
McKenna: "On a top-secret Government mission involving expenditure of thirty thousand pounds, did you not regard it as an important change of plan that they should come in by air rather than by sea?"
Kelly: "It was important that the arms should come in faster."

Mr McKenna, referring to a meeting I had with Mr Gibbons after my return, asked if I had told Mr Gibbons of the change of plan from ship to plane. I replied that I had no specific recollection but that I would have been very surprised if I had not done so. In effect, I said, I would go as far as to say that I had.

McKenna: "You are positive now that you did tell him?"

Kelly: "I am not being positive about it to the extent that I have a clear recollection of telling Mr Gibbons, 'this is coming in by plane', but I, in my reports, would not miss this out. I would certainly tell him."

At the meeting upon my return from the Continent, I had discussed with Mr Gibbons the renewed urgency of getting in untraceable arms, as emphasised by the unavoidable sending of traceable arms to Dundalk on April 2 for possible distribution in Northern Ireland. In this context, it is certain that the new plan to move the arms in by air was discussed. At that meeting also we discussed the possible involvement of the Defence Forces proper, if the situation in the North should deteriorate. In fact, the method of moving the arms was only incidental to our conversation; we both accepted that they should be brought in as soon as possible.

I described to Mr McKenna my final visit to the Continent in mid-April and told him that when I telephoned Mr Haughey's office from Vienna, Mr Fagan, a principal officer in the Department of Finance, instructed me to cancel the operation.

McKenna: "Will you tell me why you selected Mr Haughey to ask for instructions rather than the man who, in your evidence, was in control of the plan, Mr Gibbons?"

Kelly: "As far as I was concerned this was a Government plan and I had no reason to think otherwise, and as far as I was concerned any member of the Cabinet would give the instructions and Mr Fagan, as far as I was concerned, could, if he thought necessary, ring Mr Gibbons."

As regards the April 23 meeting in Blaney's office, I told Mr McKenna that after the "brazen bastard" incident, "it dawned on me that Mr Gibbons was playing some game".

McKenna: "And not Mr Blaney?"

Kelly: "No."

McKenna: "And not Mr Haughey?"

Kelly: "No. As far as I was concerned it was a completely legal movement of arms approved by the Minister for Defence and this was the first indication I got that the Minister was playing a game of his own."

McKenna: "At this meeting you were not a junior officer trying to make a case to your superiors; you were there as an equal?"

Kelly: "I was there as a person who was very much involved in carrying out this top secret operation. In these circumstances, I was there as an equal."
McKenna: "Were you surprised that what you had taken as a lawful army duty for three months was now suspect and a matter for enquiry by the Special Branch?"
Kelly: "I was surprised and wondered about it, the same as the others wondered, as to what was taking place. They were surprised at it too, as to what was taking place, as to who was misinformed or otherwise. What affected me most was Mr Gibbons taking this other attitude. The attitude of Mr Gibbons sank home and I kept it to myself."
McKenna: "Did you express your surprise at the meeting?"
Kelly: "I have very little recollection of the meeting, except what affected me personally and what annoyed me at that time very much was the attitude of Mr Gibbons, which was one of, as far as I was concerned, changing over from a man who had been responsible for an importation of arms now more or less suggesting that he had no responsibility for it. That is my main impression of the meeting and it created a very deep impression on me. I can tell you it was the impression I brought away from the meeting and it was the only impression I was concerned with."
McKenna: "Were you ever concerned with the impression your reports had on Mr Gibbons?"
Kelly: "Mr Gibbons was fully informed at all times and if he did not agree with the operation all he had to do was to say stop. As Minister for Defence his orders would have been obeyed. He did not say stop through Colonel Hefferon and he did not say stop to me directly. He fully approved and at all times he had full knowledge of what was going on and it was at this meeting of April 23 that it hit me that he was going to shirk his responsibilities."

In further reply to Mr McKenna, I told him that I had a distinct recollection of my meeting with Colonel Delaney on April 28 and agreed that the effect of what Colonel Delaney had said to me was:

"You are now getting an order to desist entirely from your present activities: you will make no more contact with anyone whatsoever, either here or abroad, in connection with these activities; you will engage yourself wholetime in the pursuit of your legal soldierly duties."

When Mr McKenna asked if I considered it an extraordinary order I replied:

> "I did, but I would like to explain a bit further concerning that order. I had met the Minister on the previous night and the Minister

> had explained to me that he had intended transferring me to a unit of the Department that would not inconvenience me in any way, so that I would have complete freedom of movement to carry out my duties, this top secret work I was on. So I left the Minister that night very happy, to find on the following morning two officers on my doorstep…
>
> I was very surprised in view of what the Minister said the previous night. As soon as I got this order I made it my business to see him again or try to get an appointment for the following night (with the Minister) and I tried to get an explanation, which I have given here in direct evidence. Then, on the third night… I resigned.
>
> He sent for me and once again tried to talk me out of it, the same ground again, waffling and wuffling about how he would look after me and he then signed the documentation."

In direct evidence I told Mr D'Arcy that I had gone to Leinster House to see Mr Gibbons about Colonel Delaney's order on the day it was issued. In the beginning of the conversation, I informed the court, Mr Gibbons had said that it was a mistake, that the army had over-reacted and had agreed that the sending of two officers to my house to collect me was a disgrace. I asked Mr Gibbons about my leave, I continued, and he said:

"I am sorry, that was probably my fault. I said you were not to get leave."

I knew then that Mr Gibbons was being less than honest with me because such an order from the Minister for Defence could only convey to the military authorities that I was *persona non grata.* I knew then that he was going to deny that he authorised the arms importation. I asked him how he could reconcile Colonel Delaney's very specific order with his instruction of the previous night that I should keep up my Northern Ireland contacts. He said that I could still continue those contacts. I felt like telling the Minister exactly what I thought of him at that stage, but, in a restrained voice, I merely asked him how was that possible or did he want me to end up on a court-martial charge because of Colonel Delaney's very specific order. Mr Gibbons gave no direct answer to this, other than saying something to the effect that everything would be all right.

As we left his room and went to the lifts he repeated that there was no question of my breaking my contacts or of the Northern people being turned away and when I pressed him on this, suggesting that someone was being hoodwinked, he said no, that John Kelly was too intelligent a man to be hoodwinked. He offered me a drink and when I accepted, I thought it strange that he brought me to the visitors' bar. In fact, the whole drink episode was a furtive exercise, hurriedly concluded, and I left Mr Gibbons convinced that he intended using me as a scapegoat.

I went home and discussed things with my wife. I told her that the only logical conclusion was that Mr Gibbons intended using the full weight of military law to place me under restraint and hold me incommunicado. Next morning, I signed my retirement papers and that evening, this time at Mr Gibbons' request, I was again in his office at Leinster House. He did not seem anxious to sign my retirement forms which were on his desk, even indicating that there would be a Government decision in a day or two which would clear up the matter. He was clearly implying that I had nothing to worry about but, unable to trust him any longer, I insisted that he sign my retirement forms there and then.

The details and the full significance of my three interviews with Mr Gibbons on three consecutive nights did not emerge in full in the rarefied atmosphere of the court. As my marathon cross-examination drew to an end, Mr McKenna asked:

"If you considered that you were under arrest, which I don't concede at all, you had the more reason to have a grievance when Colonel Delaney spoke to you?"

Kelly: "I knew the Minister was behind it after the conference with the Minister the night before. Colonel Delaney was subject to the Minister and the Minister was the man behind it."
McKenna: "Had you a grievance?"
Kelly: "Of course I had a major grievance and I went to Mr Gibbons and expressed it to him."

Obviously falling back on Defence Force Regulations, Mr McKenna asked if I had requested permission from Colonel Delaney to express my grievance. I replied that there was no point in approaching Colonel Delaney because he received his orders from the Minister, as the Minister had in effect admitted to me on the night of my "arrest".

Technically, Mr McKenna may have been correct when he would not concede that it was an arrest, but whatever it was, it was carried out by my comrades, whom I had looked upon as friends, with much less finesse and much less humanity than my actual arrest by the Special Branch on May 1.

As I looked down the court from my vantage-point in the witness-box, I had seen Colonel Delaney hide his head in his hands. Well he might.

CHAPTER 21

Mr Charles Haughey TD, former Minister for Finance, was examined by Mr McCarthy when he took the stand. After discussion in the jury's absence, Mr Justice Henchy ruled that what had happened in Cabinet was *prima facie* irrelevant. This effectively prevented Mr Haughey from giving evidence which would have shown that Mr Gibbons was aware of my existence as early as August 1969. It would also have established that my status as liaison officer had been approved at Cabinet level.

The jury returned and Mr McCarthy continued his questioning within the limits outlined by the judge.

McCarthy: "Mr Haughey, in August or September of 1969, I'm not sure of the exact month, but a committee was set up to deal with a special situation in the North?"
Haughey: "I wouldn't say it was to deal with a special situation in the North, but one of the things that was very much on the Government's mind at that time was the lack of information we had in connection with internal affairs in the six-county area. The committee consisted of myself, Mr Blaney, Mr Faulkner and Joe Brennan and we were given instructions that we should develop the maximum possible contacts with persons inside the Six Counties and try and inform ourselves as much as possible on events, political and other developments, within the six-county area."
McCarthy: "Was there any individual or person not in the Cabinet who was concerned with creating a link between you and your fellow members and the people in the North?"
Haughey: "Captain Kelly."
McCarthy: "When was the committee set up?"
Haughey: "I'm afraid I couldn't be exactly sure, but it was in August/September time. As there were many things happening at that time I couldn't put a precise date on when meetings were held to set up the committee."
McCarthy: "Did you come into personal contact with Captain Kelly then?"
Haughey: "I did, yes."
McCarthy: "Can you remember what month?"
Haughey: "It was September."
McCarthy: "When you saw him then have you any clear recollection of what he told you and what he talked about?"

Charles J. Haughey (centre) with his solicitor, Pat O'Connor (right) and friend

Haughey: "Yes, he gave me a briefing on the situation in the Six Counties as he saw it; what groups there were, what their aims and objectives were and so on. Shortly after that, in October I think, he brought along a deputation to see me."
McCarthy: "I don't know if it would be in any way wrong to state the membership of the deputation, or would you rather not?"
Haughey: "I'd rather not, yes."
McCarthy: "At or around that time, did you meet John Kelly?"
Haughey: "Yes."
McCarthy: "How did you meet him?"
Haughey: "Captain James Kelly introduced him to me."
McCarthy: "He brought him to you?"
Haughey: "As part of the delegation."
McCarthy: "Had there been any other Government decision dealing with the North? I'm not dealing now with the distress or aid fund, but in regard to the situation in the North with which other Ministers were to be particularly concerned."
Haughey: "There were two to which I would refer. One was that the Minister for Justice was instructed by the Government to send Garda offi-

cers, and I at that time thought they were to be Special Branch officers, into the Six Counties to be able to give us a first-hand account of everything that was happening within the Six Counties. Furthermore the…"
McCarthy: "Subsequently, before you leave that, were first-hand reports provided by the Minister to the Cabinet?".
Haughey: "A number of reports were read by the Minister for Justice to Government meetings."
McCarthy: "And you were going to say?"
Haughey: "The Minister for Defence was also given a general instruction from the Government to prepare contingency plans. At that time none of us knew exactly what might happen inside the six-county area, but we decided that the Army should be prepared for any possible emergency or contingency that might arise, and I was given instructions to make whatever additional monies might be required available to the Minister for Defence to procure any sort of special equipment, or anything else that we might need, so that the army might be in a position to meet any contingency that might arise."

Having stated that monies for the care of refugees were not involved in the contingency plans, Mr Haughey said in reply to Mr McCarthy:

> "At that time, none of us could visualise what the Army might be called upon to do. We knew there was no question of open hostilities with the British Army, but short of that, there were many possible contingencies that might arise. We might, by UN decision, have been asked to send troops into certain areas to patrol these areas. It is possible that if there was a completely chaotic situation, the British army or the British Government would agree to our patrolling certain areas, where we would be acceptable. There was also a question that in a complete breakdown, there was a possibility that the Army here might go inside the Six Counties on rescue operations. All these were possibilities, contingencies, that the army was asked to prepare for.
>
> It was realised that in order to prepare for them we would have to supply the army with special equipment, it might be gas masks, it might be anti-riot equipment, it might be a special type of arms. The Army was to work this out and I was to make the money available for the supply of these items."

Mr Haughey went on to explain how monies for the relief of distress were allocated to various groups in Northern Ireland.

McCarthy: "With regard to determining the *bona fide* of the applicants, had you the means of checking this?"
Haughey: Well, Captain Kelly was one of the very important people. He had a very good knowledge of who was who inside the six-county area..."

When asked if he was aware that I was concerned with trying to get arms for the Defence Committee, Mr Haughey replied:

"No, not at that time, not in February."

McCarthy: "Well, did you become aware of it at any time, or had you been aware of it?"
Haughey: "No. My first knowledge of this was on March 19 or 20, when Mr Fagan came to me and said he had an approach from Army Intelligence and said that they wished to bring in a consignment without having it subjected to the usual customs clearance. I said if I had the power to do it, I would do it. He assured me that I had the power and I said, 'OK, go ahead'. May I add that at that time, on the nineteenth or twentieth, Captain Kelly came to Mr Fagan as an official approach. Both Mr Fagan and myself had no doubt that this was an official approach from Army Intelligence through official channels.
McCarthy: "When Mr Fagan spoke to you did you learn the nature of the consignment?"
Haughey: "No, we never discussed the details of the consignment. May I also add that my decision at that time was not in relation to a specific consignment. I was giving Mr Fagan a general direction that anything Army Intelligence wanted to do about bringing in consignments through customs without clearance was to be acceded to, because I associated it with the contingency plan. It was present in my mind that these were items, whatever they were, which were needed by the Army to fulfil the contingency plans Directive."
McCarthy: "Whilst the Directive was general in application, it was arising out of a particular request relating to a particular consignment?"
Haughey: "Yes."
McCarthy: "If you had known, first, that the consignment contained arms, ammunition and bullet-proof vests, would that have made any difference?"
Haughey: "Not the slightest, no. The contingency plans naturally envisaged items of that nature and I could also envisage the provision for the Army here of special types of arms and ammunition, which would not normally be issued to them and in so far, if I had known that the consign-

ment did consist of any particular type of arms and ammunition, I would have given the sanction just the same."
McCarthy: "If you had known that they were intended for possible ultimate distribution to civilians in the North would that have made any difference?"
Haughey: "No, not really, provided, of course, that a Government decision intervened. I would have regarded it a very normal part of Army preparations in pursuance of the contingency plans that they would provide themselves with and store here on this side of the border, arms which might ultimately, if the Government said so, be distributed to other persons."
McCarthy: "Were you aware of the Directive issued by the Minister for Defence to the Chief-of-Staff on February 6, 1970?"
Haughey: "No. I was surprised to learn since the case started that the Directive was only given on February 6, because the Government's instructions to the Minister dated back to August '69. I believe that there was a question raised by some people around February as to what progress had been made with the contingency plans and perhaps as a result of that discussion, the Directive was given clearly and precisely in February."

Mr Haughey stated that on January 22 he had met Mr Gibbons and officials of both departments in his own office and that Mr Gibbons had stayed behind when the officials departed.

McCarthy: "What did you discuss?"
Haughey: "Well, Mr Gibbons said words to the effect that the estimate, which we had just more or less settled, was all right as a peacetime estimate, but that of course we were not in a peacetime situation; that there was the Northern situation to be considered. I assured him again that whatever was needed to equip the Army for any special six-county duties would be made available over and above the normal estimate."
McCarthy: "When Mr Fagan came to you on March 19 with a request for you to authorise customs clearance, did you associate that in any way with the discussion you had had with Mr Gibbons?".
Haughey: Yes, it would have been a natural sequel to the discussion, to a number of discussions which Mr Gibbons and myself had had about this very question. The army was under direction to prepare for any contingency that might arise. I had not the slightest doubt that this approach by Captain Kelly on behalf of Army Intelligence was in pursuance of the Directive.

When asked by Mr McCarthy if he recalled being asked to look for a job for me in the public service, Mr Haughey replied in the affirmative. He said that this would have been in February or March, and that Mr Gibbons had expressed the fear that British Intelligence was "on" to me. Mr Haughey continued:

"The Minister for Defence wanted to retain Captain Kelly's services. He was worried about his situation as an army officer and he wanted to find some post for him inside the public service, where he would still he able to continue with his activities. I suggested that a very good cover for him would be to become a Special Customs Officer with responsibility for pig smuggling, which was then a very serious problem."

McCarthy: "I think you were under some pressure from the National Farmers Association (NFA)."
Haughey: "Well, I was not directly under pressure from the NFA, but there was quite an agitation then about the volume of pig smuggling, which was incidentally costing our Exchequer very large sums of money. It seemed at that time that there was wholesale smuggling of pigs across the border in this direction and it seemed that it would have been very logical to appoint an additional officer with special responsibility to stop this trade."
McCarthy: "And this would enable him to operate around the border area?"
Haughey: "I'm quite certain that that was my motive and that it was also the motive of the Minister for Defence."
McCarthy: "Was there any question of the Minister for Defence wanting him out of the army, because he was involved in trying to get arms imported here for the contingency that we have been discussing?"
Haughey: "No, my view of the situation was completely different. My view of the situation was that Captain Kelly was a very valuable Intelligence Officer. I never heard any suggestion that he did not have Mr Gibbons' complete confidence, but that he was a useful person and that if at all possible we should retain him in some guise where he could pursue his activities and not be picked up as an Irish Army Intelligence Officer by the British Army."
McCarthy: "Perhaps it is a small point, but Mr Gibbons has said that you made this suggestion sometime after he had made the request and that he associated it with you having attended an army parade?"
Haughey: "Yes, I heard him say that and I must say that it is not clear to me exactly what he meant. I reviewed the St. Patrick's Day Parade in Dublin , but there was no army unit participating in that parade."
McCarthy: "None at all?"

Haughey: "Well, there was an army guard-of-honour and an army band, but there was no army unit marching in the parade as such."
McCarthy: "It is an industrial parade?"
Haughey: "Mainly industrial."
McCarthy "And at Easter I think you were down the West of Ireland?"
Haughey: "I was in Galway at Easter and in fact I took part in the Liam Mellows commemoration ceremony in Galway on Easter Sunday."
McCarthy: "Mr Gibbons's reason for referring to this was, I think, because he says that you said something to the effect that I saw your boys and seeing your boys made me think of your Captain Kelly?"
Haughey: "As far as I remember, his evidence was to the effect that I said as I saw your boys marching past or something like that. I don't know what the reference is to".
McCarthy: "At all events, you did make the suggestion to Mr Gibbons. Was it a serious suggestion?"
Haughey: "Well, the request came from him and as far as I was concerned it was something I thought of, that would answer his problem. If he did not wish to take it seriously, that was not my affair."

Cross-examining, Mr Walsh asked Mr Haughey:

"Do you remember a conversation with Mr Gibbons in which he said to you that he had an officer in the Army who had to be got rid of as quickly and discreetly as possible?"

Haughey: "No, I don't remember a conversation in those terms. I do remember us both over a period of time discussing Captain Kelly, discussing his role, and he had a very special role by authority of the Government. We discussed that role from time to time and I do remember Mr Gibbons telling me of his fears that Captain Kelly would come under the notice, must by now have come under the notice of British Intelligence and that he wanted to get some position for him where he could carry on his valuable work."
Walsh: "Did Mr Gibbons tell you that the officer in question was an army Intelligence Officer and that he considered it the most desirable and prudent thing that a position in the Government service should be found for this officer in all haste?"
Haughey: "Not in that way, but there were a number of conversations between Mr Gibbons and myself on the matter, and I knew that with the authority of the Government, Captain Kelly had a special job to do. I also knew that Mr Gibbons at that time was afraid that he might be picked up by British Army Intelligence. Therefore, he wanted to get him some other

job in which he could continue his activities. I think the very fact of the type of job that I suggested for him is proof of that."

Prosecuting counsel took up the question of arms and Mr Haughey's knowledge of them.

Walsh: "Did you have any knowledge, Mr Haughey, as to what that cargo consisted of?"
Haughey: "No. I want to repeat again: as of March 19-20, I was not concerned with any cargo. I was concerned with a general arrangement for Army Intelligence, not with any particular cargo."
Walsh: "Did you give Customs clearance knowing that a consignment of arms and ammunition was involved?"
Haughey: " No..."
Walsh: "If you had known, Mr Haughey, that what was involved was a consignment of arms and ammunition purchased with monies provided by the Government for the Relief of Distress in Northern Ireland, would you have given customs clearance?"
Haughey: "That is a hypothetical question. It did not arise."
Walsh: "Did you suspect that arms and ammunition might be the consignment?"
Haughey: "It was not a question of suspicion. This was a very normal routine matter as far as I was concerned. We, in my office in the Department of Finance, had an official approach from Army Intelligence for facilities, and as far as I was concerned -- once I ascertained I had authority to do so, I would direct the facility being afforded in the most open way."

Counsel was nothing, if not determined. He gnawed away at the arms bone.

Walsh: "Did you appreciate that it was arms and ammunition?"
Haughey: "No, I did not appreciate or know at that point of time, and, even when I spoke to Mr Berry, the words, arms and ammunition, were never used."

The phone conversation with Mr Berry, of which Mr Berry had given evidence already, took place on April 18. Mr Haughey introduced it, by asking if Mr Berry was aware of a "certain cargo".
Walsh: "So there was a conversation then, relating to a certain cargo... Was there any reference to what the consignment consisted of?"
Haughey: "No, none. And, as far as I can recall, Mr Berry did not say what it consisted of".

Walsh: "Your conversation with Mr Berry ended with your telling him, 'It had better be called off, whatever it is'?"
Haughey: "Yes. That is my recollection."
Walsh: "Did it not occur to you to ask Mr Berry at any stage what the consignment was?"
Haughey: "No, for – I just recall – the first thing Mr Berry asked me was, had I a scrambler, and he was very conscious of the need not to be talking in any careless terms on the telephone."
Walsh: "I gather from what you say that Mr Berry was totally and absolutely wrong when he says you asked, if a guarantee was got that it would go direct to the North, could it come through?"
Haughey: "I could not have had that kind of discussion. I would have it with the Minister for Justice. The question of guarantee could not arise, I can only say that Mr Berry must be mistaken in his recollection of the particular word 'guarantee'."
Walsh: "Was the North mentioned?"
Haughey: "No. As I said, we spoke about a consignment as such, not where it was going or what it was or anything of that sort."
Walsh: "Did you even question what was in the consignment?"
Haughey: "I certainly had a very shrewd idea that it was something that Army Intelligence was bringing in in pursuance of their plans."
Walsh: "You did not know for certain but you had a very shrewd idea that this was a consignment of arms and ammunition?"
Haughey: "That is quite correct. I did not know for certain, but I did not exclude the possibility that it was arms and ammunition."

On his meeting with Mr Gibbons on the same weekend, he told Counsel that he did not see Mr Gibbons until Monday afternoon; "it was a question of Mr Gibbons coming to see me about his business, to discuss it with me, to get my advice and to consult with me."

Counsel: "Did you not ask him what the consignment was?"
Haughey: "No. It did not arise. In my mind was present the fact that this was a consignment being brought in by Army Intelligence in pursuance of their own operations."

There was no talk about calling it off for a month, as Mr Gibbons had asserted, Mr Haughey told the court, but that he might well have informed Mr Gibbons, during their Monday afternoon conversation, of the Berry phone-call, and the decision taken to call off the operation.

Counsel: "If your evidence is correct, Mr Haughey, I suggest that when Mr Gibbons came to see you on Monday your reaction would have been, 'I have already called this off but now, please, tell me what it's all about'?"
Haughey: "That's not what happened. It may be what you think should have happened, but it did not happen."

Undoubtedly, there was a major conflict between Mr Gibbons and Mr Berry on their separate conversations with Mr Haughey. Mr Gibbons had not been an inspiring witness on the matter. He was too equivocal and there were many in court who accepted the contention of the Defence counsel, Mr McCarthy, that he attempted to tailor his evidence to fit in with that given by Mr Fagan. On the contrary, Mr Berry came across as a very precise witness who, in what seemed to be his usual meticulous fashion, used notes.

The core issue of the trial was whether the proposed arms importation was authorised by Mr Gibbons. In this connection, the two conversations were mere side-shows, giving undue prominence to the attempt by the prosecution to show that Mr Haughey knew that arms and ammunition constituted the cargo in question.

The central theme of Mr Haughey's response to this was a denial that he knew arms and ammunition were involved. It was false. He did know.

The Haughey denial was a big blow to the defence. If the top Minister in the Government after the Taoiseach did not know that arms and ammunition were involved, where to my defence and that of John Kelly and Albert Luykx? We contended that the importation was Government policy. If a top Minister in that Government did not know that arms were involved, it certainly did not help our case.

Fortunately, Colonel Hefferon, the chief prosecution witness after Gibbons, was an honest man. His evidence, delivered without fear or favour, confirming that my activities were fully authorised, in line with Government policy, was a major factor in countering both Mr Gibbons' wholly partisan evidence and the possible negative effect of Mr Haughey's denial. As evidence of the high standing the Colonel had among his peers as a man of integrity, it is worth quoting Lieut. General Michael J Costello, one of Ireland's more illustrious soldiers since the foundation of the State. He told me after the trial: "Once I heard Mick Hefferon's evidence, I knew where the truth lay. He's not and never was a liar. He couldn't tell a lie. Once he gave evidence, I knew whose side I was on."

So did a lot of others.

CHAPTER 22

Evidence having concluded, the order of address by the various counsel was debated in the absence of the jury. Mr Wood, in particular, argued that he had the right to address the jury last, as his client, Mr Luykx, had not given evidence and no evidence had been called on his behalf. Mr Wood put his case rather forcefully, stressing what he claimed was established practice during his long years at the bar.

Mr Justice Henchy was not persuaded, however, and he decreed that the order of summing-up speeches be as follows:

First: Counsel for Mr Haughey
Second: Counsel for Captain Kelly
Third: Counsel for John Kelly
Fourth: Counsel for Mr Luykx
Fifth: Prosecuting Counsel

Towards the beginning of his address, Mr McCarthy described the prosecution as:

"conceived in panic, nurtured on rumour and malice and born in confusion and spite... this has been demonstrated in a particular way in regard to the calling of evidence at this trial."

Later Mr McCarthy said:

> "The failure to call Colonel Hefferon, is something that marks this prosecution as something bordering on being a persecution. It didn't end there... When the evidence had been going on one day, we had the almost absurd situation that the prosecution was not prepared to go on with evidence until they called Mr Ó Moráin, the former Minister for Justice. Mr Ó Moráin's evidence was purely technical... to say that he had never given a licence to any of these defendants or to a certain named company, a licence to import arms. That's what his evidence was. That evidence had to be brought in at a particular stage, at what particular stage? At this stage, gentlemen, at the stage before Mr Gibbons gave evidence. They didn't want Gibbons contradicted again, just in case someone might ask Mr Ó Moráin some question or other that might affect Mr Gibbons' credibility. That's the reason for it, gentlemen. I suggest to you that that's an unfair tactic on the part of the prosecution. We

> can't stop them doing it. It is a matter entirely for the judge, who would normally act in accordance with a request from the prosecution. But that I suggest is the reason, because until the cross-examination of Mr Ó Moráin started, his evidence was entirely technical and not in dispute that he had ever given a licence. No one suggested he ever had, but it was other questions they were afraid he might be asked, which would implicate Mr Gibbons. I suggest that, gentlemen, was an unfair tactic for the prosecution and it is another mark of the unfairness that has been shown."

Mr McCarthy quoted what John Kelly had to say about the prosecution, when he claimed that he and the other accused stood on trial as a matter of political expediency, and not from any desire that the course of justice be impartially administered.

"It is no reflection on the course of justice," Mr McCarthy continued, "that a case had to be heard at length by juries who are, as you are now, ministers of justice or judges in the case. . . The reflection is on those who make it happen, whoever they may be. I should point out to you, gentlemen, that the conduct of criminal trials lies in the hands of the Attorney General, under an article of the Constitution. He is the person bound to conduct them."

By concentrating on the evidence, Mr McCarthy illustrated Mr Gibbons' lack of credibility. In referring to the Directive of February 6, he recalled that Mr Gibbons, when questioned about its source, whether or not he had seen it since the last trial, and if so, with whom, had claimed privilege, which was allowed. Mr McCarthy went on:

> "Now it is improper to go into questions in regard to a claim of privilege and I don't do so. I merely say, why did he claim privilege? What possible difference can it make to know who was with him when he read it? How could it affect, let's assume any number of people that might have been there, an army officer, the Chief-of-Staff, the Attorney General, the Minister for Justice, the Taoiseach, who? What does it matter? How could that affect State security? He claimed it, he did and we are bound by that, but it tends to excite some suspicion. What's behind all this? Why was the claim made?
>
> There were other matters Mr Gibbons dealt with evolving from a Government decision, which necessarily involved a conclusion by anyone listening to him that they had come from a discussion at Cabinet level. No claim of privilege made! Nothing at all! Everything was free and open! Except when it came to this one

thing! I don't know why, gentlemen. I can't suggest a reason, other than that there was something to conceal, something that lies somewhere behind or beneath the prosecution. But it excites suspicion about the veracity or the reliability of the person who gave the evidence and, gentlemen, it was this witness who was maintained as a witness for the prosecution, while Colonel Hefferon was discarded."

Mr McCarthy concluded his address with the words:

"I referred, gentlemen, yesterday to the nature of this prosecution as some ill-conceived monster. I suggest that it's time it was buried."

The judge called on Mr Finlay. Decisively and analytically, disdaining histrionics, Mr Finlay got to the heart of things, starting with what he described as basic agreed facts, the first of which was that I was a fully employed serving officer, attached to Intelligence, during the relevant period.

Finlay: "He was never transferred, he was never shifted, he was never moved and he was never dismissed and he was never put into any other position in the army during that time. That fact is agreed.

"As a soldier, gentlemen, he had a necessary discipline, which is much more strong and much more stringent than the discipline needed as a civil servant or as an ordinary employee. Those in authority over Captain Kelly could at any moment of time, with even greater facility than applies to a managing director in a factory, or a political master in the civil service, shift or move Captain Kelly, stop him from doing anything or make him do anything that they wanted. Not one stir was made during the entire time from August of 1969, till after the events we are investigating, to move Captain Kelly or to remove him from his position as an Intelligence Officer. That is an agreed fact and it is a good solid fact from which to start your investigations of this case."

Because what was the next agreed fact? The next agreed fact is that during the entire of the time up to April 9 1970, his immediate and direct superior was the Director of Intelligence, Colonel Hefferon. That is not in dispute. That during the entire of that time, in detail, he told his immediate superior officer what he was doing. That is not in dispute. That during so much of that time, which at the very best from the point of view of the State commenced at the end of January or beginning of February 1970, and I am using a neutral tone, because I am still talking about agreed facts, the Minister for Defence, in broad terms as to all of it and in detail as to a great deal of it, knew what Captain Kelly, was doing."

And the next agreed fact comes from the mouth of the Minister for Defence himself, that in a series of conversations, in a series of meetings he had with this Captain in Intelligence, not only did he not order him to cease what he was doing, not only did he not direct him to be removed to other duties, not only did he not transfer him to any other unit in the army, but during the entire of those conversations, up to the rather interesting meeting of April 23, on the Minister's own admission, no hint of disapproval, no note of criticism, no warning or advice to cease, came from the mouth of the Minister for Defence."

Those are basic and agreed facts, which are not in dispute in this case and I suggest to you, gentlemen, that if you like to look at the case in its broadest possible terms, to adapt a phrase which I think applied to a book, which some of us may have read: this is the case in which nobody shouted stop. Wouldn't that in itself, if we had not to go through the weary details of all the evidence, leave you, gentlemen, with no reasonable conclusion in this case but that what Captain Kelly did, during the entire of that time, was done with the authority of the Minister for Defence?"

As to authorisation, Mr Finlay said:

"Now, the word 'authorisation', as if it was a golden word, talking about licences and the production of a civil servant with a log book, has nothing to do with this. What you have got to solve is a good, hard, common-sense problem, namely, were these acts done under the authority of the Minister for Defence?"

Mr Finlay then used his gardening analogy to illustrate what authority actually meant, and he continued:

"The only conceivable conclusion is that what was done by Captain Kelly during the entire of the relevant period was done under the authority of the Minister for Defence."

Mr Finlay then referred to the details of the case. Here the jury had a double burden, he said. In the first place they had to examine dispassionately the evidence of people who held, or had held, high office.

"And the second burden is this, that I think you will have found almost inevitably, gentlemen, that in regard to the details of evidence there is a sort of precision which borders on evasion when persons who hold high office come to give evidence. The answers of Mr Berry and Mr

Fleming which have been illustrated here by Mr McCarthy with regard to the Special Branch, show such a precision. The answers of Mr Gibbons in regard to Fort Dunree training and in regard to the emerging of concrete facts in relation to the importation of guns show such a precision."

Mr Finlay went on to deal with the Bailieboro meeting and the Dunree training in chronological order.

> "I think the other thing you must have regard for, gentlemen, is that whilst Mr Gibbons, in a way that you may or may not have accepted, stated that this (the Dunree training) was a sort of empty gesture to the people of Derry, but to anyone else, it must have appeared as if the Irish Army amongst its contingency plans was concerned to provide protection in the event of a breakdown... and there isn't any sense, meaning or idea in training a man in the use of a gun unless you envisage that in the Doomsday situation and on the breaking up of peace and order, you might provide that man with a gun to use."

Mr Finlay, referring to the February Directive, stated:

> "I don't mind what the Government meant Mr Gibbons to do. All I'm concerned with is what Mr Gibbons did, as communicated to Captain Kelly. Mr Gibbons gave this Directive and Colonel Hefferon, the superior officer of Captain Kelly, discussed it with Captain Kelly and told him that a necessary part of it would be the availability to the army of surplus arms for the contingency of distribution in Northern Ireland.
>
> Indeed, that appreciation of what this contingency plan and the Directive meant was wholly and entirely confirmed by Mr Haughey, on the matter of which no challenge or cross-examination was made to him. Mr Haughey, in my note, said that it would be an integral part of the contingency plan that the army would supply itself with arms, which it could supply to people in the Six Counties, if that decision were ever taken by the Government.
>
> So Colonel Hefferon's appraisal of the Directive of February 6 is to that extent fully confirmed by another Minister, then in the Government and very much concerned with this matter. That was the information which Captain Kelly had and it provided the manifest reason why the Minister for Defence was authorising him in the rather unusual duties upon which he was then embarking. If that was part and parcel of one of the things which the Army had to do

> in order to provide for all contingencies, then the expedition to vet arms on the Continent of Europe made sense, as part and parcel of one of the things someone had to do for the Minister for Defence."

I can only highlight some aspects of Mr Finlay's address, which was a precise, detailed and comprehensive rebuttal of the prosecution case against me, but from a legal viewpoint the case hinged on whether or not the attempted importation was under the authority of the Minister for Defence for the use of the Defence Forces. Mr Finlay had done much to prove that such was the case, but under the disadvantage that the State had the last word, he suggested that the prosecution might concentrate on attempting to prove that the arms were not "for the use of the Defence Forces".

> "That would be tantamount," he pointed out, "to saying that the Minister for Defence had authorised something which the Statute did not permit him to authorise. The words in the Statute are 'for the use of the Defence Forces'. 'Use' is a word which we all know and constantly employ. I suggest to you, as Mr McCarthy did, the definition, 'applied to a purpose'.
>
> It is clear on the evidence that the Army in 1970, in the spring or early in 1970, had as an obligation imposed upon it by the Minister for Defence the making of plans and the taking of steps to put itself into preparedness for all sorts of contingencies. It is equally clear, I suggest to you, that one of those possible contingencies which no one wanted to happen, which everyone hoped wouldn't, but which might yet break by reason of events in Northern Ireland, was that the Army might be called upon by the Government to distribute arms to civilians in Northern Ireland. If it was so called upon, it would be a poor Army and a poor Defence Department that would turn around to the Government at the last moment and say, 'we haven't got any suitable arms'.
>
> Such a decision, if it were ever taken by the Government, would be in an emergency and as a matter of extreme rapidity, and I think it is as clear as the noon-day sun, that if the Army wanted to be prepared for that situation, then one of the desirable pieces of equipment was appropriate surplus arms. What I say to you, on all the evidence in this case, was what Captain Kelly was assisting to import. If he was importing arms so that the Army might be in a position, in the event no one wanted but which might occur, of the Government deciding to distribute arms, is anyone to say by any

> law of common sense applied to the ordinary use of words that those arms were not for the use of the Defence Forces?"

Mr Finlay went on to give further analogous examples in relation to equipment purchased by the Defence Forces and concluded his dissertation on use by arguing that if permission had been given to distribute the Dundalk rifles in the North, it could not be said that they were not being used by the Defence Forces.

"Mr Gibbons' attempt to deny or revoke the authority he had given may well be explicable," Mr Finlay said, "by the meeting of April 23, a meeting described by both Colonel Hefferon and by the accused, and described with some indignation by Captain Kelly, having been told by the Minister that he was brazen and was in the hot seat."

Mr Finlay brought his address to a close with the words:

> "Indignation should not be a part of evidence in a case, but I feel sure that you find it within yourselves to forgive Captain Kelly that indignation. That meeting, so inappropriately held on the day of the celebration of St Enda's, appeared to be the first indication of a change of mind by the Minister for Defence.
>
> To change one's mind used to be said to be the prerogative of a woman. To change one's mind, gentlemen, is, I think, probably a virtue in a politician, given certain circumstances. But I confidently entrust to you the duty under your oath as jurors to ensure that a change of mind by the Minister for Defence could never form the basis for the conviction of Captain Kelly."

Opening his address to the jury, Mr Sorahan referred to the envelopes, marked "Secret" and "Top Secret", to which he said there had been reference. "Walking back and forth through the halls of the court to the Law Library, one could not but…"

Judge: "What happened going to and from the Library is irrelevant. I told the jury at the commencement of this trial that they must confine themselves to what happens within this courtroom in evidence and you must keep to that ruling."
Sorahan: "My Lord, it's a pity your Lordship feels…"
Judge: "You accept that ruling, Mr Sorahan, or not."

The judge pointed his finger at Mr Sorahan, who was half-turned towards the jury, in a gesture of admonishment, but turning quickly and sharply Mr Sorahan said:

"I object to a finger being pointed at me in a threatening manner by so courteous a judge as your Lordship."

Caught out in an involuntary action, Mr Henchy jerked back the offending finger as though stung by a scorpion. It was a little bit of gamesmanship, a side-issue, but it added its own spice to the trial.

Mr Sorahan said that the jury would be satisfied that anything John Kelly did, he did for no base motive, not for gain, not for personal, commercial or social advantage:

"John Kelly's defence is that everything he did, he did it because he considered it his duty. He did it believing, and for good reason indeed, that this was completely official. It was *sub rosa*, it was underground, it was secret; it was kept as far as possible from the glare of publicity and public knowledge, but he says that he did it sincerely thinking that it was a completely official Government-sponsored project. Could anyone blame him?"

They were not looking to shoot any member of the Stormont Government, Mr Sorahan continued, or to shoot police. Delegations composed of a wide spectrum of anti-Unionist opinion in the North were looking for guns for the lawful purpose of defending their homesteads, their wives and their children, lest there should be a recurrence of the pogrom that occurred on the night immediately following August 15 in the Ardoyne and Falls Road areas of Belfast.

John Kelly was brought openly to Government Buildings, Mr Sorahan said, and if there was a conspiracy, if Captain Kelly was not satisfied that it was an official matter which had the sanction of the Minister for Defence, Mr Gibbons, would Captain Kelly not deserve to be severely reprimanded for negligence in bringing with him his "co-conspirator", John Kelly? But there was no conspiracy. They had come openly, Mr Sorahan added.

In conclusion, Mr Sorahan said that it only remained that the jurymen, thinking of Magna Carta, the great charter of 1297, should do their duty and "give the judgement of those four men's peers on this, and for God's sake, gentlemen, throw out this smelly, shameful, disgraceful prosecution."

Mr Wood, on behalf of Albert Luykx, stated that Mr Luykx had in fact committed no crime in assisting Captain Kelly who was acting with the knowledge of three Ministers of the State. He asked emphatically why Albert Luykx should have been dragged into the humiliation of a criminal trial? "I don't know the reason. All I know is what I can see before my eyes, a silly, senseless pantomime. There is no case against Mr Luykx and I am not going to let him go into the witness box to explain away a case which does not exist."

Referring to Mr Gibbons, Mr Wood told the jury:

> "Forget that he is a Minister of State. He is now down in a court of justice, one man against others. Remember, gentlemen, what were to me at any rate and I am sure to some of you, some of the things, shocking things he said. I give as one example: he was cross-examined by Mr Finlay and he asked Mr Finlay to tell him what he was driving at before he would answer the question. What manner of Minister is this? This is the man who took the oath to swear the truth, the whole truth and nothing but the truth and he wants to know what has the cross-examiner got in his mind before he would risk answering the question. Does that shock you? Does that indicate to you the sort of man I suggest Mr Gibbons to be?"

In regard to the record of the Dáil debate, Mr Wood told the jury:

> "Don't let's mince words, he's a liar and his excuse for being a liar is that it was a Dáil debate…
>
> This is the man upon whose evidence you must act and whose evidence you must accept as the truth beyond all reasonable doubt, when he swears he did not authorise the importation of arms. This is the man, you will remember, this is the man who told Dáil Éireann and the populace of this country that although he had certain suspicions in his mind, no concrete evidence had emerged.
>
> Mr Gibbons, said counsel, had been told over and over again by Colonel Hefferon and by Captain Kelly just what Captain Kelly was doing. He made his own classical remark that comes from his own mouth, that when the Army turned up to collect the official consignment of arms that he supposed Captain Kelly melted into the shadows. This man, to use his own adjective, had the brazen effrontery to tell Dáil Éireann that no concrete evidence of importation had emerged… You and I know what it means to take five hundred rifles along the border. Everyone who sat in this court knows what it meant and what it involved save the man, Mr Gibbons. Gentlemen of the jury, isn't it obvious Mr Gibbons was subscribing to the actions being taken, because, and I would be the last to blame him, of the terror of many people of an Orange cloud?… What is this trial about? I don't know whether it is an exercise in democracy or all of the other things Mr Sorahan said. I think it is an asinine pantomime, sheer waste of your time and everybody else's time, except the lawyers like me who are paid for it… I am still baffled

> and Mr Luykx must be baffled as to why he must be dragged in here to the humiliation of a public trial in a criminal court. Look at the criminal, gentlemen of the jury. What has he got out of this case only tears, blood and sweat and now the humiliation of being an actor in this silly pantomime by which you have been wearied?"

Mr Wood had got to the heart of the matter. It all hinged on the credibility of Mr Gibbons. Mr Gibbons was the man whom the court was asked to believe when the prosecution made its claim that the importation was not fully authorised.

Authorisation and use, the two key words in the relevant sub-section of the Firearms Act, had already been elucidated and clarified by Mr Finlay and, indeed, the weight of the evidence made it abundantly clear that not only had the importation enjoyed Government backing, but that it was authorised by the competent authority, the then Minister for Defence, Mr Gibbons. The evidence even showed that Mr Gibbons had been briefed to the extent that he knew where the arms were to be stored in the Republic pending a Government decision. That Mr Gibbons should do an about-face somewhere between April 18 and April 20 might be conceded to be his prerogative as Minister for Defence, but, to paraphrase the words of Mr Finlay, why did he not shout stop even at that late stage? I suggested earlier in this book that political in-fighting in Fianna Fáil took such precedence over integrity that State security was put in jeopardy by Government leaders. It is still the only feasible explanation.

On the direction of the judge, the prosecution had been given the last word, but despite this major advantage, Mr Walsh had an impossible task when he stood up to address the jury on the morning of October 22. It was not his fault that his address was full of inconsistencies.

In order to import arms legally without a licence, Mr Walsh said two conditions had to be fulfilled: the importation must be for the use of the Defence Forces of the State and it must be under the authority of the Minister of Defence. He continued:

"Now it is the State's case that neither of these conditions was complied with. But both have to be complied with."

"The fundamental point of the defence is that these were not arms that were to be brought in and broadcast wholesale, but arms to be brought in under army custody against the contingency that they might be released."

Mr Walsh suggested that had the arms arrived on *The City of Dublin* on March 25, they would have been off-loaded, handed over to John Kelly and myself and transported to God knows where. Here, he chose to ignore the evidence of Colonel Hefferon, who knew precisely where they were going and who had stated that he had so told the Minister for Defence. In reference to the bullet-proof vests that had arrived on March 25, Mr Walsh said:

"We don't know where they are now, but we do know that wherever they are they are no more under the control and custody of the national army than they are in the custody and control of the IRA, and if the ammunition had come in, we are entitled to ask ourselves where the ammunition would be now?"

Mr Walsh was scarcely entitled to equate the bullet-proof vests with the arms and ammunition without first explaining that the importation of the vests was not contrary to law and second, without reminding the jury that I had told the court they were directly under my control when I was a serving officer, and that I had also told the court why they passed out of my control. In cross-examination, Mr McKenna had asked me if up to the date of my retirement I had kept the vests under my control as an Irish army officer. This was a disingenuous red herring introduced by the prosecution. It had nothing to do with the case. The intention could only have been to confuse the jury.

Mr Walsh's insinuation that the arms would have gone to God knows where if they had been off-loaded on March 25 was questionable, to put it mildly. Certainly, there was no basis for it in the evidence.

Mr Walsh argued that "the very careful edifice Mr Finlay had built for Captain Kelly had been undermined because neither Colonel Hefferon nor Mr Gibbons had said he had been kept informed of the expenditure out of the bank accounts for the purchase of arms". One very good reason why the financing of the operation was not put forward was because *it was irrelevant to the charge before the court* and this was substantiated by Mr Justice Henchy in his summing up when he told the jury that the manner in which the importation was to be financed should be left out of their considerations in fairness to each of the accused, and in particular in fairness to Mr Haughey. Accountability in that matter might lie elsewhere, he added.

Further, because Northern people, relying on the good faith of the Government here, had financed the operation and because I had no intention of divulging the names of those people, I had instructed my counsel to avoid, as much as possible, any concentration on the money question. It was later to be the subject of an intensive investigation.

I have referred to Mr Walsh's statement that Mr Gibbons could have legalised the whole operation by writing his name on a piece of paper. This was inconsistent with what the evidence showed authorisation to mean; again, it could only have been thrown in to confuse or mislead the jury.

It was not what Mr Walsh said, however, that underlined the paucity of the prosecution case, but what Mr Walsh did not say. Why did he not produce the Directive of February 6, or to be precise, the version of it that existed at Army Headquarters as attested to by Colonel Hefferon, the genuine one that the prosecution could not find in the first trial? Why did he not refer to the five hundred rifles sent to Dundalk? There could be only one reason. The two events taken in association would have shown that the arms importation was fully and duly authorised.

That was the crux of the matter, which Mr Walsh attempted to circumvent. Indeed, in an effort to give the prosecution some credibility he indulged in further inaccuracy on occasion, as when he stated that I had made a direct approach to Mr Haughey to obtain customs clearance. He did not go to his superior officer in Military Intelligence, he did not go to the Minister for Defence, he went direct to the Minister for Finance, said Mr Walsh. This was untrue, as the evidence showed.

At one point, Mr Walsh, speaking of John Kelly, referred to the subterfuges in which he had undoubtedly engaged and at another point he commented upon "this elaborate hoax to bring in arms". In both cases, he was denigrating secrecy, while, within half-an-hour, he was deploring the lack of secrecy, when he referred to my "broadcasting on the Dublin docks information too secret to be whispered in the ear of the Chief-of-Staff of the Army". Accepting the hyperbole, Mr Walsh should have been at least consistent in his presentation. He could condemn either secrecy or the lack of it, but not both in the same, short speech.

Attempting to counter suggestions that the State case had been unfairly presented, particularly by dropping Colonel Hefferon, he made the rather extraordinary comment that, in the case of a material witness the defence would have a real grievance if the witness were sent to South America and were not made available. Having recalled that Colonel Hefferon was on subpoena to the defence, Mr Walsh continued:

"Having said all that, I make this concession, that if the State was wrong in the decisions it took not to put him forward as a reliable witness, the defendants have in that respect, a legitimate grievance. What harm can it have done them, as matters turned out, I don't know, but I'm prepared to concede they have a grievance." It seems Mr Walsh felt that the case was lost. Maybe that explained, if not excused, his presentation.

Towards the end of his address, Mr Walsh admitted that it was possible he had overstated points in favour of the prosecution. As a wag in the Four Courts Hotel bar put it later that evening:

"Sure, if he hadn't overstated it, he might as well have made a defence speech and be done with it."

Mr Justice Henchy opened his charge to the jury at eleven o'clock on the morning of Friday, October 24 . Having outlined the principles and rules of law that applied to the case, he went on:

> "This case ended on a note, on the part of the accused, or some of them, that this has been an unfair and unnecessary prosecution... There were many suggestions, such as 'born in malice', 'brought in spite', 'an ill-conceived monster', 'this prosecution borders on persecution'; it was referred to as a 'smelly, shameful, disgraceful prosecution'; it was referred to as 'a silly pantomime' and there were other uncomplimentary expressions used that I am not going to repeat to you. In order that you shall form your own verdict as to whether this was a justified prosecution or not, it is proper that I should assist you with my view. My opinion, gentlemen, for what it is worth, is that this was a proper prosecution to bring."

Mr Henchy gave three reasons, taken from the statements of Mr Gibbons, Mr Berry and Mr Fagan respectively, which he saw as justifying the bringing of the prosecution by the Attorney General. To me, one of the accused, it seemed that there could have been only one reason to justify bringing the case. That is, had there been concrete evidence to show that Mr Gibbons had not authorised the arms importation. As far as I was concerned there had been no such evidence other than that of Mr Gibbons. But the Government inspired Directive, the movement of the rifles, the association of Mr Gibbons with the importation by the head of the Special Branch, Chief Superintendent Fleming, on May 2 and the inclusion of Mr Gibbons' name on Mr Cosgrave's famous (or infamous) document called this evidence into question.

Still, Mr Henchy was merely expressing an opinion and he made this clear to the jury, assuring its members that it was not binding on them. If they thought that the prosecution should never have been brought, then of course, he told them, they would bring in a verdict of not guilty against each of the accused.

There was one other point in the judge's summing-up which I did not and never will accept. He said that it was not in dispute that at a certain stage I proposed to resign from the army and throw in my lot with my associates in the North. He qualified that assertion later by basing it on the correctness of Mr Gibbons' evidence. Certainly, I sympathised with the minority in the North and my ambition is to see a thirty-two county

Ireland, but I never have seen, and I still don't see, that ambition being achieved without the assistance and co-operation of the Government in the South. In carrying out my liaison intelligence duties, I became aware that that assistance and co-operation were forthcoming and, when I, personally, put the proposal to import arms to Mr Gibbons, not only did he approve, but as I said in evidence, he was enthusiastic. When it was put to me by Colonel Hefferon that I might have to retire from the army to carry out my duties with greater facility, I agreed, but implicit in my acceptance was that my activities had Government backing and Mr Gibbons impressed on me that this was the case.

Mr Henchy referred to the part of John Kelly's statement where he said that until he was arrested, everything that happened led him to believe that what was being done had the full knowledge and consent of the Minister for Defence and the Government.

That in itself was not a defence, Mr Henchy explained. The full knowledge and approval of all the Government Ministers, he said, could not make a matter legal if the Statute said it was illegal. He went on to say that Acts of Parliament were binding on everybody from the Government down, and the law, whether they agreed with it or not, could only be changed by an Act of Parliament.

In referring to me, he said that I had admitted that I did not know that arms could not be brought in except with a licence or with the authority of the Minister for Defence and that I considered that, if the Government agreed, it was all right. He might also have added that I had repeatedly claimed that I had been acting with the authority of the Minister for Defence.

That may have been an explanation for the conduct of John Kelly and Captain Kelly, the judge conceded. They may have been given reason to believe, by certain Government Ministers, that what they were doing was all right, but he had to direct the jury that that was not the law. If that happened, he said, and if they were in agreement to breach the Section of the Act, that amounted to guilt. At this point, the judge should have pointed out to the jury that both John Kelly and I had claimed we were operating with the agreement of Mr Gibbons.

Mr Gibbons was the chief witness for the prosecution and Mr Henchy dealt with him in some detail.

"Now, Mr Gibbons was cross-examined for the purpose of showing that his evidence was not worthy of belief," Mr Henchy said.

> "It was pointed out to him, for example, that in Dáil Éireann on May 8 he made a statement to clarify the position and he said that

all he had was suspicion; that nothing concrete had emerged. It has been suggested that that was less than the truth; that it was a half-truth and should be treated as a lie. And Mr Gibbons said, no, as far as he was concerned all he had was suspicion of an intended, or knowledge of an intended importation; that he hoped Captain Kelly would be out of the Army before any consignment would come in from Trieste, and that he was not telling a lie, when he said he had only suspicion. He denied he knew any arms had been purchased in Hamburg… It was suggested to him in effect that he had gone along with this idea of an intended importation of arms and that only when it became clear that the matter had been referred to the Taoiseach he backed out. He was cross-examined about many of the events that I have referred to here and he recounted deputations that he had met and so forth. He was cross-examined about the rifles he sent to Dundalk, about the training given to civilians from the Bogside who were inducted into the FCA at Fort Dunree in Donegal and there trained by the Irish army, and it was suggested to him that the statement he made in the Dáil about this was untrue, half true and, in fact, a lie. And he said, no, it was not, that technically, training was not given to any civilian; that before training was given to people who came from Derry, the nine people or so were all inducted into the FCA and thereby became technically members of the Defence Forces, so that his statement was technically true. And when pressed on the point, he said that this was a statement in Dáil Éireann, thereby implying that statements of this kind, which are not the literal truth, are frequently made in Dáil Éireann."

Mr Henchy, who is one of the most punctiliously correct of judges, had indicted not only Mr Gibbons but also Dáil Éireann.

The jury retired at twenty-eight minutes past three in the afternoon. Immediately, defence counsel were on their feet. They felt that there were several points on which the jury should be redirected and with good reason. To the background of a hum of excitement from the lobby of the court, counsel made their various submissions. The jury was recalled. The judge redirected them, but the foreman was on his feet. He wanted to clarify one point. It was difficult to get his exact words in the shuffling, heaving, overcrowded courtroom, but the sense was clear enough. What had Colonel Hefferon told about the Directive and surplus arms?

Mr Finlay shuffled through his papers. The other counsel shuffled through their papers. Mr Finlay was on his feet and pushed his glasses back on his nose with what seemed to be a habitual jab of his forefinger.

There was some cross-talk with the judge, but it was certainly conveyed to the jury that one of the matters arising from the Directive was the provision of surplus arms which might, in certain events, have to be made available to people in Northern Ireland and that this was one of the things which Colonel Hefferon had discussed with me.

The jury seemed to have got to the heart of the matter and by their very pertinent question suggested that they were basing their deliberations on the crucial issue of whether or not the operation had been authorised by the Minister for Defence and, incidentally, by the Government. They finally retired at ten minutes to five o'clock.

Someone suggested that the prisoners might leave the courtroom and Judge Henchy graciously remarked that there were no prisoners as such in his court. Mrs Moynihan, my solicitor, Peter Sutherland and I, found ourselves downstairs in the small overcrowded bar of the Four Courts. We were happy. That the jury had posed such a pertinent question was indicative, but... the vagaries of juries were discussed, but people were shaking hands, offering congratulations. Were they premature? If the jury came out quickly, it was a sure sign of a "not-guilty" verdict, someone said. They won't be out for an hour at least, someone added, didn't you see their tea going in? Tea or not, there was a bustle on the stairs and before I knew what was happening I was being ushered back to the courtroom.

The jury had returned to court within the hour and I had to squeeze through a mass of people, all well-wishers it seemed, to get back to my seat.

Mr Peadar O'Reilly, the clerk of the court, asked the jury:

"Gentlemen, have you agreed on a verdict?"

"Yes, we have," the foreman replied and passed across a sheet of paper.

Someone's hand descended on my head in a heavy, if friendly pat, before, in a hushed silence, Mr O'Reilly made his formal announcement:

"Mr Albert Luykx – Not Guilty."

"Mr John Kelly – Not Guilty."

"Captain James Kelly – Not Guilty."

"Mr Charles Haughey – Not Guilty."

Immediately the court erupted into a wild scene of cheering and shaking hands. People jumped for joy and I pushed through the exuberant crowd to arrive on the street, battered and in disarray. John Kelly was carried out shoulder-high and the crowd burst into wild, uninhibited song. There were television cameras everywhere and I answered the quickly thrown questions as best I could. I put my arm around my wife and we walked quietly away.

The crowd caught up with us and an evening of celebration had begun. Old friends; new friends; people I had not seen for twenty years and people who knew my father; newspapermen, friendly and understanding, as always; photographs, handshaking and more handshaking; drinks and autographs; the verdict was not guilty and the night was ours.

CHAPTER 23

When the trial verdict was announced, Mr Lynch was in New York, where he had addressed the Twenty Fifth Anniversary Commemorative Session of the United Nations on the general theme of "peace, justice and progress". On Saturday morning, the day after the trial ended, he called a press conference of the Irish correspondents at the United Nations. He did not issue a formal statement, but in replies to pressmen, he gave his opinion on various aspects of the trial.

The Taoiseach made it clear to the assembled newsmen that, despite the fact that those accused at the Arms Trial had been acquitted, be believed there definitely had been an attempt to import arms illegally. He appeared to base his allegation on the difficulty of proving a conspiracy charge but, in fact, the case as it had developed in court revolved around whether the importation was legal or otherwise. The Taoiseach was therefore rejecting the court decision and impugning the integrity of twelve jurymen. To do so, especially on foreign soil, seemed scarcely worthy of the Prime Minister of the country.

Mr Lynch went on:

"Members of the Government know how arms can be imported on behalf of the Army or Gardaí and they know that it can only be by means of a duly-signed certificate."

That was a false statement. Mr O'Grady gave the lie to it in the trial.

"I had no knowledge whatever of any involvement of Mr Gibbons at the time I took action," Mr Lynch said.

"It appears from the evidence that he became aware of this attempt to import arms very late in the day and took steps to have this importation stopped. That came out in the evidence. That was the position."

Perhaps Mr Lynch considered February late in the day, when Mr Gibbons admitted that he knew or at least suspected that I was going to Frankfurt to vet arms under cover of a visit to my sister. Perhaps he considered March very late in the day also, when Mr Gibbons, unequivocally for once, made it clear that he was aware of an intended importation of arms. Further, the Taoiseach's choice of words suggested that Mr Gibbons had taken action to stop the importation when he first became aware of it, but the evidence showed that no steps were taken until April 17 at the earliest, a lapse of some weeks from Mr Gibbons's indefinite March date and a lapse of two months from February. In fact, when the evidence of Colonel Hefferon and Mr Ó Moráin was taken into consideration, Mr Lynch's interpretation of the Gibbons involvement became still more suspect.

In a reference to John Kelly's unsworn statement, in which he claimed that nobody from the Taoiseach down had indicated that arms would not be available, Mr Lynch said that a number of delegations came to him from the North and that the delegation which was referred to as coming to the Dáil on March 3 came to him as well.

"To that deputation and all others," Mr Lynch told his New York audience, "I specifically stated that the Government would not provide arms. There was no equivocation whatever about this. That deputation came to me early that day and afterwards saw a number of Ministers. There would be no need to see other Ministers if I had told them that arms would be provided."

On various occasions since, John Kelly has repeated what he said in his court statement, and in sworn evidence, to which the Taoiseach did not refer, I substantiated what John Kelly said. The facts are and were that Mr Lynch in both February and March had neither unequivocally refused nor unequivocally promised arms and, in the circumstances, the delegates would have been remiss if they did not take the opportunity to press their suit on as many members of the Government as possible. Actually, by making use of such phrases as "my heart is in the right place", Mr Lynch seemed to me to give a very strong impression to the delegations that in extreme circumstances he would give them arms. As one delegate said to me, Mr Lynch had gone as far, or had committed himself as far, as anyone could have expected the Taoiseach of the country to do.

In New York , Mr Lynch went on to say that he had been criticised for the way he had treated the Northerners and that it was said at one press conference in May that he had "thrown them to the wolves". They talked about being thrown to the wolves, Mr Lynch said, because they had got no promise whatsoever from him that arms would be supplied.

When I was arrested on May 1, the Northerners strongly suspected that they were thrown to the wolves, and when, on May 6, Mr Lynch announced in the Dáil that he had information about an alleged attempt to import arms illegally, they were convinced that this was the case. It was only two days later at a press conference called by the Northerners that the expression "thrown to the wolves" was used in relation to the actions of Mr Lynch.

After May 1, any denouncement by Mr Lynch of representatives of the minority in Northern Ireland could in no way be conceived of as an indication that Mr Lynch had not promised arms. On the contrary, because of its timing, which Mr Lynch himself placed in May, the accusation of being thrown to the wolves only emphasised disappointment at broken promises.

It was suggested that Mr Lynch was under severe strain and was not well when he gave his New York press conference. Certainly, his performance did little to enhance his credibility, but neither did a statement he made to the Dáil on May 9:

> "I want to say, since the Minister for Defence will not be intervening again and the Minister for External Affairs has not intervened in this debate, that neither of them gave any indication whatever that our Army was standing at the ready to go into the North of Ireland. I have that categorically from them. I told successive groups that we could not and would not send troops across the border. I said to do so would be an act of war and only this House, not the Government, is entitled to make an act of war. I told successive groups too – and they came, I am sure, in genuine fear and in the conviction that they needed guns – that we could not supply any guns either, because I felt possession of arms on any side would be dangerous."

This was an outrageous statement in its calculated and audacious falsity. Whatever the Minister for Defence or the Minister for External Affairs may or may not have told Mr Lynch, the Army had been instructed to prepare for incursions into Northern Ireland and was told that surplus arms were to be set aside for possible distribution in Northern Ireland, as the uncontested court evidence of Colonel Hefferon indicated. Mr Gibbons issued the Directive on the authority of the Government. Was it possible that he did not give any indication whatever to the Taoiseach that the Army had been instructed to prepare for incursions into Northern Ireland? If he did not, he was surely guilty of a dereliction of duty, which could only have merited his dismissal as a Minister, even on the Taoiseach's own terms.

Also, as has emerged since the trial and, as I have detailed in this book, Mr Lynch himself, realising that the original Directive, put in evidence by Colonel Hefferon, undermined the prosecution case, was party to the preparation of a substitute, fake or forged Directive, even to the extent of monitoring the changed wording. By doing this and destroying the original record, Mr Lynch and the other members of his Cabinet involved, were sailing very close to criminality, if not actually indulging in it.

In New York, Mr Lynch said that Mr Haughey had not been informed of a vital matter, adding: "a government must exist on complete mutual trust and confidence". He said of Mr Gibbons, on the same occasion:

"He did not come to me after I had taken action. I think he is a loyal Minister. He knows his present job very well. He is a successful farmer, is highly intelligent, and now that the trial is out of the way, I think he will be a very effective Minister for Agriculture."

In the Dáil on May 9, Mr Lynch was very specific that the first indication he got of the arms importation was on Monday, April 20. If the Taoiseach's dubious claim of being totally unaware that our Army was standing at the ready to go into the North of Ireland was plausible, this could only mean that Mr Gibbons had issued the Directive of February behind the Taoiseach's back. If Mr Gibbons did not come to the Taoiseach until April 20, was he not, on his own evidence in court alone, at least equally guilty with Mr Haughey of not keeping Mr Lynch informed on a vital matter?

On Monday, October 26, on his return from New York, Mr Lynch was greeted at Dublin airport by the majority of the Fianna Fáil party.

Dermot Mullane of *The Irish Times* described the occasion:

"The members of the Cabinet, with other Deputies, Senators and party supporters, ranged behind the Taoiseach at the airport, roared approval when Mr Lynch asserted: 'Fianna Fáil is not at a cross-roads. There is a by-road on the way, but we are not going to go up it. We are going to go straight on.' At another point, when Mr Lynch was asked if he was going to step down from the leadership, the faithful roared as one man: 'NO'."

He then repeated his earlier allegation that despite our acquittal, unquestionably there had been an attempt to import arms illegally and then announced an investigation into the money that was paid for the arms. He said that the investigation had been hindered by the closure of the banks due to an industrial dispute, and that he had no idea when it would be completed but "it is being pursued and the investigation will be pursued".

The investigation was to culminate in an Inquiry by the Dáil Committee of Public Accounts, which had its first sitting on January 7, 1971. Meanwhile, from the windy sweep of Dublin Airport on October 26 1970, Mr Lynch could look forward with certainty to a successful outcome when the inevitable *Motion of Confidence in Taoiseach and Government* came before Dáil Éireann.

When the confidence motion was debated, Mr Gibbons, as was to be expected after his performance in the Four Courts, was the prime target of the Opposition and it was on November 3, during a speech by Dr Garret FitzGerald of Fine Gael, that he made the extraordinary remark:

"A lie is one thing, perjury is another," to take its place, side by side with his Four Courts classic

"This was a Dáil debate."

As Dr FitzGerald cut closer and closer to the bone, Mr Gibbons found it more and more difficult to contain himself.

FitzGerald: ".... He was given the full detailed knowledge of this affair by Captain Kelly..."
Gibbons: "That is not true."
FitzGerald: "He was told the next port they were to come from. He was not told of the name of the ship apparently, if that is the detail that was missing."
Gibbons: "That is not true and the Deputy has not a scrap of evidence to show that is true."
FitzGerald: "I have read out to this House every word I could find that the Minister said on this subject...You found out what port he was trying to bring them from next, Trieste."
Gibbons: "Yes, and it was wrong."

Mr Gibbons was deliberately misinterpreting Dr FitzGerald. He knew that the arms were destined for Trieste and were only intercepted in Vienna to be flown in by plane, because of the urgency inspired by his movement of the rifles to Dundalk.

FitzGerald: "It was wrong?"
Gibbons: "Yes."
FitzGerald: "Captain Kelly never went to the Port of Dublin?"
Gibbons: "That was the first time."
FitzGerald: "I see. Let us be clear about this. Deputy Gibbons suggested that arms were not attempted to be imported to Dublin port on March 25 and that all the people who gave evidence to that effect, customs officials and so on, were perjuring themselves."
Gibbons: "The Deputy is trying to mislead the House. I suggest he is back on his slander track."
FitzGerald: "I am trying to get at the truth."

This went on for some time and it was a sure sign that his protégé was making heavy weather of it when Mr Colley, Minister for Finance, found it necessary to intervene.

"Gibbons' account," he said, "was rather more accurate than the Deputy's version of it."

FitzGerald: "I read out every word before and I am happy to read it out again."
Colley: "And the Deputy can then give his own version of it again."
Mr Desmond (Labour): "And the Minister never thought of telling the Taoiseach about what was going on."
Gibbons: "I shall deal with that point, too."
Desmond: "Credibility, how are you."
FitzGerald: "I want to get the right papers together again... Let me read rather more fully than I did before the end of the cross-examination here:

> 'Mr Sorahan handed to Mr Gibbons a copy of the Official Report of the Dáil debates and asked him to read it. Having read it, Mr Gibbons said the relevant piece of his speech was that it was suggested in a Radio Éireann interview that any participation by Captain Kelly in an attempt to smuggle arms could only have been made with his (Mr Gibbons) knowledge and consent.'
>
> 'Mr Sorahan asked Mr Gibbons to read the next sentence and Mr Gibbons read: 'I wish emphatically to deny such knowledge and consent.'
>
> *Mr Sorahan:* 'You did have knowledge, did you not? I am not suggesting at the moment that you consented but did you have knowledge from March?'
> *Mr Gibbons:* 'I had vestigial knowledge.'
> *Mr Sorahan:* 'What do you mean by that? Would you use perhaps a more mundane or down-to-earth word than that ?'
> *Mr Gibbons:* 'I had been given to understand previously by Captain Kelly in the most vague and nebulous way that he proposed to leave the Army in order to take part in the assistance of the people in Northern Ireland and I understood that this could very well embrace the importation of arms. But the fact that he recognised that his resignation from the Army would be necessary to do this...'
> *Mr Finlay (for Captain Kelly):* 'The witness is not answering any question that was put to him. He is not giving an account of any conversation...'
> *Mr Sorahan:* 'I agree. He has gone off the rails. Not for the first time.'
> *Mr Sorahan then asked:* 'You had vestigial knowledge, is that right?'
> *Mr Gibbons:* 'Yes.'
> *Mr Sorahan:* 'But you had knowledge *simpliciter*, is that not right?'
> *Mr Gibbons:* 'Yes.'"

Deputy FitzGerald continued:

"What more can anybody say?... Is there one person in this country, Deputy Gibbons included, who would raise any question or shadow of a doubt that he had knowledge? He has admitted in the fullest sense to his knowledge."

Gibbons: " I have not."
FitzGerald: "Do not let us waste time with this man."

Dr FitzGerald still had to listen to Mr Gibbons make a speech, however, in which he went back to the Dáil debate of May 8 and 9, treading once again over well-worn ground. Captain Kelly had merely told him, he said, that his allegiance had shifted from army duties to *the beleaguered people in the Catholic ghettos in Belfast and elsewhere in the North* and, in reference to my trip to vet arms in February, he claimed to have said to the Director of Intelligence:

"Is it not the most reasonable thing in the world for an officer, whom you tell me is an honourable and high-principled man, to make such a visit to his sister?" Directors of Intelligence do not report to Ministers when an officer, no matter how high-principled or honourable, wishes to visit his sister in Frankfurt or San Francisco.

Mr Gibbons went on to explain what he had meant by "vestigial knowledge" in his reply to Mr Sorahan:

> "What I meant by that was that I knew both from Captain Kelly himself and from Colonel Hefferon, who was then Director of Intelligence, that Captain Kelly was up to something in the matter of the importation of arms, but beyond that I knew very little. Now there is a hiatus here. Except for this vital thing, I had a pretty good idea for some months that the Special Branch of the police was on to Captain Kelly and on to this arms conspiracy generally. I had confirmation of this from the then Minister for Justice about that time too; as I have already said, I felt that since this was the case, it relieved me of the distasteful task of acting as policeman..."

This was one of the most crucial statement made by Mr Gibbons either in the Four Courts or in Dáil Éireann, since the arms crisis broke on the country. In the Four Courts, he had intimated that he knew I was under Special Branch surveillance, because of information he had obtained from the then Minister for Justice, Mr Ó Moráin. This was confirmed by Mr Ó Moráin in evidence when he said he recollected obtaining some informa-

Captain Kelly (left) and General M.J. Costello

tion associating me with arms. Mr Ó Moráin also said that at some stage before April 18 he was under the impression that it was an official operation, and went on to say that there seemed to be a grave lack of co-operation between Military Intelligence and the police, and that in the few months before April he had made the suggestion to Mr Gibbons and the Taoiseach that a cabinet sub-committee should be set up for the purpose of co-ordinating matters.

In dealing with Mr Ó Moráin's evidence in the first trial, I have already referred to the probability that the Taoiseach knew of the arms importation before April 20, but when Mr Gibbons indicated in Dáil Éireann that the Special Branch knew for some months, he was in effect confirming Mr Ó Moráin's evidence.

Taking all the evidence into consideration, it is hard to understand how Mr Lynch was unaware of an important aspect of Government contingency plans until April 20. The head of the Special Branch had suggested to me on May 2 that the Taoiseach knew all along, and Mr Gibbons, by his disclosure in Dáil Éireann, seemed to confirm that this was the case. Where did that leave Mr Lynch? Colonel Delaney confirmed that the importation only became unofficial on April 17 when in his statement to the police he said:

"On April 17, 1970, Captain Kelly came under notice as being concerned in an attempt to import arms from the Continent, and a military and Garda investigation into his activities began." If the Special Branch were aware of my activities for some months, why should an investigation only begin on April 17, unless the Special Branch, in common with its political head, Mr O' Moráin, believed I was carrying out an official operation?

Out of the miasma of contradiction it seemed as if at last some hard truth was emerging.

Having exposed his leader in a desperate attempt to cover his tracks, Mr Gibbons went on:

"With regard to the hiatus, between then and April 17... what happened in that period I was not informed about at all, and I so testified in court."

How could he have had such a good idea for some months that the Special Branch were on to me, if he had not a good idea what they were on about? Anyhow, Mr Ó Moráin testified in court that he had discussed the matter with him.

"I will proceed further now with the analysis of this short statement of mine," Mr Gibbons continued, "because I want to assist the House as best I can." He quoted from his evidence:

"I was aware, through the Director of Intelligence, that attempts to smuggle arms were a constant danger and these attempts were kept under surveillance at all times." Mr Gibbons explained:

"It is evident that when I said that, I depended *in toto* on the good faith of the then Director of Intelligence. What has emerged subsequently would naturally change my view on this, but to assert that this particular statement at that particular time is or was in any way misleading is in itself a misleading assertion."

Colonel Hefferon, of course, had contradicted Mr Gibbons's evidence in the Four Courts.

On the following day, Mr Colley rose to speak. Having tried to perpetrate the *canard* that a certificate was necessary under the Firearms Act, he went on to say of Mr Gibbons:

> "If, as alleged in this House, he is untruthful and a perjurer and a man who could not care less about the truth, could he not have made life easy for himself by telling untruths and committing perjury in the court? Is it not clear that most of his trouble has developed because he was so scrupulous in telling the truth? We know him. I know him. I know how scrupulous he is and I know that that is what has been the cause of a lot of the trouble he has suffered. If

he is the liar and perjurer that has been suggested, why on earth would he get himself into that kind of difficulty? It would have been too easy for him to say more or less than he did and avoid all that trouble. It is perfectly obvious that he was not prepared to give a glib explanation but rather to be as accurate as it was humanly possible to be."

In closing the debate, the Taoiseach said that it was an undeniable fact that he had told all the Northern delegations that had come to see him that the Government could not overtly or covertly make arms available. In speaking of Mr Gibbons, he said:

> "I am dealing with the references made here last May to the alleged complicity of Deputy Gibbons, then Minister for Defence, in the arms importation affair. I told the House then that I had no information on this at the time I took action against two other Ministers. I also told the House that I subsequently had enquiries made following which my confidence in him had not changed. Evidence has since been adduced that Deputy Gibbons, on learning of the attempted importation of arms, not only took steps to try to stop it, but refused specifically to sign a certificate that would have facilitated the importation of these arms."

Mr Lynch was perpetuating the certificate *canard* also; another act of typical Lynch duplicity under Dáil privilege.

One man who refused to accept the situation was Mr Kevin Boland who said:

> "Clearly the Minister, who denied any knowledge of or consent to the operation, actually admitted discussing the importation of arms with his junior officer. He described it, of course, as *vestigial knowledge,* and I do not know whether it was vestigial knowledge or not, but he did discuss the importation of arms in which Captain Kelly was personally involved with Colonel Hefferon. The judge when dealing with this later said that:
>
> 'The jury might say that Mr Gibbons should have put his foot down and told Captain Kelly that he must not import arms in any circumstances, that that was a matter for the proper army authorities and that when he (Mr Gibbons) got information about the attempted importation into the port of Dublin and the projected importation

from Vienna, and when he, Mr Gibbons, did not say no in categorical terms, Captain Kelly was entitled to presume that Mr Gibbons was saying yes. That is the view that is open to you. I will say no more about it.'

This is the view which the judge said was open to them, which the jury, having heard all the evidence, clearly decided to take. It was obviously the only reasonable view to take. They could not have taken any other view in view of the oath they had sworn to bring in a just and true verdict. They were ordinary, reasonable, intelligent men and they would know that if this importation of arms was a breach of Captain Kelly's duty as an army officer it was not a minor breach of conduct such as not paying his mess bill, but a major breach, which was just about as serious a breach of conduct or as serious a misdemeanour as any army officer could commit. However, the Minister who admitted being told about it, and that the attempt was to continue, also admitted that he did not even tell his army officer to stop doing it. He did not have him transferred, he did not ask him to resign and he did not do what, if his story was true, was his absolute minimum duty to do, have him dealt with by military law. There is only one possible explanation for it and that is that he knew of this, that he approved of it and that he was part of it.

It was only when to his surprise he discovered that the Taoiseach was not prepared to stand over what was being done in pursuance of a Government decision… it was only then that he did a deal and the deal was to put on the performance that he put on in the High Court.

So the evidence of the Minister for Agriculture and Fisheries in court made the jury's task simple. They naturally decided that the two tried and trusted army officers were honourable men. They decided that the army's estimation of these people was vindicated. They decided that the man who had been serving as a junior officer in the most trusted branch of the army, the Intelligence service, was properly assessed by the army authorities as being fit for that job. They decided that the man who had progressed to the highest rank he could reach in the army, the highest rank that can be reached by anyone in the army except the Chief-of-Staff, Colonel, and had held the position of maximum trust in the army, Director of Intelligence, they decided that the army's assessment of these people was the correct assessment; that it was vindicated. They decided also that, in this business, it was the then Minister for Defence who was the weakling.

So far as I am concerned, then, the decision I have to make seems to be very clear-cut. The Taoiseach and the Minister for Agriculture and Fisheries are one. If there is culpability, the major culpability is that of the Taoiseach. In view of all that has happened and particularly in view of the jury's verdict, there can be no question of my supporting this Motion of Confidence."

Before the motion was put, Kevin Boland's resignation as a member of Dáil Éireann was dramatically announced. In the closing words of his speech, Mr Boland said that he had nothing left to him but his personal honour and "I propose to retain that". He was a lonely figure as he left the Dáil chamber. Conviction had forced him to resign his ministerial office in the previous May. As he walked now into at least temporary political obscurity, his colleagues in the Government party sat apparently unmoved. An honest man had gone. Immediately, Mr Lynch was on his feet to ask if the House would agree to his moving of the writ to fill the vacancy.

The Motion was put and Dáil Éireann reaffirmed its confidence in the Taoiseach and the other members of the Government by seventy-four votes to sixty-seven.

The Irish Times of October 30, 1970 summed up the situation in the last line of its editorial:

"They are hanging together – Fianna Fáil is a great organisation. So is the Mafia."

The end of the month was near and Sheila and I looked forward to receiving my gratuity and accumulated pension, now that I was acquitted. November 1 passed and no money arrived. Enquiries to the Department of Defence got the usual reply. The Government would not permit payment. Michael Connolly's loan was running out fast and, anyhow, as a loan, I would like to pay it back as soon as possible; he had a young family also. Sheila took matters into her own hands. She rang Dick Walsh of *The Irish Times* , the man who had befriended us in May. He arranged to get her into Dáil Éireann and meet her there. He felt that if he could contact Mr Hillery, Minister for Foreign Affairs, a fellow-Clareman, with whom he was on friendly terms, something might be done about the money.

Dick brought Sheila to the Visitors' Bar in Leinster House, where she accepted a drink to fortify her for the forthcoming interview. In fact, she

Department of Defence letter refusing payment of entitlements.

OIFIG AN AIRE COSANTA

BAILE ÁTHA CLIATH, 8.

12.X.70

37 SP 5654

A Chara

With reference to your recent enquiry about the question of your husband's entitlement to retired pay and arrears of pay, An tAire Cosanta desires me to say that a decision on these matters has not yet been taken.

Mise le meas

RÚNAÍ AIRE

Mrs. J.J. Kelly,
98 Wainsfort Road,
Terenure,
Dublin 6.

was on her second when Mr Hillery appeared and, being an abstemious social drinker, she was more than ready for the fray. She started off quietly enough, but in the end, she was very scathing about the injustice the Government had perpetrated on me, on her, and, in particular, on her family.

"I'll fix that straight away," Mr Hillery told her and left.

A short while later, he put his head around the door of the bar and called over to Sheila: "Tá se deanta."*

A day or two later, a cheque for the full amount due, arrived in the post. As a family, we much appreciated Mr Hillery's kindness and promptness in dealing with the matter.

* *Irish for "It is done".*

CHAPTER 24

If a Government buys arms, it pays for them. This is the usual practice. It was the situation in Ireland in 1970. Arms were bought under Government authority for use in Northern Ireland if the situation demanded. They had to be paid for and who else to pay for them but the Government which organised the operation? And that is the way it was, with the arms that were the subject of the arms trials. James Gibbons, Minister for Defence, was the statutory authority on behalf of the Government for the importation and Charles Haughey, Minister for Finance, supplied the necessary funds.

The initial authority for the expenditure of the monies was the Government decision of August 16, 1969, which decreed that "a sum of money – the amount and the channel of the disbursement of which would be determined by the Minister for Finance – should he make available from the Exchequer to provide for the victims of the current unrest in the Six Counties."

By any criterion, this gave major latitude to Mr Haughey, as to how the money should be used and, in the context of Northern Ireland at the time, it is inconceivable that the Government did not consider the possibility of providing arms for defensive purposes. Most reasonable people could envisage the possibility of providing arms for protection, for example, in a case of the razing of Belfast's Bombay Street. The possibility of similar and, indeed, worse atrocities reoccurring could not be ignored. Consequently, it was incumbent on the Government to formulate contingency plans to deal with the situation. It did exactly that, finally formalising such plans in its Directive to the Army on February 6, 1970.

It was over seven months after the August Government decision to authorise money for relief in the North that the matter was brought before Dáil Éireann for sanction. On March 18, 1970, the necessary retrospective sanction for money which was nearly all spent at the time was granted unanimously by Dáil Éireann. In fact, it looked very much as if the parliamentarians, by voting the money through on the nod, without discussion or question, were quite happy to close the stable door after the horse had bolted.

Nevertheless, this did not deter the resourceful Mr Lynch, who, when he failed to secure the result he desired in the arms trials, tried a ploy designed to show that the money used to pay for the arms was not properly authorised.

At his behest, the following resolution was passed by Dáil Éireann on December 1, 1970:

> "That the Committee of Public Accounts should examine specially the expenditure of the Grant-in-Aid of Northern Ireland Relief issued from Subhead J, Vote 16(Miscellaneous Expenses) for 1969/70 and any monies transferred by the Irish Red Cross Society to a bank account into which monies from the Vote were, or may have been lodged and shall furnish a separate report on this expenditure as soon as possible."

Two days later, twelve parliamentarians were nominated to the Committee of Inquiry. They were Deputies Sylvester Barrett, Ben Briscoe, Hugh Gibbons, Ray McSharry, Thomas Nolan and James Tunney of Fianna Fáil; Richard Burke, Edward Collins and Garret Fitzgerald of Fine Gael; and Justin Keating and Sean Tracey of Labour. Deputy Patrick Hogan of Fine Gael was appointed Chairman.

This august collection of individuals set to work with a will, but, perhaps inevitably, the Inquiry degenerated into a rehash of the arms trials, with each member of the Committee having his own axe to grind, which meant that the arms trial evidence was reground, with varying degrees of intensity on at least twelve occasions. Nevertheless, after a year or so, with Deputy Keating substituted by Deputy Frank Cluskey and Deputy Briscoe by Deputy Joe Dowling, a Final Report was produced.

One of the principal witnesses to present himself before the Committee of Inquiry was Mr Gibbons. Something of a sensation was caused, when the Chairman referred to a letter Mr Gibbons had sent to the Committee, stating that I had told him that the money for the arms came from the Fund for the Relief of Distress.

Chairman: "...You discovered that the money for the operation came from the Fund for the Relief of Distress in Northern Ireland?"
Gibbons: "Yes, that is what I understood Captain Kelly to say. I do not purport to quote him verbatim, but that is what I understood him to say."
Chairman (referring to Dáil Éireann debate): "The Taoiseach, in replying to the source of the money for the purchase of arms, stated: 'I do not think the House could expect nor could I give any further information about the disposal of Secret Service Funds. However, I want to add that I made specific inquiries as to whether any monies could have been devoted or could have been paid out of Exchequer funds or out of any public funds in respect of a consignment of arms of the size we have been dealing with and I am assured that there was not or could not have been.'

That was the 14th May, yet in the document you sent you say you were aware of this?"
Gibbons: "I had been told by Captain Kelly."
Chairman: "You had been told by Captain Kelly that this fund was the source of the money?"
Gibbons: "That is right."
Chairman: "Had you informed the Taoiseach at that stage?"
Gibbons: "The Taoiseach had not asked me that question, as far as I can recall."

This was vintage Gibbons. He might be a Minister in Government, but he was not going to accept any responsibility for not informing the Taoiseach of a vital matter that would have prevented Mr Lynch misleading the Dáil. The Taoiseach had to ask him first. Otherwise, the Taoiseach was left in the dark. At best it was an unusual way to run a government, which was constitutionally bound to operate on the principle of collective responsibility. Basically, Mr Gibbons was refusing to answer a very direct and simple question by the Committee Chairman: did he or did he not tell the Taoiseach of his knowledge of the money?

Chairman: "When it was being discussed in the Dáil and the Taoiseach said that he could not find out where the money came from and that he was satisfied that it did not come from public funds did you not, at that stage, inform the Taoiseach?"
Gibbons: "The communication between me as a member of the Government and the Taoiseach is a matter of privilege… "

Again, typical Gibbons evasiveness, but was there a slight but subtle shift there; a suggestion, maybe, that he might have told the Taoiseach?

Later, Deputy Keating took up the issue.

Keating: "Did he (Captain Kelly) indicate this to you clearly – that it was money voted by the Dáil for the relief of distress?"
Mr Gibbons confirmed that this was the case.
Keating: "Did you tell the Taoiseach in Dáil Éireann after the 14th May what Captain Kelly had told you?"
Gibbons: "I had several conversations with the Taoiseach. I am certain if the Taoiseach denied any knowledge of the expenditure of the money that Captain Kelly had said was expended – I had not told him. In other words, I will accept without reservation what the Taoiseach said as being true as far as he knew it."

Keating: "Did it occur to you in the months between the May debate and the opening of the trial that you possessed information which was contrary to the statements of the Taoiseach and contrary to the opinion of all those who were concerned to find the true solution?"
Gibbons: "No, because so many statements had been made all through the summer, let us say from May onwards, that this had receded in my mind. I am being subjected to such a tremendous battering that it had receded in my mind. When I was asked by the Committee to say all I knew about this Fund I did it immediately. If I had any intention of concealment I would have continued to conceal it."

He did not continue to conceal it for the very good reason, that it was substantial and significant evidence linking the money to the Department of Finance. Consequently, it suited the Government to introduce what I had told Mr Gibbons about the money at the Inquiry. Mr Gibbons was wrong, however, about the date on which he and I discussed the money. It was several weeks earlier. And it still was not clear whether he had informed the Taoiseach. He accepted what the Taoiseach said as being true as far as the Taoiseach knew it, but it was the truth as he knew it with which the Committee was concerned.

Keating: "Are you telling us now that until the Committee's request you had no thought of the significance in the whole story of what Captain Kelly told you on April 30?"
Gibbons: "No, nor am I telling you that I am certain that I have not disclosed it to the authorities. What I am telling you is that I cannot recall when I did it, if I did it at all."

Who or what were the authorities Gibbons might have told? How close were they to the Taoiseach or did the term embrace the Taoiseach? Remember, both Lynch and he colluded in concealing the Bailieboro meeting and its significance from the court at the arms trials: Gibbons telling the lie and Lynch condoning it. Both also colluded in producing the substitute, forged Directive at the second arms trial. Had they colluded in concealing the information on the money to facilitate Mr Lynch's misleading of the Dáil on the basis of a statement submitted to him on May 14, 1970 by Mr CH Murray, Secretary of the Department of Finance, as a possible answer to a query whether public funds had been used for the purchase of arms:

"I am perfectly satisfied as a result of inquiries which I have made that every penny of State funds has been spent for the purpose for which it was voted by the Dáil."

This statement could be interpreted as covering the purchase of arms as legitimate expenditure sanctioned by the Dáil. When cognisance is taken of the fact that officials of the Department of Finance and its Minister placed the money at the disposal of the Northern Defence Committees to use as they saw fit, it is difficult to arrive at any other interpretation in the circumstances of the time.

Mr Lynch chose to read it otherwise, however, telling Dáil Éireann on May 14:

> "... I made specific inquiries as to whether any monies could have been voted or could have been paid out of Exchequer funds or out of any public funds in respect of a consignment of arms of the size we have been dealing with and I am assured that there was not nor could not have been."

The Inquiry acknowledged that "the actual words used by the Taoiseach to the Dáil were somewhat different from those suggested by Mr Murray". It did not feel, however, that the terms of the assurance suggested to the Taoiseach by Mr Murray were justified, but accepted without quibble the interpretation put on them by the Taoiseach, stating that Mr Lynch had acted in good faith. On Mr Gibbons' failure to inform the Taoiseach of his knowledge of where the money came from, it contented itself with stating that if Mr Lynch had been briefed by Gibbons, "the Taoiseach would not have been put into the position of unintentionally giving wrong information on this matter to the Dáil on May 14, 1970."

Peter Sutherland,* who represented me before the Inquiry at a scheduled cross-examination of Mr Gibbons, was more forthright on the integrity and honesty of Mr Gibbons, not only on his knowledge of the money issue, but on his evidence in general. Mr Gibbons refused to turn up for cross-examination to explain his defamation of me before the Inquiry. Nevertheless, Mr Sutherland went ahead. In his introductory comment, he referred to a Supreme Court judgement:

> "With reference to this Committee that judgement stated among other things that 'a person whose conduct is impugned must be afforded reasonable means of defending himself'. One of such reasonable means is the right of cross-examination... The Constitution of the State guarantees that the State, as far as practicable, will, by

* *Later Attorney General, European Commissioner, Director General, GATT and WTO, non-executive Chairman, BT, Chairman and Managing Director, Goldman Sachs Int.*

> its laws, vindicate the citizen's good name... But Mr Gibbons, by his non-appearance, has effectively precluded my client from exercising these rights. Not alone has he defied the Constitution, but the Minister has contemptuously dismissed this Committee which was set up by the parliament of which he is a member."

In comparing Mr Gibbons evidence to the Committee to that which he gave at the arms trials, Mr Sutherland made it obvious that Gibbons committed wholesale perjury at one place or the other. Having given examples of this contradictory evidence in respect of me, Mr Sutherland, in the restrained manner of the legal profession, asked how can Mr Gibbons equate his evidence at the arms trials with "his evidence to this Committee on oath? I submit that he either misled this Committee or he misled the Court."

This analysis of the quality of Gibbons' evidence went unchallenged by any member of the Committee of Inquiry, quite simply because the Sutherland presentation, based on undeniable and ascertainable statements made on oath by Mr Gibbons himself before either the Court or the Inquiry, was irrefutable.

In relation to the source of the arms money, Mr Sutherland referred to Mr Gibbons evidence to the Committee that I had told him about it on April 30. Mr Sutherland continued:

> "The reality is that the money and its source were discussed by Mr Gibbons with Captain Kelly in March, 1970. Mr Gibbons on that occasion leant back in his chair and laughed, making some comment about Charlie's (Mr Haughey's) money... The reason that Mr Gibbons misled this Committee was that in his own interests it was essential for him to show that his knowledge was after the event."

It was not the only time, Mr Gibbons switched the date of events before the Committee. On April 21, 1971, he testified that he had been informed by Mr Peter Kearney, Permanent Secretary of the Department of Defence, almost a year before, on April 17, 1970, of my presence abroad, stating:

> "The first knowledge that I had of his presence abroad was when Mr Kearney came in with hurriedly jotted notes that he had obviously taken down as he listened to a telephone call about a man representing himself as Commandant Kelly of the Irish Army making Irish Army purchases and various other things as well."

All that was wrong with this evidence was that it did not happen on April 17. It happened in April 1 and could only have happened on that day. That was the day I travelled to Antwerp, with Albert Luykx as interpreter when he was stopped by immigration. I sat on a bench outside the office where he and the immigration officer had a conversation. I had only a limited knowledge of French, but listening through the unclosed door, I realised that the name, Commandant Jim Kelly, was figuring prominently, with an odd glance thrown in my direction by both parties through the large, single-paned window. Albert may have been gilding the lily by upping my rank, although I had an impression, from my time with United Nations, that it was common Belgian practice to designate senior Captains as Commandants. It was a matter of little import, however, and Albert and I joked about it as we sat in the airport lounge, while officialdom made the inevitable phone calls.

As was to be expected, the Department of Defence was contacted to verify my identity and the purpose of my visit to continental Europe. Mr Kearney, quite correctly, brought the strange, and, to him, probably outlandish query to the attention of his Minister with all due haste. The end result was that the Belgian authorities rescinded the ban on Albert Luykx entering the country to permit him accompany me on my stated business of concluding an arms purchase. This could only have happened because Mr Gibbons had authenticated my visit by confirming that I was abroad on official business related to such a purchase..

Obviously, when Mr Gibbons granted clearance to me as working on behalf of the Government on April I, he was, as I accepted at the time, endorsing the Government authorisation of the arms operation. It was only afterwards, by falsely switching the date of the incident forward, that he attempted to use it to give some colour and a degree of verisimilitude to his attempt to portray me as an unreliable person to the Committee of Public Accounts. Also, as Mr Sutherland put it in the case of the money, "the reason that Mr Gibbons misled the Committee was that in his own interests it was essential for him to show that his knowledge was after the event." If Mr Gibbons had indicated to the Committee that he had authorised my presence on the Continent to purchase arms on April 1, weeks before the Taoiseach admitted to any knowledge of the affair, it would have been another nail in the coffin of Mr Lynch's credibility.

At one point during his evidence to the Committee, Mr Gibbons, in replying to Deputy Fitzgerald, stated:

"I did not know anything about Captain Kelly until after Christmas."

Fitzgerald: "All we are discussing for the last five minutes arises because you said you had reason to suspect Kelly"
Gibbons: "My knowledge of Captain Kelly's existence did not take real shape until 1970."

Mr Gibbons also told Deputy Fitzgerald that he had given his approval to a meeting Colonel Hefferon had with Mr Haughey – "I think it was round October, 1969."

In referring to this meeting, Colonel Hefferon told the Committee:

> "Deputy Gibbons' recollection as to the date is slightly at fault, not very much, just slightly. The date is, according to a diary I kept at the time, September 24, and as the Minister has indicated I received his sanction and approval beforehand. My record also indicates that I reported back to Deputy Gibbons that very evening after returning, and gave him a verbal report of the meeting.
>
> It will be recalled that this meeting was the one to which Deputy Haughey had asked that I bring Captain Kelly along with me and at which Captain Kelly requested and received sanction for financial support for the forthcoming meeting held on the week-end 4th/5th October. You have the evidence of the lead-up to this meeting in Bailieboro in some detail already, so I do not propose to go any further into it. The whole point that emerges from it is that the meeting with Deputy Haughey, approved of by Deputy Gibbons, almost entirely centred around Captain Kelly's briefing of Deputy Haughey, and his recommendations for getting a meeting of representatives of the Northern Defence Committee organised as soon as possible.
>
> I saw Deputy Gibbons again, according to my record, some time around 5.30 pm, and put him completely in the picture. To suggest that I would give him an account of the proceedings and omit to mention Captain Kelly by name in reporting to my own Minister on such an important meeting is absolutely irresponsible.
>
> In conjunction with the timing of this meeting of September 25, I would remind the Committee that the very weekend following, the Derrymen assembled at Fort Dunree for the course... So, on September 25, the Minister did hear of Captain Kelly and was aware of the fact that the Minister for Finance had sent for him and what was discussed there... Though in my own mind quite certain that Captain Kelly, as well as his role, was known to Deputy Gibbons as far back as mid-August, I would need to have access to

the Intelligence archives to prove this. I am confident I could do so."

This evidence, verified by contemporaneous notes in the Colonel's diary, conclusively established that Mr Gibbons was fully briefed about me and my role from September and from mid-August as verifiable from Intelligence records. Consequently, Mr Gibbons was misleading the Inquiry, when he stated that I only took real shape for him in January, suggesting that I was "a very nebulous figure" skulking in the background until then. Much more crucially, however, the Colonel established that through him, Mr Gibbons had been party to the planning of the Bailieboro meeting and had been briefed on the fact that it was funded by the Minister for Finance, Mr Haughey. Thus, both Ministers charged by the Government with handling the Northern situation, had co-operated in organising the meeting, which has been described "as the genesis of the arms importation".

This new evidence about Bailieboro was of utmost significance because it showed that Mr Gibbons was briefed not only on the meeting after it took place, but was briefed on it prior to the event. Quite simply, he, in conjunction with Mr Haughey, was party to the seminal meeting that sparked the aborted arms importation. It was important corroborative evidence in that it further established that Mr Gibbons had given false evidence when he denied knowledge of the Bailieboro meeting.

This vital evidence emerged when Colonel Hefferon sought to cross-examine Mr Gibbons on the grounds that the Minister had defamed him when giving evidence to the Committee. Mr Gibbons not only refused to present himself for cross-examination, but saw fit to pre-empt whatever presentation the Colonel might make by mounting a vicious and venomous attack on him under parliamentary privilege. In early November 1971, just weeks before the proposed cross-examination, he told Dáil Éireann of "the perfidy" of the former Director of Intelligence, classing him as a man "unworthy to hold his high position in the army".

He concluded his tirade against Colonel Hefferon by stating that his actions "supplied to me the missing pieces of this horrible jigsaw puzzle and, in my eyes, he stands in line with Iago, the false friend of Othello in Shakespeare's tragedy".

He seemed to base this cowardly attack on the false grounds that the Colonel had joined Kevin Boland's political party, Aontacht Éireann, which was formed in 1971 to promote the Republican ideal of a United Ireland by democratic means. It was a perfectly respectable political organisation, registered like other political parties in the State such as

Fianna Fáil, Fine Gael and Labour. Its aim was to achieve the National ideal of a United Ireland by constitutional and peaceful means and, as such, opposed to violence as the means of doing so. I was the vice-President of this party, but Colonel Hefferon was not even a member, contrary to what Mr Gibbons stated. He was merely a guest at the inaugural meeting of the party and was invited on to the platform, where he was acclaimed by the large crowd present. The reason for the acclamation was the recognition that, as a prosecution witness in the arms trials, he stood by the truth, exposing Mr Gibbons as a perjurer and a knave. Hence, Gibbons left no stone unturned in his attempts to calumniate him. He could not do so in public, because he would be held to account for his defamatory scurrility. Instead, he wrapped himself in the protective cloak of parliamentary privilege to spit his bile and venom with impunity.

Loyalty and honour were two traits, which Michael Hefferon valued highly: loyalty to the Army, the State and his friends; honour based on personal integrity, with the easy condemnatory lie foreign to his nature. All who knew him during his Army career could testify to that. It was these personal characteristics of loyalty and honour that led him to testify with straightforward honesty as a prosecution witness in the court and as a witness before the Committee of Inquiry, despite establishment pressure to do otherwise. It was sad and, indeed, nauseating, that his erstwhile political leader, should spew forth his vile vilification of him in a slimy burst of vitriolic vituperation, just because he was an honest man.

At the Committee of Inquiry, Colonel Hefferon merely reminded the members that Mr Gibbons "very recently… took occasion to launch a bitter attack on me when under parliamentary privilege. I would have welcomed very much a chance to get him here and to jog his memory, which he has admitted before the court at times as being defective, and to jog it on many matters which are at issue between us."

Essentially, the Colonel's evidence not only confirmed, but reinforced the Sutherland contention that Mr Gibbons had either misled the Inquiry or the court on several vital matters, backing his accusation by reference to court and Inquiry records. He pointed out that Mr Gibbons had told the Inquiry that he did not know I was going to vet arms when I made my first trip to the Continent in February 1970 and that the expression "cover story", in connection with it, was "absolutely new" to him, whereas, the following exchange took place in the High Court between counsel and Mr Gibbons:

Counsel: "Did the Director of Intelligence also tell you that his (Captain Kelly's) real reason was to go and deal with this question of arms?"

Gibbons: "He suggested this in a rather critical way. He said: 'I have an idea his real purpose may be to vet' – that is the expression he used – 'to vet arms'."
Counsel: "To vet arms?"
Gibbons: "Yes."
Counsel: "So that the Director of Intelligence told you and I suggest that this would have been sometime about the middle of February…"
Gibbons: "Probably."
Counsel: "… that Captain Kelly he believed was going to vet arms and that he was giving as cover or ostensible reason for that, the vacation to his sister – a trip to his sister in Frankfurt?"
Gibbons: "Yes."

If Mr Gibbons, was telling the truth in the High Court, he was obviously misleading the Committee of Inquiry.

On the question of my plans for future action in relation to the arms importation after March 1970, Mr Gibbons in evidence to the Inquiry, stated:

"Captain Kelly told me towards the end of March of an abortive attempt that had been made to import guns through the port of Dublin, but he was talking about a thing that had already occurred. He told me nothing of his intentions in the future."

Colonel Hefferon pointed out that in the High Court my counsel, Mr Finlay, had queried Mr Gibbons:

"Did Captain Kelly also inform you on that occasion that the importation of the arms was being arranged in some other way?"

Gibbons: "Yes. I said to him at the time and I hoped as well that this would be true, but I said something like this: 'I suppose that consignment is gone west anyway' and he said: 'No, it is not. It will be possible to retrieve it in one way or another'."
Finlay: "Am I right in understanding he made it clear to you that he was going on assisting in the attempted importation?"
Gibbons: "That was clear at that stage, yes."

The Colonel pointed out other examples of where Mr Gibbons had given contradictory evidence in the High Court and to the Inquiry, giving false testimony under oath in either one place or the other. Describing Mr Gibbons statements about me to the Inquiry as "all bunkum", he declared that "Mr Gibbons is telling one story to the court and another, the direct opposite, to the Committee of Inquiry."

CHAPTER 25

On August 24, 1971, Mr Haughey, the former Minister for Finance, appeared before the Committee.

Chairman: "It has been suggested that the Fund was manipulated...?"
Haughey: "... that some of the monies were taken out of this Fund to purchase arms?"
Chairman: "Yes. When did you first hear about that?"
Haughey: "In the High Court."
Deputy Keating:"... Can I take it, in your thinking as the Minister at the time charged with the disbursement, that the use of the monies for the provision of arms, even if that were for defensive purposes, was totally excluded from the terms of that decision?"
Haughey: "Absolutely".

This was *absolutely* untrue, as I indicated during the arms trials and as confirmed by Kevin Boland later. In fact, Mr Haughey was aware that arms were involved from the very beginning. As early as September 1969, he met a delegation from Belfast to whom he promised money for the relief of distress, including the purchase of guns. When the Belfast Fund for the Relief of Distress was formed in conjunction with the Defence Committees, I, as a person closely concerned with its formation and as one who attended the first meeting between Mr Haughey and its representatives, can state it was clearly understood by all, including Mr Haughey, that, at the discretion of the Defence Committees, a major portion of the money was intended for the purchase of arms.

Mr Haughey was questioned by Chairman Hogan on the financing of the Bailieboro meeting:

"You gave £500 to Captain Kelly for the Bailieboro meeting, or at least you gave it to Colonel Hefferon and he passed it on?"

Haughey: "I did not give it to anybody; I authorised the payment of it to Colonel Hefferon, yes."
Chairman: "This money was provided, we understand, to organise what they now call the Bailieboro meeting?"
Haughey: "No, that is not my recollection. My recollection is that the Director of Intelligence sought this money for use for refugee purposes, to assist refugees."

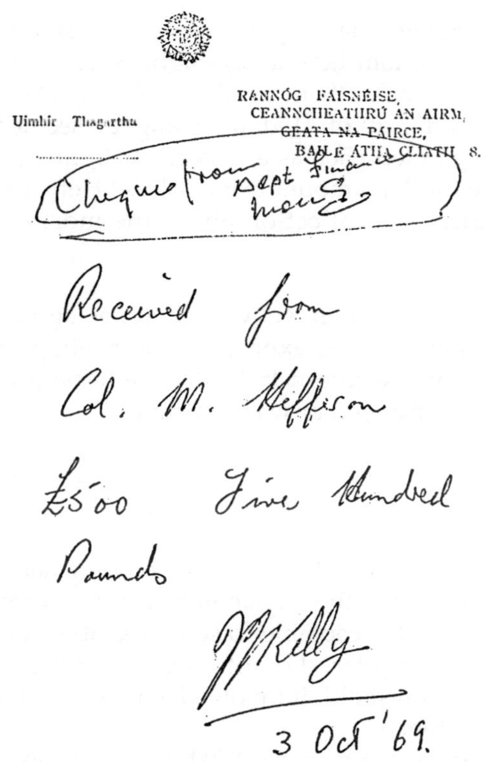

Uimhir Thagartha ....

RANNÓG FAISNÉISE,
CEANNCHEATHRÚ AN AIRM,
GEATA NA PÁIRCE,
BAILE ÁTHA CLIATH 8.

Cheque from Dept Finance money

Received from

Col. M. Hefferon

£500 Five Hundred

Pounds

J Kelly

3 Oct '69.

Author's receipt for £500

Chairman: "There was a second £500 which I thought was for the refugee purpose. I thought this was for the Bailieboro meeting?"
Haughey: "No, that is not my recollection, Mr Chairman. I can only tell you, as honestly as I can, what I remember about this affair and I understood that the Director of Intelligence sought this money for expenditure in refugee circumstances, to help alleviate the situation of refugees."
Chairman: "Yes. Were you aware that the money was passed on to Captain Kelly in its entirety?"
Haughey: "No, I did not know that. I did not know that."

There was some suggestion that Mr Haughey's recollection on the matter was at fault because he had allotted a second £500 to Colonel Hefferon for refugees and got mixed up between the two. This was possible, but Colonel Hefferon was very positive that £500 was approved for Bailieboro and subsequent meetings; that the cheque was issued to him by the Department of Finance; and that it was handed over to me prior to the Bailieboro meeting. My evidence to the Committee substantiated this.

At the meeting with Mr Haughey, I had explained that the purpose of the Bailieboro meeting was to ascertain how arms might be used in the North, if the Government was to make them available. The question of cost came up and I mentioned a figure of £150. Mr Haughey seemed to think this was too little and suggested £500 as a reasonable figure. Some days afterwards, I got a cheque for that amount from Colonel Hefferon.

Whatever about Mr Haughey's recollection about the money, the Committee's Final Report stated:

> "The sum of £500 was given to Captain Kelly to cover, as agreed with the then Minister for Finance, the expenses of a meeting or meetings, at which people from Northern Ireland were to be present, which Captain Kelly had arranged or was to arrange."

"The Committee has failed to secure a satisfactory account of the expenditure of this sum from Captain Kelly," the report added.

This, despite the fact that I explained how I spent it, although, when giving evidence, I got the impression that the explanation for the expenditure of a major portion of it was not acceptable to some members of the Committee. One aspect of it, in particular, did not seem to impinge; did not seem to cross their credibility threshold. It involved a man, whom one can only describe as a political refugee.

One weekend, not long after I was given the £500, I got a phone-call from a political figure in Belfast, requesting that I meet him at the Border that evening as a matter of urgency. I did so and, to my surprise, I was introduced to a former British soldier, who, because of his "heroic action" in defending his friends and neighbours against an onslaught from the Protestant Shankill Road area, was not only a target for Loyalists, but the RUC were looking for him as well. The politician gave me £100 to sustain the "refugee" until he got to Canada, where, it seemed he had a girlfriend, whom he was anxious to join.

I brought him back to Dublin, where I secured accommodation for him and set about obtaining a visa, which was necessary to enter Canada at the time. The Government, at my request, did not hesitate to contact the Canadian Embassy and, within a week, I was in possession of the vital travel document. The fare to Canada was about £90, the "digs" cost something similar and I subsidised my friend's eight or nine day stay to the tune of £100, which he needed, having arrived more or less in the clothes "he stood up in". There was some other minor expenditure on incidentals. This accounted for about £200, when the Belfastman's £100 was taken in to consideration.

98 Rathfarnham Rd
Terenure
Dublin 6.
12. 1. 71

Dear Mr. Murray,

Yours of Jan 8 refers.

The £500 received by me in October was received for Intelligence duties – expenses etc and was used for this purpose.

Expenses outstanding prior to October	£23. 0. 0.
Oct to April – Meetings with groups, delegations, individuals etc, two and three times per week	£250. 0. 0.
Telephone – October to June (verified)	£62. 12. 9
Bailieboro Meeting	£35. 0. 0.
(x) Refugee / Contact – Accommodation 10 wks, Air Fare	£200. 0. 0
Est. mileage outstanding Jan to May '70	£150. 0. 0.
	£720. 12. 9.

(x) Reimbursed £100

Est. Total outstanding £120. 12. 9.

Re recovery from Dixon and O'Brien a/cs no recovery as yet.

James J. Kelly Capt.

Letter to Sec., Department of Finance outlining expenditure of £500.

I estimated that meetings with groups, delegations and individuals cost me £250 from October to May and I also had a verifiable telephone bill from October to May for £62. 12s. 9d. The Bailieboro meeting cost £35, while I was owed £23 by the Department of Defence for expenses prior to October 1969. There were also mileage expenses outstanding from January to May, which I estimated at £150. This added up to a total of £720. 12s. 9d., leaving the Government owing me £220. I2s. 9d. I have taken these figures from correspondence I had with Mr CH Murray, the Secretary of the Department of Finance, in January 1971.

Possibly, I did not go into the same detail with the Committee, but I certainly gave them an outline of how the money was spent. Also, the information on the matter had been conveyed to the Secretary of the Department of Finance, with whom they were in a position to check. Certainly, they had no reason to suggest that I did not give a "satisfactory account" of how the money was spent.

An admission by Mr Haughey that he had given the £500 for the Bailieboro meeting, would have simplified matters for both Colonel Hefferon and me, while an admission that he had known about the arms, would have been equally helpful. At the arms trial, when he denied knowledge of arms, he had created a big doubt in the mind of at least one juryman, who told me afterwards:

"You had it won hands down, but Haughey let you down. When he said he knew nothing about the arms, he set you back twenty-five per cent."

Whatever effect Mr Haughey's denial of his knowledge of the arms may have had on the Inquiry members, it was he who arranged for the money to be transferred to the Defence Committee on the understanding that some, if not all, of it would be used for the purchase of arms. In essence, Mr Haughey handed over unfettered authority to the Northerners to use the money as they thought fit. As I have indicated already, I was aware of this, but there was no way that I could have my knowledge substantiated, because, as I told the Committee of Inquiry, I had no intention of calling, or even naming, residents of Northern Ireland especially, whose lives would undoubtedly be put at risk in the circumstances of the time, if it were officially confirmed that they had negotiated for arms with the Dublin Government.

The Inquiry seemed to accept the validity of this, stating in its Report:

> "The possibility cannot, however, be excluded that a desire to avoid implicating some person or persons in authority within the jurisdiction and/or some person or persons outside the jurisdiction with

> whom he was in contact at the relevant period might have influenced Captain Kelly in giving his evidence."

Referring to my authority to handle the money, the Committee commented:

> "... Captain Kelly himself at no stage suggested in evidence that he had sought the consent of any person in authority for the use of money from Baggot Street for the purchase of arms."

That was incorrect. Under Mr Haughey's authority, the Defence Committee through the Relief Fund was charged with managing the Baggot Street monies from the disbursement viewpoint, with Mr Haughey feeding in money on demand. Apart from his delegated blanket authorisation at the start, Mr Haughey did not involve himself in the day-to-day running of the Baggot Street accounts. Responsibility for doing so had been assigned to the Central Defence Committee. Consequently, any dealings I had with the bank in Baggot Street was with the consent and under the authority of that Committee.

On numerous occasions, I told the Leinster House Inquiry that this was the case. The members may have chosen not to accept such authority as valid, but it was the factual position.

Indeed, the method used by the Government, through its Minister for Finance, to fund the arms importation was not of major importance to me. It was only because I was trusted by both sides, the Minister and the Central Defence Committee, that I became a conduit for the movement of the money. This was superimposed on my real duty as a Military Intelligence Officer, which was to bring the arms importation to a successful conclusion. In fact, it was only when this seemed likely with the arms scheduled to arrive in Dublin airport on the State carrier, Aer Turas, in the third week of April 1970, that the Government gave the first positive indication that it was rescinding its authority for the importation. It did so by mounting a major security operation at Dublin airport. When the security cordon was in position, Peter Berry, Secretary of the Department of Justice, entered his Minister's office, triumphantly announcing: "There's a ring of steel around Dublin airport." Mr Ó Moráin's reply was laconic, but succinct: "You'd think we were in fucking Casablanca."

There was absolutely no necessity for the histrionics. Even at that late stage, all the Government had to do was to shout STOP and that would have been the end of the affair.

Another finding of the Inquiry was:

> "It must be added that had Colonel Hefferon taken appropriate action when he learned from Captain Kelly about the proposed arms importation and his drawings from the account, much of the money might not have been misappropriated. Had the then Minister for Agriculture and Fisheries, Deputy Neil T Blaney, the then Minister for Finance, Deputy Charles J Haughey, and the then Minister for Defence, Deputy James Gibbons, passed on to the Taoiseach their suspicion or knowledge of the proposed arms importation, the misappropriation of part of the money which is now known to have been spent on arms might have been avoided."

This conclusion could only have been based on the false premise that the Taoiseach, Mr Lynch, had not been party to the arms importation from the time it was first mooted at the Bailieboro meeting in October 1969. Further, the Inquiry members must have realised that such was the case when Deputy Michael Ó Moráin, the former Minister for Justice, appeared before them as a witness.

In his opening statement, he said:

> "I wish to reiterate my position that I have conveyed to this Committee in my letter. I need these particular files, firstly, the files comprising the reports from the Garda dealing with the alleged attempted importation of arms and sums allegedly offered to procure arms. There were at least three of these. The final one being the report discussed by me with Garda Commissioner Wymes and Mr Fleming (Head of the Special Branch).
>
> … there are a number of reports sent me by members and/or ex-members of the Gardaí as a result of visits to the North of Ireland on my instructions. These reports were discussed from time to time by the Government. As their existence was denied by Deputy Gibbons, I want those files produced…
>
> Mr Chairman, you have statutory authority to get these files. I have quoted you the authority from your own Act establishing this body and I suggest to you that it is your business to get the best evidence on this matter and to get these files made available to me…"

Deputy Fitzgerald: "Are there any documents other than those that would be in the files mentioned which would assist your recollections in regard to any communication you had with the Taoiseach on these matters – any

other documents that we should look for which would assist your recollection of that?"
Ó Moráin: "There may have been communications between Mr Berry and the Taoiseach… There may be written communications between him and the Taoiseach. I had a number of interviews with the Taoiseach in connection with these matters from time to time…"
Deputy Collins: "In your report to the Taoiseach, was Captain Kelly's name involved?"
Ó Moráin: "Yes, any information I had from any source, the Taoiseach got both from myself and from Mr Berry."
Deputy Burke: "Mr Ó Moráin, you said you had a number on interviews with the Taoiseach. Could you say approximately how many?"
Ó Moráin: "Of course, I was meeting the Taoiseach regularly, but I have specific recollections of three special interviews about these matters."
Burke: "At approximately the December/January period?"
Ó Moráin: "Yes, but I would be able to pinpoint it better if I had these files."

Mr Ó Moráin seemed particularly anxious to obtain access to the file dealing with a meeting he had with Commissioner Wymes and Chief Superintendent Fleming in December 1969. In his later evidence to the Inquiry, Mr Fleming mentioned the meeting. Peter Berry, Secretary of the Department of Justice, also knew of it and his recollection of it was described in some detail to *Magill* magazine:

> "There was one crucial meeting involving Ó Moráin and this was on December 10, 1969. On that date, he met Commissioner Wymes and Chief Superintendent Fleming of the Special Branch and they gave him a complete run-down on the activities of Captain Kelly, his promises of arms, his offers of money and his involvement over a period of time with known subversives. They also told them that two Ministers, Haughey and Blaney, were involved in a plot to import arms. Ó Moráin says he asked them to recheck their sources as he continued to be unhappy with information coming from one of the IRA Deep Throats."

Mr Ó Moráin was obviously as cynical of information emanating from the IRA as Colonel Hefferon and, indeed, the Government, which rejected it at the time of the Bailieboro meeting. Nevertheless, Mr Ó Moráin was adamant that he reported on the meeting to Mr Lynch.

> "The position as far as I'm concerned with these reports," Mr Ó Moráin said, "is that I need them to refresh my memory... They were refused to me before although I would like to point out that counsel for the Attorney General in the arms trials stated publicly that he was waiving all questions of privilege with any matters, touching that trial. They made an exception to that rule on my case and refused me permission to have access to these files... They are the best evidence. They are a contemporaneous record of my knowledge of these events. Therefore, I think it would be more satisfactory from everybody's point of view if I had them here available to me."

Despite the former Minister for Justice's very reasoned and rational plea to have the files made available, his successor in that office, Desmond O'Malley, just as he did in the case of the arms trials, refused to comply. The only possible reason for this was to conceal Mr Lynch's calculated deception about the arms issue. It would seem that fellow Fianna Fáil members on the Committee of Inquiry were imbued with the same spirit of devotion to their leader, to judge by the efforts made by some of them to demonstrate that the files were not necessary to arrive at the truth, "best evidence" or not.

At the conclusion of what was the one and only – and a comparatively short one at that – session with Mr Ó Moráin, undoubtedly a key witness, the Inquiry Chairman suggested that they go into "a private session for a quarter-of-an-hour and then let the witness come back again."

That was the last of the "best evidence" of the files and of Mr Ó Moráin as a witness, as far as the Committee of Inquiry was concerned.

Not to pursue the matter was distinctly odd, if not negligent, behaviour for a Committee of Dáil representatives charged with seeking to establish the truth without fear or favour on behalf of the people of Ireland. It was too much for one of them, Deputy Justin Keating, who resigned a few days after Mr Ó Moráin's appearance. His stated reason for doing so was his firm belief that there was "an organised arrangement between the Government and the Committee of Inquiry's Fianna Fáil members to prevent a full investigation of the Grant-in-Aid expenditure, in direct violation of promises explicitly given in the Dáil."

He claimed that the objective of the Fianna Fáil members of the Committee was to block it from documenting the fact that the Taoiseach, Jack Lynch and the then Minister for Agriculture, James Gibbons, "knew of Captain Kelly's activities in relation to the attempted arms importation long before the crisis of May, 1970."

He quoted "the recent letter" of Justice Minister O'Malley confirming "his refusal to make available to the Committee all the relevant information in his possession". He pointed out that testimony before the Committee indicated that Mr Gibbons and Mr Lynch had prior knowledge of the "arms conspiracy". He also believed that Mr Gibbons, and more seriously, the Taoiseach had misled the Dáil.

He said it was impossible to conclusively prove this, while the Committee was deprived of the powers required to obtain the files. To remedy the matter, he stated, it was necessary to apply to the Dáil, but "this course of action was voted down by the Fianna Fáil members of the Committee", in the days after Mr Ó Moráin's evidence.

He was convinced that if the Committee of Inquiry was to arrive at the truth, that files in the Department of Justice and Defence must be produced; and that Mr Ó Moráin should be recalled as well as Mr Gibbons and Mr Haughey.

"I cannot escape the conclusion," Mr Keating declared, " that Ministers of Government and the Fianna Fáil members of the Committee are acting in collusion to make a proper investigation impossible.

"The events of the past few weeks have convinced me that it was essential for someone to explain to the Irish People the nature of the manoeuvre in which the Government and the Fianna Fáil members of the Committee were and are engaged."

This indictment of the Government and the Fianna Fáil element of the Committee did not take place under cover of Dáil privilege, in the way Mr Gibbons and Mr Lynch seemed to have patented. Instead, Mr Keating chose to come out in the full public glare, unprotected by privilege, at a press conference in the seat of power itself, Dublin's Leinster House.

It was an impassioned plea for a wrong to be righted and he expressed the hope that as a result of his resigning and of his criticisms, there would be a rethinking on the Government's part. He concluded that he could only gain the freedom to express himself openly and honestly by resigning from the Committee of Inquiry and that "this I have regretfully done".

As far as officialdom was concerned, the Keating denouncement fell on deaf ears. The Government continued to stonewall and the Inquiry sailed on for another year or so, before producing its Final Report, which included the finding based on the premise of Mr Lynch's ignorance of the whole arms affair until April 20, 1970. It was bizarre that it should do so in the light of Mr Ó Moráin's evidence, the missing files, the Fianna Fáil blocking tactics in relation to their availability, and the resignation and comments of Mr Keating.

The Inquiry went up many by-ways and plunged down various cul-de-sacs during its peregrination on the money trail for a year and the best part of a second, from December 1970 to July 1972, until, it reached a conclusion on the issue that brought it into existence: whereto the Grant-in-Aid of £100,000, administered by the Minister for Finance and authorised by Dáil Éireann? Finally, with the aid of the banks where the money was lodged, all the money at issue was fully accounted for, plus several thousands more.

Out of the £100,000, £29,166. 12s. 0d. was paid for refugee work undertaken by groups and individuals, who had no association with the Belfast Fund for the Relief of Distress, and the money was paid direct to them without reference to the Belfast Fund. A total of £4,227. 4s. 3d. was not spent and thus recovered, as the Committee of Inquiry phrased it. This left £66,606. 3s. 9d. available to the Belfast Fund.

The expenditure from the Belfast Fund was shown by the Committee as follows:

A. Not Spent On Relief Of Distress

	£.	*s.*	*d.*
Captain Kelly	500	0.	0.
George Dixon account	35,149	13.	9.
Ann O'Brien account	5,850	0.	0.

It has already been explained how the payment of £500 to me was spent. As regards the Dixon account, it was spent on arms, while the O'Brien account was used to fund the production of *The Voice of the North*, a newspaper which put the Nationalist case, while some money from the account found its way to Belfast.

It was suggested that *The Voice of the North* had its origins in the Propaganda Unit set up by the Government in August/September 1969, although this has been disputed, like much else that happened at the time. Seamus Brady, a member of the Unit, in his book, *Arms and the Men*, referred to the formation of the Unit:

> "The Propaganda Unit, which was being set up in the Taoiseach's own Department, was the reason why I had been asked to return from Derry (in August). Some twenty public relations men, all but two seconded from State companies, were being assembled under Eoin Neeson, ex-journalist and Director of the Government Information Bureau...

> For the initial meeting of the members of the Unit I wrote a 5,000-word background briefing on the Battle of the Bogside, which was also circulated to members of the Cabinet. We were an eager-beaver team as we sat around the big table in the conference room in Government Buildings for an explanatory pep talk from George Colley, the Minister for Industry and Commerce, who was to control this propaganda campaign.
>
> Colley spoke with authority... The Government was determined to mount an international campaign in a bid to force Britain to the conference table on the partition question. More significant, he said, the Government was keeping all its options open..."

When this is taken in conjunction with the Government authority given to Mr Haughey to make money available to provide for the victims of the current unrest in the Six Counties, one wondered how the possibility of providing arms could not have arisen. Certainly, it was not excluded, as it was not excluded by the Dáil when it gave retrospective sanction to the expenditure of the Grant-in-Aid. Events, such as the Bailieboro meeting, the February Directive and the Gibbons movement of rifles to the border in April, merely confirm that the Government did not exclude the possibility of providing arms. It could be deduced from this, that the provision of arms, not to mention a newspaper or £500 given to me in connection with the arms, were not outside the scope of the Grant-in-Aid, contrary to what the Committee of Inquiry suggested when it classified expenditure in relation to them as "Not Spent on the Relief of Distress". It was a question of semantics and definition. In the last analysis, Mr Haughey should have clarified the matter because, as described earlier, he authorised the money for the purchase of the arms and knew what was going on from the start. By choosing to deny this, he left Colonel Hefferon and me in an exposed and awkward position, just as he had left his co-defendants at the arms trials.

B. Possibly Related To Relief Of Distress

This concerned a refugee problem in Monaghan.

	£.	s.	d.
Colonel Hefferon	250	0.	0.

C. Possibly Spent In Belfast – Undetermined

	£.	*s.*	*d.*
Purposes	34,850	0.	0.
Total:	76,599	13.	9.

This money was used for the relief of distress in Belfast. In fact, it emerged at the Committee of Inquiry that £72,250 had been used for the relief of distress in the Belfast area. This was vouched for by two well-known and highly reputable Belfast citizens – accepted as such by the Inquiry – on behalf of the Belfast Committee for the Relief of Distress.

The over-expenditure of the amount of the Grant-in-Aid available to the Belfast Fund is explained, because other monies were subscribed as follows: £5,000 from The Red Cross and £4,993. 10s. 0d. from USA, totalling £9,993 10s. 0d., giving a total of £76,599. 13s. 9d.

The Inquiry commented:

> "This sum purports to account more or less for all the money transferred… from the Grant-in-Aid. Thus, on the one hand, the total sum available to the Belfast Committee is stated to have been spent on relief of distress while, on the other hand, a sum amounting to more than half of it seems to have been spent on other purposes.
>
> "It has been suggested to the Inquiry that both propositions may be reconciled on the basis that there might have been what was called a 'switching' of money, that is, that while the money transferred to the George Dixon and Ann O'Brien accounts was spent other than on relief, an equivalent amount might have been made good to the Belfast Committee for the Relief of Distress from other monies available in Northern Ireland."

It was common knowledge at the time that thousands of pounds had been contributed by people and organisations, both at home and abroad, to the Defence Committees in the latter half of 1969 for the defence of beleaguered Nationalism in the six-county area. Undoubtedly, enough money was available to put a "switching" operation into effect. The Inquiry was aware of this, but took refuge in stating that "no first hand evidence of a switch was received" by it. In fact, there was no physical "switch" of money from Belfast to Dublin. Instead, as the Inquiry itself admitted, the distress money might have been reimbursed in Belfast, while the Dublin money was used to purchase arms. From a security standpoint, this arrangement made perfectly good sense, especially to people in Northern Ireland. It would have been extremely foolish of them to operate an arms account in British-occupied Belfast, in conjunction with the "foreign" Irish Government, thus immeasurably increasing the risk of being charged with a serious crime such as treason by the British regime.

The switch theory seemed to absorb the Inquiry greatly, with some members returning to it again and again.

"... But where did the money come from?" Deputy MacSharry questioned me.

"Where did the money that was in Belfast come from?" I responded.

MacSharry: "Yes. Where was it lodged to any of these accounts? Can you tell us any of the lodgements?"
Kelly: "Excuse me. I will put a hypothetical situation to you. Supposing you had a bank account here with £10,000 in it and somebody else had a bank account in Belfast with £10,000 and you wanted to buy something in Belfast and he wanted to buy something in Dublin. You were friends and you said to the fellow in Belfast: 'Buy that stuff for me at £10,000' and he said to you: 'You buy the stuff in Dublin for me at £10,000' and you do it. What would this amount to?"
MacSharry: "Bank Giro."
Kelly: "What would it amount to?"
MacSharry: "This is hypothetical".
Kelly: "You do not need Bank Giro, just word of mouth, telephone."

Eventually, the Inquiry seemed to accept the switch theory, declaring:

"Even if the monies transferred to the George Dixon and Ann O'Brien accounts had been reimbursed to the Belfast Committee for the Relief of Distress from funds outside the jurisdiction of the State it would be irrelevant to and could not make legitimate the expenditure of the Grant-in-Aid monies for purposes other than those intended by the Dáil."

Whatever about the legitimacy of the jurisdiction argument or the unorthodoxy of the money handling methodology, the end result, spelled out by the Inquiry's Final Report, was as follows:

1. £72,250 spent on the relief of distress in Belfast.
2. £250 by Colonel Hefferon of refugee related work.
3. £500 by me on Bailieboro meeting and related activities.
4. £35,149. 13s. 9d. on arms.
5. £5,850 on "Voice of the North", with a small proportion going North.
6. £29,166. 12s. 0d. spent on relief of distress, primarily in Belfast.

It is evident that the total expenditure far exceeded the Grant-in-Aid of £100,000; that the expenditure on the relief of distress also exceeded £100,000; that the total monies available to the Belfast Fund in the Republic was accounted for in full; that no personal gain accrued to anyone from the Fund.

CHAPTER 26

Mr O'Malley, the Minister for Justice during the arms trials and the subsequent Committee of Inquiry, was a brash young man with something of a sarcastic, biting edge to him. These attributes came quickly to the fore, when only fourteen days after taking over as Minister from Mr Ó Moráin in May 1970, he wrote a letter to Peter Berry, his long established departmental secretary. It was published in the June 1980 edition of *Magill* magazine:

éire

ROINN DLÍ AGUS CIRT
(Department of Justice)
BAILE ÁTHA CLIATH
(Dublin)

22nd May 1970

Dear Mr. Berry,

Ireland has survived for 24 hours without you. Please feel humble.

I forgot **last** night to tell you a charming story that will enliven your weekend. Senator F. McElgunn is a secondary teacher in Carrick-on-Shannon. He caught a youth doing some minor misdemeanor but did not actually see him. On accusation the youth queried "How do you know, sir?" McE replied "If I say you did a thing, you did it".

"Oh, no, sir", chimed in another boy from the back of the class. "It's not <u>you</u>, sir. It's if Peter Berry says you did a thing, you did <u>it</u>."

No longer are you the faceless one, just known and feared in the corridors of power. You are now spoken of in hushed tones by the peasantry of even a backward county like Leitrim.

D. O'M

<u>DESMOND O'MALLEY</u>
Minister for Justice

Mr Berry, who had started work in Justice in 1927, over ten years before Mr O'Malley was born, was not amused. The people of Leitrim were not too happy either with the "peasant... backward county" epithet.

Mr O'Malley had been Parliamentary Secretary to Mr Lynch from July 1969. In this capacity, he attended Cabinet meetings, where the Bailieboro meeting was discussed. Also, he was comprehensively briefed on the matter, *inter alia*, by the punctilious Mr Berry, when he became Minister.

Yet, Mr O'Malley, as Minister for Justice, did not intervene to set the record straight when Mr Gibbons, in the High Court, denied knowledge on oath of the Bailieboro meeting.

Some months later, on April 21,1971, at the Committee of Public Accounts Inquiry, Mr Gibbons reiterated his sworn denial about Bailieboro:

> "This meeting was mentioned at the arms trials. As I recall it, I said I had no recollection of any description of having been told about that meeting. I have thought a good deal about that since; I racked my brains for any detail about it, the purpose of it, the people who attended it, what was decided, and I am absolutely certain that I was never informed of the Bailieboro meeting and that the reference to it in the Four Courts is the first reference I can recall."

Once again, Mr O'Malley stood mutely by as Minister for Justice, giving, by inference at least a false gloss of truth to what he knew to be false evidence on a vital issue in relation to the arms saga.

In his Papers, published by *Magill* in July 1980, Peter Berry revealed that when he was invited to appear before the Committee of Public Accounts Inquiry, he, even though he had retired from the Civil Service at that stage, wrote to Mr O'Malley enquiring what his response should be.

Magill continues:

> "The Minister's private secretary replied saying that the Minister considered that anything which Mr Berry might usefully say would be contrary to the Official Secrets Act and that Mr O'Malley would not agree to release him from his obligations under the Act.
>
> He was then invited by the Committee of Public Accounts if he would 'consult' with it and decided to agree, in spite of ministerial objections, and he so informed the Department of Justice. He then enquired of the Minister if he should reveal to the Committee the fact of his meeting with Mr Lynch on October 17, 1969 at Mount

> Carmel Hospital, where he informed the Taoiseach of information he had received concerning the involvement of Captain Kelly in the arms plot.
>
> Mr Berry goes on to say in his Papers: 'The reply I received back was that the Taoiseach had no recollection of what was discussed. I pointed out that this did not deal with the point as to whether he had come on a social call or in answer to a request. I received another call to say that the Minister was reluctant to speak to the Taoiseach again; that the Taoiseach deprecated any reference to this visit…'"

Despite this ministerial attempt to put him off doing so, Mr Berry appeared before the Committee and "revealed the fact that he had informed Mr Lynch of Captain Kelly's activities and of the arms plot on October 17, 1969".

Thus, on another vital arms trial issue: the contemporaneous knowledge of Mr Lynch and his Government of the arms importation, Mr O'Malley's sense of justice again seems to have been put in abeyance when he attempted to block Mr Berry giving evidence before the Committee of Inquiry which confirmed that Mr Lynch was lying when he told Dáil Éireann that the first he knew of the importation was on April 20, 1970.

It is fair to assume that it was in pursuit of the same ignoble and dubious objective, the very antithesis of justice in that it involved covering up Mr Lynch's duplicity in mounting the arms trials, that caused Mr O'Malley, both in the courts and at the Committee of Inquiry, to deny access to departmental files to his predecessor as Minister for Justice, Mr Ó Moráin, who had cited them as "best evidence" on the very issue of Mr Lynch's credibility.

If Mr O'Malley attempted to block Mr Berry giving evidence to the Committee of Inquiry, he made it his business to ensure that Chief Superintendent Fleming of the Special Branch did so. As reported by *Magill:*

> "It emerges from the Berry Papers that Fleming was specifically instructed by the Minister 'to be totally frank at the Committee of Public Accounts hearing'. The instruction to do so was given through Mr Berry. In spite of this Mr O'Malley failed to either defend Mr Fleming in public or even to inform the Garda Commissioner that he had so instructed Mr Fleming."

Certainly, Fleming needed defending after his appearance before the Committee of Inquiry, simply because the vast bulk of his evidence was hearsay, fed to the Gardaí by the Sinn Féin operatives, of whom Mr Fleming's superior officer boasted to Colonel Hefferon that there were two; the same people to whom Mr Ó Moráin had referred as "IRA Deep Throats" at his meeting with Mr Fleming and Commissioner Wymes in December 1969.

Peter Sutherland, on my behalf, describing Mr Fleming's evidence, stated:

> "It is impossible for this Committee or for anybody else to test the veracity of this information, quite simply, because it is all hearsay. This must be taken into account in relation to evidence which appears to be directly contradictory to that evidence: the evidence of Mr Ó Moráin, the evidence of Captain Kelly and the evidence of Colonel Hefferon. I respectfully submit that, in your deliberations, the Committee must accept that this alleged evidence of Chief Superintendent Fleming cannot seriously be taken as refuting any evidence given by a witness on oath before this Committee."

In my submission to the Committee of Inquiry on Mr Fleming's evidence, I expounded further on his hearsay:

> "In every security service in the world, one of the primary aims is to obtain 'an inside source', that is an informant inside the illegal or subversive organisation under surveillance. That is elementary, but what is also elementary is that any illegal or subversive organisation realises this and, in consequence, it is part of any such organisation's purposes to plant its own inside man or men to feed selected or false information to the investigating agency. That is the only explanation – that Chief Superintendent Fleming was and is being used by his informants – that presents itself to me as to why he should come in here and swear to hearsay, which is absolutely and utterly false to my definite knowledge.
>
> This would explain why other witnesses before this Committee should refer to the sources of information available to the Chief Superintendent as being dubious and why, for example, the former Minister for Justice, Mr Ó Moráin, should describe the supposed information as being of the 'Duirt bean liom go nduirt bean lei'* variety, also stating: 'The source I believe he is referring to – cross checking – is a source that was not reporting direct to his section at

* *A woman told me that a woman told her…*

> all and a source which was regarded as very doubtful by Commissioner Wymes and myself.' "

I also pointed out that there was evidence before the Committee of Inquiry showing that Mr Fleming not only purveyed hearsay as truth, but that he also gave what he knew to be false evidence, specifically in relation to liaison between Army Intelligence and the Garda authorities. I referred back to Mr Sutherland's cross-examination of Mr Fleming:

Sutherland: "Would you accept that at this time, from your own knowledge, there was a liaison between Army Intelligence and the police?"
Fleming: "I expect there was, yes."
Sutherland: "Don't you know quite well that there was – ?"
Fleming: "Yes, there – ?"
Sutherland: "There were regular meetings?"
Fleming: "I am not aware of that?"
Sutherland: "You are not aware of that?"
Fleming: "Regular meetings?"
Sutherland: "In the Castle (Dublin) between the police authorities and Army Intelligence?"
Fleming: "If I may ask, who would represent the police authorities?
Sutherland: "I am asking you whether or not you are aware of the fact that there were regular meetings?"
Fleming: "I am not aware of regular meetings."
Sutherland: "Are you aware that Chief Superintendent, as he then was, Pat Malone was in regular contact with Army Intelligence?"
Fleming: "Chief Superintendent Pat Malone was never in the Castle until he was promoted to Deputy Assistant Commissioner some months ago."

"To put it quite bluntly, Chief Superintendent Fleming was not only being evasive, he was being dishonest, when he gave this evidence," I told the Committee of Inquiry,

> "From my own knowledge as an officer of Army Intelligence over a period of ten years, I know, and Chief Superintendent Fleming knows, that he reports directly to Section C3, Crime Section C3, in Garda Headquarters. That section is the responsibility of a Chief Superintendent and, during the period in question, the Chief Superintendent in charge was Chief Superintendent Pat Malone, now Assistant Commissioner Malone... Chief Superintendent Fleming knows this quite well. He knows it as well as I do, and the

reason he did not tell the whole truth to this Committee on this question of reporting was because he knows that his superior in security matters generally, did not bring the hearsay, which he attempted to put forward as truth here, to the notice of the army authorities. Specifically, Mr Malone did not bring it to the notice of the Director of Intelligence."

The only conclusion one can reach from this, is that Mr Fleming, and possibly Mr Malone, did not accept the hearsay evidence as credible because of its source; that they were at one with their Minister, Mr Ó Moráin and with their Commissioner, Mr Wymes, in rejecting it and that it was only after the arms trials – where there was no mention of it – that it had come to the forefront under the jurisdiction of Mr O'Malley, who, unlike his predecessor, seemed to accept that it was fit and proper 'evidence" to place before a parliamentary Committee of Inquiry.

On the issue of liaison between the Garda authorities in the Castle and Army Intelligence, Mr Fleming said he was not aware of regular meetings.

"This is a downright lie," I told the Committee.

"In my capacity as personal staff officer to the Director of Intelligence during the period in question, there was regular liaison between a senior officer in Military Intelligence and the Special Detective Unit – Special Branch – of which Chief Superintendent Fleming has charge, and, on occasion, that army officer met none other than Chief Superintendent Fleming. Yet, this man comes in here and states: 'I am not aware of regular meetings'. In fact, contact at this level was routine and has been going on, to my knowledge, at least since I joined Military Intelligence in 1960...

These are the facts and Mr Fleming knows them as well as I do, and he also knows as I know, that every tittle-tattle of information concerning army personnel *vis-á-vis* the security situation in particular, whether hearsay or otherwise, is conveyed as a matter of urgency to the Director of Intelligence through the channels I have mentioned.

The crimes against National Security – and that is what they are in effect – of which Chief Superintendent Fleming now accuses me are so outrageous in the security context that not alone would they have been reported to the Director of Intelligence, but they would have caused a major sensation in that office leading to a major and thorough investigation.

That is why Chief Superintendent Fleming was not willing, or hesitated, to tell the truth to this Committee concerning the chain of command in the Gardá and why he denied knowledge of the very specific links by which security information is co-ordinated between Military Intelligence and the Garda. He knows that the hearsay, which he attempted to put forward as truth here, if it had any basis in fact whatsoever, would have been investigated long before my retiral from the army in May, 1970."

The security crimes of which Mr Fleming accused me were listed by him when he gave evidence to the Inquiry as follows:

"At the outset I would like to point out that all this information has come from confidential sources and I am not at liberty to reveal the sources from which the information came.

First, in about the last week of September 1969 Captain Kelly met Cathal Goulding, Chief-of-Staff of the IRA, in Virginia, Co. Cavan, and he agreed to get him a regular supply of arms and ammunition for use in Northern Ireland. He also promised to provide training facilities for Northern members of the IRA in Gormanston Camp. Captain Kelly attended an IRA meeting in Cavan in the first week of October, 1969 and he then promised the IRA to give them £50,000 by instalments. To prove that he was not bluffing he promised to pay the first instalment within three days.

On or about October 7, 1969 he paid over £7,000 at Cavan Town to Cathal Goulding. During the last week of November 1969, he paid over a further sum of £1,000."

Chairman: "To whom on this occasion?"
Fleming: "As far as I know it was to Cathal Goulding. I cannot swear to that, though. In the early part of December 1969, he paid over a further £1,500. Again, I am not sure, but I think it was to Cathal Goulding. Those are the sums which as far as I know Captain Kelly paid over."
Deputy Collins: "Captain Kelly said in one statement to the Committee that he never met any members of the IRA as such. In fact, that was in reply to a question from myself?"
Chairman: "If he did say that, it would be incorrect?"
Fleming: "It would be incorrect, because I know of, at the very least, four or five occasions where he attended meetings with IRA members. One of these meetings took place at a certain hotel in Monaghan – I will not mention the hotel – some time at the end of October or early November 1969."

In answer to Deputy Fitzgerald, Fleming said that he knew "for a fact" of at least one meeting attended by Rory Brady, a senior colleague of Cathal Goulding's at the time and, later, President of Provisional Sinn Féin.

All the above evidence was false. It was assumedly fed to Mr Fleming and his confreres by the IRA "informants", because it suited the purposes of an element of the IRA to do so in the fraught circumstances of an impending split in that organisation. It is worthy of note that all the "crimes" of which the Chief Superintendent accused me, allegedly took place during the pre-Christmas period of 1969 in the run-up to the end of year, the time of the IRA split. From then on, this particular, well-nurtured line of disinformation went out of operation. One could speculate and come up with many answers as to why that happened, but, one thing is certain, Chief Superintendent Fleming's aptitude for peddling hearsay as genuine straightforward evidence was not as avidly fed, if fed at all, from then on.

It is ironic that when Mr Fleming was giving false evidence about my meetings and my supplying of money to Cathal Goulding, the reality was that I had met Mr Goulding on three occasions in Dublin in September and early October 1969, under instructions from the Director of Intelligence, who notified the Security Branch, C3, at Garda Headquarters of the meetings. The meetings were initiated by an influential member of the Nationalist community in Northern Ireland, who suggested that it might be beneficial to meet Mr Goulding. There was nothing secretive about the meetings, at one of which I invited Mr Goulding to have a drink. We had it in Coman's pub on Dublin's Rathgar Road. Our conversations were friendly and straightforward. We talked about events in the North, with which we both had familiarity, but Cathal Goulding was too astute to give anything away and I expect I was equally circumspect. As regards giving him money, the issue did not arise, because quite simply, and as emerged at the Inquiry, no such money was at my disposal at the time. I reported back to Colonel Hefferon, who told the Inquiry, "out of it emerged absolutely nothing".

It struck me as exceedingly strange that the Chief Superintendent did not mention the fully authorised meetings with Mr Goulding – the only ones Mr Goulding and I had – which were referred to his superiors at C3, while spilling out details of totally fictitious meetings. The only conclusion I could come to at the time was that he had been sent to do a hatchet job by someone in Government and that mention of the genuine meetings might cut across his efforts to mislead. When I learned of the circumstances under which he appeared before the Committee of Inquiry, with the Minister for Justice instructing him "to be frank", I was more convinced than ever that he was under serious pressure to act as he did.

Similarly, when he denied to the Inquiry that he had named Haughey, Blaney and Gibbons to me as the three Ministers involved in the arms importations on May 2, 1970, substituting Boland for Gibbons in his evidence to the Inquiry, it seemed to me that he was under severe pressure.

From my arrest on May 1, 1970, I had got to know John Fleming very well, finding him well disposed to me throughout that Summer prior to the arms trials. During the court proceedings, I had several quick and friendly chats with him and there was never any suggestion but that Gibbons and, indeed, Lynch himself, were involved in the arms importation; in other words that it was an authorised Government operation. But it also came across that he was a worried man; that he was not sure what way the ball would hop.

"My job could be on the line," he told me more than once, dry-washing his hands, in what seemed to be a nervous habit.

Uncertainty simmered in him. A comparatively young man, he was on the way up, with the Commissionership beckoning; an essentially decent man, with ambition lurking and it tripped him up. In the end, he did what he was told, not what he should have done

Chief Superintendent Fleming had backed himself into a corner. Basically, it there had been any truth in his allegations against me, it was his bounden duty to have brought them to the notice of the Army. By not doing so, if there was any semblance of truth in them at all, he was in grave dereliction of his duty as a top security figure in the State. As I knew from my years in Intelligence, any hint of any association with subversives by an officer or soldier was brought to the notice of the army authorities as a matter of urgency. Indeed, at that time, a young officer, whose alleged offence was in going to places of entertainment where he might be seen as associating with alleged subversives, was unceremoniously thrown out of the army without a trial of any description.

Either, the Chief Superintendent had attempted to foist false evidence on the Committee of Inquiry, or he was in neglect of his duty in not bringing evidence, which he told the Committee he "checked and double-checked", to the notice of the army authorities through the proper channel, C3, over a year earlier. In either case, he was guilty of a serious offence. There was no investigation into this. On the contrary, his reward for being "totally frank" was to be promoted.

In another respect, it could be argued that Mr O'Malley was not totally frank in relation to the arms trials. This concerns a secret meeting which he had with Mr Haughey on September 9, 1970, at 2.30 pm, two weeks before the commencement of the first trial on September 22.

To quote Vincent Browne in *Magill* on the Berry Papers:

"O'Malley volunteered that he had met Haughey at Tralee Races and Berry said he knew. O'Malley said that he had arranged to see Haughey again at his home in Kinsealy later that week. Berry strongly advised against this, pointing out that the Special Branch had Haughey's house under observation. Berry also remarked that O'Malley might be enticed into indiscretions by drink and that their conversation might be tape-recorded by Haughey.

Berry said that if O'Malley was intent on going ahead with his meeting with Haughey, it would be better to have it in Leinster House in the Minister's own office...

Following the meeting which lasted for only half an hour, O'Malley returned to the Department of Justice where he had a conversation with Peter Berry...

The Berry Papers state:

'Mr O'Malley told me that he had seen Mr Haughey from 2.30 to 3.00 pm in his room in Leinster House. He said that Mr Haughey's principal worry was over my evidence and that he had asked if I could be *induced, directed or intimidated* into not giving evidence or changing my evidence.

'I asked the Minister what was meant by induced, did it mean could I be bribed? The Minister did not answer me directly. He was biting his knuckles.

'He said that he had reminded Mr Haughey of my statement in the Book of Evidence and he didn't see how I could withdraw or substantially change. I said, has he in mind that I could become forgetful or absentminded or muddled? I asked what had he meant by could I be directed?

'The Minister went on to say that Mr Haughey had threatened that I would be roasted by Counsel Seamus Sorahan who would question me on a case in January '70 in which proceedings had to be squared by me.

'I said to the Minister that this was a load of nonsense, that the charge on indictment had been preferred on the instructions of the Taoiseach against my advice and that the charge had been withdrawn, subsequently, on the instructions of the Attorney General, who had instructed the local State Solicitor. I told the Minister that this particular case was well documented and that I would get him the file.

'The whole nature of the meeting and the fact that the Minister had even listened to that kind of talk left me in no doubt, that he was pretending to Mr Haughey that he was a friend.

'It gave me a touch of nausea.'

> Quite clearly, these revelations have the most serious significance for both Mr O'Malley and Mr Haughey. For Mr Haughey they suggest he was attempting to pervert the course of justice. For Mr O'Malley there are even more serious issues at stake; they suggest that he, the Minister for Justice, collaborated with Mr Haughey, if only to the extent of passing along the message, in attempting to pervert the course of justice. They also suggest that he was behaving in a manner totally disloyal to Mr Lynch, for as the former Taoiseach has revealed, Mr O'Malley did not tell Mr Lynch either before or after that the meeting had taken place or what the purpose of the meeting was."

Another matter within the orbit of the Minister for Justice was the major injustice perpetrated against me in the run-up to the arms trials. This was the deletion in the Book of Evidence of the penultimate sentence in Colonel Hefferon's statement to the Gardaí that anything I had done had been done with the authorisation of the Minister for Defence. Peter Sutherland brought the matter to the attention of the Committee of Inquiry when cross-examining Chief Superintendent Fleming.

Sutherland: "Did you conduct personally, or did officers on your behalf conduct an interrogation of Colonel Hefferon during April or May, 1970?"
Fleming: "As far as I remember, some of the members of the Detective Branch took a statement from Colonel Hefferon at that time."
Sutherland: "You, I presume, at that time examined the statement which had been taken by Inspector Doocey particularly?"
Fleming: "I would have read it at that time, yes."
Sutherland: " Do you remember reading the last sentence of that statement in which Colonel Hefferon said, 'any acts which Captain Kelly..."

The Committee of Inquiry Chairman interrupted to express worry about the introduction of new evidence.

Sutherland: "It is merely the authorisation of Mr Gibbons that I am referring to... I must suggest to you, Chief Superintendent, that the last sentence of the statement was..."
Fleming (interrupting): "I am prepared to accept what you say..."
Sutherland: "I merely want to put to the Chief Superintendent that while a sentence in that statement was that Colonel Hefferon said that anything

that Captain Kelly had done he had done with the authorisation of the Minister for Defence. Do you remember reading that?"
Fleming: "He possibly did say that, but I can't swear to that at the moment..."

There were further interruptions by the Committee.

Sutherland (persisting): "... I merely want to put this question finally to Chief Superintendent Fleming. Do you remember at any stage any statement being made by Colonel Hefferon to the police or to the Special Branch specifically that Captain Kelly had at all times acted with the authorisation of Mr Gibbons?"
Fleming: "I don't know. That may have been in his statement..."
Sutherland: "I am suggesting to the Committee that this evidence can be given to the Committee by Colonel Hefferon."
Fleming: "Yes."

The changing of Colonel Hefferon's evidence was another piece of official deception indulged in somewhere between the taking of the deposition and its appearance in the Book of Evidence with the vital penultimate sentence removed. This pernicious act took place on the initiative of someone at Government level or close to it and its purpose was to suppress and delete evidence of such significance that it would simply not have been possible to mount a case if it was allowed to stand.

Peter Sutherland posed the question to the Committee:

"If that statement was included in the Book of Evidence, wouldn't it in fact have meant that there was no case against Captain Kelly?"

The Committee chose to ignore Mr Sutherland, however, and did not even bother to call Colonel Hefferon, who was standing by to clarify the matter. Mr O'Malley, under whose aegis as Minister for Justice the statement was altered, did not choose to clarify the matter either. Instead, he let the false record stand in the Book of Evidence and, by doing so, left himself open to the charge of colluding with his political master, Jack Lynch, in plotting to bring persons before the courts on false charges, surely, a most serious crime for any Minister in any country or State, especially one claiming to be a democracy.

During the second arms trial, there was a major debate in the foyer and corridors of the Four Courts on the changing of the Directive and the dropping of Colonel Hefferon as a prosecution witness. It later emerged into the public domain through Kevin Boland that Taoiseach Lynch was involved in changing the terms of the Directive. Were other members of the Government involved and, if so, whom? Which members of Government, for example, were present at the crucial meeting in the Rosslare hotel between the two arms trials, where the niceties of changing the Directive and dropping Colonel Hefferon were worked out? The names on everyone's lips at the Four Courts were Gibbons, O'Malley and the Attorney General. It is noteworthy that when Mr Haughey's counsel, Niall McCarthy, who might be expected to know, was summing up, he suggested that the people who might have met with Mr Gibbons were an army officer, the Chief-of-Staff, the Attorney General, the Minister for Justice and the Taoiseach.

Tom McIntyre, in his book, *Through The Bridewell Gates*, put his own unique construction on the matter:

> "... The (prevailing) south-east wind, however, does murmur of a weekend meeting in a coastal resort – not so long ago – involving the witness (Gibbons), the Attorney General, and the present Minister for Justice, the Directive – that which was lost and hath been found – large in their considerations. No commencing prayers, we may assume, for Colonel Hefferon's well-being. What can we do with this Directive? And after much deliberation, continues the south-west wind, there was a famous journey to the far West Cork, to the removed spot where broods the Taoiseach, far from enemies. Can you hear him, greeting the visitors – 'Welcome, gentlemen' – about him his usual air of a man who is thinking of going to confession. Into the cottage. The wives – it's a respectable weekend – follow, one of them (much travelled) remarking on the rocky surrounding landscape that it bears a remarkable resemblance to Mexico, were it not for the rain. Women, as the poet says, get under things."

To date, Mr O'Malley has not clarified the part he played in changing the Directive and dropping Colonel Hefferon. It would seem that neither could have been done without his knowledge as Minister for Justice and, even if this was attempted, he was not the man to blithely stand back and have his authority usurped in this way.

Ever since, Mr O'Malley has filled the role of the White Knight of Irish politics, cutting a swathe on the white charger of moral uprighteousness and flying the banners of integrity, honesty and probity in public life. He claims to be the soul of honour, but what is honour?

Maybe it was honourable to stand by as Minister for Justice and take no action when his colleague, Mr Gibbons, misled the courts twice and the Committee of Public Accounts once on the Bailieboro meeting. Mr O'Malley knew as well as I knew; as Colonel Hefferon knew; as Peter Berry knew; as Kevin Boland knew; as many of his colleagues in Cabinet, inclusive of Mr Lynch, knew of the Bailieboro meeting.

Maybe it was honourable to refuse access to Departmental files, cited as "best evidence", to his predecessor as Minister for Justice, Mr Ó Moráin, which would have clarified when Jack Lynch first knew of the proposed arms importation, a crucial factor in the defence case.

Maybe it was honourable to stand by as Minister for Justice and not even query if the evidence of Colonel Hefferon that appeared in the Book of Evidence was bowdlerised, even when Peter Sutherland brought it into the public domain at the Committee of Public Accounts inquiry.

Maybe it was honourable on December 21, 1997, nearly thirty years after the event, for the former Minister for Justice to announce to *The Irish Times* on the occasion of Mr Gibbons death:

"Mr Jim Gibbons was a gentle Irish patriot, who had suffered for many years because he insisted on telling the truth on oath during the arms trials."

There was something obscene about Mr O'Malley using Mr Gibbons' death to again mislead the Irish people. He knew what he said was false, just as I knew it was false, and all the people who knew about the Bailieboro meeting knew it was false. It was a new low in Irish public life that one should use the death of another in such a perverse fashion. If he wished to honour the man he claimed as friend, and his family, he should have let sleeping dogs lie on such an occasion.

Maybe it was honourable that the former Minister for Justice should go on the BBC television *Spotlight* programme on March 10, 1998 and suggest that the accused in the arms trials should have been convicted, adding, "but that is the price we pay for democracy", before casting doubt on the integrity of the jury in the case and decrying juries in general.

Eleven months later, on Wednesday, February 10, 1998, the same Mr O'Malley, still a public representative for his native Limerick, chose to lecture Dáil Éireann on probity in public life. He spoke in the context of the money dealings, possibly involving fraud, of some politicians. At the time of writing, the dealings are the subject of various Judicial Tribunals of Inquiry, which each day seem to unearth fresh scandals, primarily related to Fianna Fáil, the main Government party. Mr O'Malley, of course, had been expelled from that party in the early eighties, having failed in his attempts to take over leadership from Mr Haughey, who had successfully made the transition from the dock in the High Court in 1970 to the leadership of Fianna Fáil and Taoiseach in 1979.

In a speech that was widely lauded, Mr O'Malley reserved most of his ire for Mr Haughey, who was the main political figure under investigation for the conduct of his financial affairs. Claiming that Mr Haughey had cast a "long dark shadow" over Irish political life, Mr O'Malley said:

> "It is nearly twenty years since he became Taoiseach, seven since he left public life, but our political system is still struggling to come to terms with his legacy... We do not expect people in public life to be saints or paragons of virtue. All we ask is that those in public life, and especially those in high political office, abide by normal and reasonable standards of honesty and decency in dealing with affairs of State. If we are to be criticised for holding that position, then this democracy is in more trouble than any of us realise."

No reasonable person could criticise Mr O'Malley for his enunciation of the standards expected in public life, but did he maintain those high standards when he cast his own "long dark shadow" as Minister for Justice during the Arms Trials? Did he abide by normal and reasonable standards of honesty and decency in dealing with affairs of State during that time? The record provides the answers.

Mr O'Malley spoke of "the cancer of corruption" of Fianna Fáil under Mr Haughey, but nobody knows better than Mr O'Malley that the roots of that cancer run longer and deeper and go further back than the money scandals currently under investigation. They run right back to the arms trials when he, as Mr Lynch's Minister for Justice, was party to the prosecution cases.

An aspect of the arms trials was the alacrity with which the concept of Cabinet confidentiality was produced. It seemed to be pulled out on demand like a rabbit out of a magician's hat. Maybe it was honourable for it to be maintained by members of the Lynch Cabinet even in the face of gross injustice. Mr O'Malley was not the only one to remain mute about the Gibbons' perjury concerning the Bailieboro meeting. The majority, if not all of Cabinet, knew where the truth lay.

Maybe Cabinet confidentiality is the proper creed for honourable men. Maybe all the tight-lipped men surrounding Jack Lynch who obeyed without question, as perjury and double-dealing prospered, were honourable men.

But there were other men who saw honour elsewhere: men like Kevin Boland, who did not see concealment of truth or the acceptance of falsehood to pervert justice as having anything to do with honour; men like Pat Murphy, whose conscience would not let him rest and who concluded it was his duty as a man of honour to let his former boss as Minister for Defence, Kevin Boland, know of the forging of the substitute document to replace the original Directive of February 6, 1970; men like Michael Ó Moráin, a man who had recovered from the illness that led to his resignation when he gave evidence to the courts and the Committee of Inquiry. He emerged as a man of integrity. He was only thwarted from exposing the whole charade by the O'Malley refusal to give him access to relevant files. He knew where honour lay; Justin Keating also knew where honour lay when he went public to expose the shenanigans of some members of the Committee of Public Accounts; last, but not least, Michael Hefferon, a man who stood firm and told the trust despite pressure placed on him to do otherwise, a man who was proud to be an army officer and was as such the most loyal of men; a man, who by his insistence on telling the simple, unvarnished truth, became the main figure in securing a just verdict of Not Guilty in the arms trials. He also knew where honour lay.

Within a week of the arms trial verdict being announced, the following motion was put to the Dáil, on Thursday, October 29, 1970, by the Taoiseach, Mr Lynch:

"That Dáil Éireann reaffirms its confidence in An Taoiseach and the members of Government."

On November 4, 1970, the vote was taken. Kevin Boland refused to support the motion. It was his political swan song. At the height of his powers, he took a principled decision to walk out of public life. In *Up Dev,* he described his departure from Dáil Éireann in the following terms:

> "I was drinking my last cup of tea in Leinster House with my wife and a few friends downstairs in the restaurant when the vote was taken, with Blaney and Haughey in the Government lobby. Victory for the Republican party, the party founded by Eamon de Valera in the La Scala Theatre, Dublin, in 1926, the party of principle and honour, the continuation of the National Movement, victory by 74 votes to 67. *Vae victis*! A solemn declaration by the majority of the elected representatives of the people that the Taoiseach, Mr Gibbons and the other members of Government were worthy of the people's confidence. If this were true, could Blaney and Haughey also be fit representatives of the people?
>
> ... Even if I was somewhat the worse for wear as I stepped from the smoky corridors of power into the clear, crisp November night air, I felt that my wounds were on my front and I could still look my own height in front of me...".

Years later, I had a few drinks in Sligo with a good friend of mine, Dave O'Regan, another army officer. At least I could look my own height when I left the court, I told him at one stage of the evening. I am five foot, nine at a stretch, and that was when I had my hair. He looked down at me from his six foot plus, his eyes twinkling.

"That's not a bad height, Jim," he grinned mischievously.

"Not bad at all," I grinned back at him. "After all, I was the tallest of the four defendants".

APPENDIX

CHRONOLOGY OF EVENTS

1969	
12 August	Apprentice Boys' parade in Derry.
13 August	Violence in Derry continues.
	Barricades go up in Belfast.
	Taoiseach makes "not stand by" speech.
14 August	British troops arrive in Derry.
	Violence erupts in Belfast – four people shot dead.
15 August	Violence in Belfast continues.
	British troops arrive in Derry.
16 August	Sniping in Belfast continues.
3 October	Training of Derry citizens in Irish Army camp at Fort Dunree, Co. Donegal, interrupted.
4/5 October	Meeting at Bailieboro, Co. Cavan, between Captain Kelly and representatives of the Northern Ireland Defence Committees.
1970	
1 May	Captain James Kelly retires from army and is arrested. Released the following day.
4 May	Michael Ó Moráin, Minister for Justice, resigns from the Cabinet on grounds of ill-health.
6 May	Charles Haughey, Minister for Finance, and Neil Blaney, Minister for Agriculture, sacked from the Cabinet. Kevin Boland, Minister for Local Government, and Paudge Brennan, Parliamentary Secretary to the Minister for Local Government, resign.
	Dáil adjourns in the morning and meets in the evening. Taoiseach tells the House he has received information connecting the sacked Ministers with an attempt to import arms illegally.
8 May	Marathon Dáil debate begins.
9 May	Thirty-six hour debate ends at 10 pm.
27 May	Captain James Kelly, John Kelly of Belfast, and Albert Luykx arrested on arms conspiracy charges.
28 May	Charles Haughey and Neil Blaney arrested on arms conspiracy charges and released on bail.
10 June	John Kelly released on bail.
2 July	Informations refused against Neil Blaney.
	Charles Haughey, Captain Kelly, John Kelly and Albert Luykx returned for trial.

22 September	Arms trial opens in the Four Courts before Justice Andreas O'Keefe.
29 September	Jury discharged and trial stopped.
6 October	New arms trial before Justice Seamus Henchy opens.
23 October	Acquittal of four defendants.
25 October	Taoiseach holds press conference in New York.
1 December	Announcement that Dáil Public Accounts Committee will investigate the spending of the moneys of the Northern Ireland Relief Fund.

1971

6 January	First sitting of Public Accounts Committee.

LEGAL REPRESENTATIVES

For the State
Mr Seamus McKenna, SC
Mr. Eamonn Walsh, SC
Mr Aidan Browne, BL
Instructed by the Chief State Solicitor

For Mr Charles Haughey
Mr Niall McCarthy, SC
Mr Peter Maguire, SC
Mr Patrick Connolly, BL
Instructed by JS O'Connor & Co.

For Mr Albert Luykx
Mr EM Wood, SC
Mr Frank Martin, BL
Instructed by Gore & Grimes

For Captain Kelly
Mr James D'Arcy, SC
Mr TA Finlay, SC
Mr Peter Sutherland, BL
Instructed by James F. Fitzpatrick & Co.

For Mr John Kelly
Mr Seamus Sorahan, BL
Mr Kevin O'Higgins, BL
Instructed by Ciarán Mac an Aili.

BIBLIOGRAPHY

Holy War in Belfast, Andrew Boyd, Anvil Books.

Drums & Guns: Revolution in Ulster, Martin Wallace, London.

Ulster, The Sunday Times Insight Team, Penguin.

Magill: May, June, July & December 1980. Edited by Vincent Browne.

Disturbances in Northern Ireland, The Cameron Commission, HMSO.

Low Intensity Operations, Frank Kitson, Faber & Faber.

We Won't Stand (Idly) By, Kevin Boland, Kelly Kane.

Up Dev! Kevin Boland, Kevin Boland.

Violence In Ireland, Cahal B. Daly, Veritas.

Orders For The Captain, James Kelly, Kelly Kane.

The Genesis Of Revolution, James Kelly, Kelly Kane.

Through The Bridewell Gate, Tom McIntyre, Faber & Faber.

The Cosgrave Legacy, Stephen Collins, Blackwater Press.

Arms And The Men, Seamus Brady, Dublin.

The Autobiography of Edward Heath, Hodder & Stoughton.

Dail Éireann Reports (Dublin) 1970.

Dail Committee Reports (Dublin) 1971/72.

Hearings – Committee of Foreign Affairs, US House of Representatives, (US Government Printing Office).